Portrait of a Bonaparte

Portrait of a Bonaparte

The life and times of Joseph-Napoleon Primoli 1851–1927

Joanna Richardson

QUARTET BOOKS
London   New York

First published by Quartet Books Limited 1987
A member of the Namara Group
27/29 Goodge Street, London W1P 1FD

Copyright © 1987 by Joanna Richardson

British Library Cataloguing in Publication Data
Richardson, Joanna
    Portrait of a Bonaparte: the life and
    times of Joseph-Napoleon Primoli, 1851–1927.
    1. Primoli, Joseph-Napoleon   2. France—
    Biography
    I. Title
    944.081'092'4   CT1018.P/

    ISBN 0-7043-2638-8

Typeset by MC Typeset Limited
Printed and bound in Great Britain at
The Camelot Press plc, Southampton

Contents

List of Illustrations

leave her.' Primoli with his afflicted mother at the Villa Taverna, Frascati.

43. The Villa Cyrnos, Cap Martin, 7 May 1912. Frederik VIII of Denmark (left) talks to Lucien Daudet. The Empress Eugénie, in black, talks to the Court Marshal of Denmark and the Comtesse de Wimpffen.

44. 'An exquisite refuge against the sullen winter.' Primoli in his library in Rome.

45. Primoli in his apartment in Paris: 19, avenue du Trocadéro (later avenue du Président-Wilson). This photograph was taken in the latter years of his life.

Introduction

Joseph-Napoleon Primoli – Gégé to his many friends – was born in Rome in 1851. His father was Pietro Primoli, an undistinguished Italian nobleman. His mother, Charlotte Primoli, was a Bonaparte princess. Joseph-Napoleon Primoli therefore spent his life largely between Paris and Rome.

He was educated in Paris, and there, in the 1860s, he began to keep a diary. Highly intelligent, sensitive, observant, introspective, he treated it almost as a confidant. It was an illuminating record of his adolescence. It was also an unparalleled commentary on the last decade of the Second Empire, for Primoli's Bonaparte connection allowed him to move in Imperial circles, and to meet Flaubert and the Goncourts, Sainte-Beuve and Mérimée, Gautier and Taine: to be, in the words of Ferdinand Bac, the godson of Parnassus.

He also described – from the inside, so to speak – the effects of the Franco–Prussian War, and the downfall of the Imperial Family. In his manhood, he recorded the post-war world: Maupassant and Dumas *fils*, Renan, Gounod, Daudet and his *romans à clef*. He was a friend of Anatole France, of Proust, La Duse and d'Annunzio. He entertained Sarah Bernhardt; in time he entertained Colette. It would be difficult to find a celebrated figure in the cultural and social life of France and Italy whom he did not meet. Intensely devoted to his mother, Primoli remained a bachelor; he was happiest, it seems, as a son and an adopted son. He became, increasingly, the confidant of his great-aunt, Princess Mathilde, and he became a devoted friend of the Empress Eugénie. He had once discussed the Liberal Empire with Émile Ollivier; at the end of the nineteenth century, he recorded the aggressive diplomacy of the Kaiser, and, early in the twentieth, he witnessed the solemn signing of the Peace Treaty at Versailles. Before he died in 1927, he had seen the March on Rome and the advent of Benito Mussolini.

Primoli knew everyone; he also had a gift for being in the perfect place at the perfect time. He was a vivid writer. Sometimes, it is true, he seemed more concerned with anecdote than history; sometimes (for he had a taste for practical jokes) he indulged in feckless invention. Nonetheless his diary is a new and splendid source-book for the student of the period. It is a Goncourt *Journal* written by a Bonaparte.

Occasionally, in later life, Primoli would enlarge on his original comments: publish an article or two in *La Revue de Paris*, *La Revue hebdomadaire* or *La Revue des Deux Mondes*. He published a number of letters from his massive archives. Often he thought of writing a book: perhaps his memoirs, perhaps a life of Princess Mathilde, or a study of the Princess and her friends. His indecisive nature, his inherent idleness, and even his discretion, prevented him. He left the material for a panoramic view of his age. Some of it has appeared in the original French. Now, for the first time, a substantial part of it appears in English. Since he was both a diarist and a famous amateur photographer, this book is illustrated largely with his own photographs.

I gladly record my gratitude to the late Count Lanfranco Campello, who generously gave me permission to consult the Primoli Papers, to publish an English translation of the diary and to illustrate it with Primoli's photographs. I much regret that, despite this permission, the President of the Fondazione Primoli has refused me further access to the archives. This unnecessary obstruction has naturally restricted the scope of the present book. One day I hope I may translate all the Primoli journals. In the meanwhile, I have attempted to give an impression of Gégé Primoli and his times. It might be more true to say that I have let him do so. I have used substantial extracts from his published and unpublished diary, his articles, and the correspondence in his archives. I have linked these extracts with the minimum of commentary. M. Claude Popelin (grandson of Claudius Popelin) has generously allowed me to use the Popelin Papers, and M. Serge Grandjean has kindly let me consult the family letters in his possession. I am most grateful to the late Professor Marcello Spaziani, for his published work and for his personal kindness and advice when I was working on the Primoli Papers at Spoleto. As always, I warmly appreciate the encouragement of Dr Alan Raitt. I must record my debt to M. Pierre Janin and his colleagues in the Département des Manuscrits at the Bibliothèque Nationale; I owe much to the resources of the British Library, and to the expert and sympathetic help which, as usual, I have received at the Taylor Institution, Oxford.

JOANNA RICHARDSON

One

1

One day in 1801, in Santa Maria del Popolo, in Rome, a young bride was waiting for her unpunctual bridegroom. She was praying fervently; but 'the congregation would have been very surprised if they had known the ardent desire which the girl was expressing beneath her bridal veil. She was not imploring God to make her husband come, she was entreating the Madonna to turn him from his path and prevent the marriage.'[1] The bridegroom still failed to appear; the congregation grew anxious, and, finally, some of his friends set out to find him. They discovered him on the Ponte Sant' Angelo, contemplating suicide. He thought that the waters of the Tiber might be less perilous than matrimony.

Luigi Primoli duly married Teresa Modetti.

> I am [wrote Joseph Primoli] the grandson of these two Irresolutes, who have bequeathed to me their dual uncertainty of soul. Their continual hesitations have troubled the course of my blood at its source by an alternating ebb and flow; they have made me this false *strapazzo* Hamlet, this miserable talking reed, without stability, without direction, bending to every passing wind, unable to take root where fate has cast it. That is why I have been unable to decide to be somebody, or something; that is why I have no determination, and no energy. I am neither good nor bad, neither young nor old, neither industrious nor idle, neither French nor Italian, neither submissive nor rebellious . . . And that is also why I have hesitated to bind myself by a lasting liaison or a fragile marriage. And, when death comes to find me, I shall have had my share of grief in this world, and yet I don't know that I shall be anxious to go and see what lies in the other.[2]

* * *

Luigi Primoli, who had married with such hesitation, enjoyed a long and happy marriage until his death in 1840. His widow survived him until 1878. Her comfort was her only child, Pietro. The family had been accorded the title of Counts of Foglia, but they could hardly claim to match the distinction of the family from which Pietro was to choose his wife. Charlotte-Honorée-Joséphine was a Bonaparte twice over. Her father was Charles Bonaparte, son of Lucien, Prince of Canino. Her mother (who had married a first cousin) was Zénaïde Bonaparte, a daughter of Joseph, King of Spain.

Teresa Primoli 'was not dazzled by the birth and fortune of her future daughter-in-law; she was terrified by such advantages, she thought that she would never dare to live an ordinary life with a princess whose mother had been born on the steps of a throne: a princess whose family might still be called upon to reign. To her great surprise, she found a very simple child who adored her husband and was naturally full of respect for her mother-in-law.'[3]

The future Charlotte Primoli was indeed a child: she was only fourteen when Pietro met her. Innocent, reserved, but ardent, she refused all the grander suitors who were offered. She determined to marry him; her parents waited until her fifteenth birthday before they announced her betrothal. On 4 October 1848 Charlotte Bonaparte and Pietro Primoli were married by Cardinal Franzoni at the Palazzo Bonaparte in Rome. The bridegroom was twenty-eight, and the bride had just turned sixteen.

The following year she gave birth to a son, who died almost immediately. On 30 April 1851, Pietro explained to a friend at Fiumicino that he could not, alas, shoot quail with him, as he was kept at home by his wife's confinement.

At last [Joseph Primoli was to write], on Friday, 2 May 1851, at noon, a French regiment, headed by a band, marched across the piazza dell'Orso in Rome, to go and mount guard at the commander-in-chief's. The cannon of the Castel Sant' Angelo shook the windows of the little Palazzo Primoli which stood on the banks of the Tiber . . . This detonation and fanfare were answered, from the first-floor room hung with green silk, by the wailing of a new-born child.[4]

* * *

The salutation was appropriate. Joseph-Napoleon Primoli was born in Rome, the son of an Italian count; he was, in law, Italian by birth. But he was drawn to France by the aura of his maternal ancestry, and by his intense devotion to his mother. He would always consider himself a Frenchman, and a Bonaparte.

2

He was, in time, to become a Bonaparte historian. Ferdinand Bac, who was thought to have a touch of Bonaparte blood, declared that Primoli 'knew nothing but *the idle tales* of History. He had the ignorance of all his race, who had acquired the habit of saying: "Why know? *We exist*." Like his family, he had learned only to glorify and hate, but never to verify.'[1] Primoli was not beyond embroidering the facts, and, on occasion, even improvising; but he had known Napoleon III and all the members of the Imperial Family. In the final years of his life, when he had inherited the papers of Princess Mathilde, and enjoyed hours of conversation with the Princess and the Empress Eugénie, he set down his own version of certain Imperial events. It has its place here, as it presents the central characters of the Second Empire; it helps to explain their personal relationships. It is a useful, indeed essential, prelude to a study of Joseph Primoli and his times.

In 1924, he published his account of the Emperor's broken engagement to Princess Mathilde. She was the daughter of King Jerome and Queen Catherine of Westphalia, and, therefore, the niece of the first Napoleon.

One may follow all the phases of this arranged and broken engagement in the unpublished letters from the young man to his mother, and in the *Souvenirs* – also unpublished – of Princess Mathilde.

In 1835, on the death of Queen Catherine, Louis-Napoleon had been summoned to Lausanne by his uncle Jerome; on 5 December, he wrote to his mother: 'Mathilde is charming, but don't think that I'm in love with her. Not at all. I have a quite different feeling for her. If I weren't afraid of marriage, I should be glad to have her as

6

my wife, but her visit to Stuttgart will spoil her. [Her uncle] the King of Wurtemberg is extremely good to them all, he wants to treat her like a daughter, and you know that Courts are like coquettes: you always malign them, but you can't leave them once you have known them.'

Princess Mathilde writes in her *Souvenirs*: 'Two days after my departure from Stuttgart I reached Arenenberg, where my father had preceded me. I was welcomed with open arms by Queen Hortense. It was not long before she spoke to me about the plan for the marriage which had been arranged. My father gave his consent wholeheartedly. He bought Gottlieb, an old castle very near Arenenberg, in which John Huss [the reformer] had been imprisoned, and he wanted to have it restored, so that he could live in it and be near us. The marriage was to be celebrated there, six months later.'[2]

While they thought that Louis-Napoleon was absorbed in preparations for his marriage, he was in fact plotting the first of his *coups-d'état*. The Strasbourg skirmish was a wild, abortive attempt to seize power in France, and to restore the Bonaparte dynasty. He was arrested, and exiled to America.

The Princess [continued Primoli] recalls in her *Souvenirs*: 'The news of this adventure reached us by public rumour, we didn't need any more in order to understand my cousin's neglect, or the delays in solemnizing the marriage. I must say that, on this occasion, none of his family took Prince Louis' part . . . My father wrote us several letters in which he burst out with virulent indignation against the Prince; he overwhelmed him with reproaches for having deceived him by asking him for my hand at the moment when he was meditating such an act of madness; he forbade me to write to either the son or the mother, and he declared that henceforward the marriage would be quite impossible.'

The Prince, however, was wounded to the heart. He had not forgotten. On 14 December, in sight of the Canaries, from the ship which was taking him to America, he wrote to his mother: 'When I was coming back through the park, a few months ago, after seeing Mathilde on her way back to Florence, I found a tree that was shattered by the storm. I said to myself: our marriage will be shattered by fate . . . The event which I vaguely imagined has come to pass. Have I exhausted . . . all my share of happiness?'

* * *

7

... After that [continued Primoli] the destinies of the two cousins had diverged; Louis-Napoleon had pursued his adventurous career, in spite of his successive reverses. His eyes had always been fixed on his star. The Strasbourg skirmish had been followed by his deportation to America; the landing at Boulogne by the imprisonment at Ham, then the dramatic escape of 'Badinguet' and finally the triumphant return to France, the election as a deputy, the presidency ...

As for Mathilde, in 1840 she ... had allowed herself to be married to an immensely rich Russian nobleman, Anatole Demidoff ...

The marriage was not happy, and, after six years of continual troubles, the ill-matched pair had finally separated; the young Princess was able at last to settle in Paris. She was there in 1848 to receive her cousin on his return from exile ...

Love – if indeed there was love – turned easily into solid friendship ... The Emperor's niece warmly supported her cousin's cause, and, on the eve of the *coup-d'état*, she pledged her jewels for him; after 2 December, she contributed to the President's success by doing the honours of the Élysée with a grace which soon became famous; she made personal friends for him, even beyond the circle of his partisans. The latter therefore found it quite natural to try to make her marry the prince. She was married already, it is true, but her husband belonged to the Orthodox Church, and as husband and wife had each been obliged to promise to give their own religion to any children that might be born, the marriage could easily be annulled. But the Princess refused; she had won her freedom, and did not want to lose it. As she explained in her *Souvenirs*: 'In 1850, there was a question of my obtaining a divorce so that I could marry the President of the Republic. I refused outright, for I preferred the situation I had to the quite exceptional one which I was offered. I did so without any hesitation, and without the least regret. I could not have forfeited my independence, when I felt that my heart was not involved. I have since congratulated myself on my decision.'[3]

There was another, unrecorded, reason for Mathilde's decision. For some years she had been the mistress of the strikingly handsome sculptor, Alfred-Émilien de Nieuwerkerke. She refused to leave him for an unattractive cousin.

On 2 December 1852, the forty-seventh anniversary of Napoleon's victory at Austerlitz, the Second Empire was proclaimed in Paris, and Napoleon III rode into his capital through the Arc de Triomphe.

* * *

By an irony which she was unlikely ever to forget, Mathilde herself had presented the future Empress Eugénie to her cousin. She had first met Eugénie de Montijo at her uncle Prince Paul of Wurtemberg's, in the place Vendôme, in September 1845. Eugénie had been sitting at a lansquenet table. Mathilde had thought her beautiful.

> Her skin was very white and matt, her red hair seemed even redder since the colour was not then in fashion. She had a slender waist, and an ample bosom; she was distinguished-looking, though she had a very pronounced foreign air. She was also free in manner, with a decisive tone in conversation, full of spirit, like a woman well accustomed to homage from men.[4]

Eugénie was not drawn to Mathilde, but in 1849 she had begun to frequent the rue de Courcelles. It was in this *salon*, where she professed to be extremely bored, that she was presented to Louis-Napoleon; and, after that first presentation, she had often met him there. She was not unaware of the attractions of an unmarried head of state, a Bonaparte who might well become an Emperor.

A few days after the proclamation of the Second Empire, so Primoli recorded,

> the whole Court moved to Compiègne, to inaugurate the famous *séries* which were to continue for the eighteen years of the Empire. The honours were done, as usual, by Princess Mathilde; and, as usual, Eugénie de Montijo was the queen. Riding through the forest, she found herself back in her element.
>
>> Unfortunately the rigours of December did not always allow long expeditions. One day, when the weather had been too bad for them to hunt with hounds [wrote Princess Mathilde in her unpublished memoirs], I had retired to my big drawing-room, where I was reading, when the Emperor came in. He sat down beside my fire and talked for a few moments, like a man who does not want to reveal his preoccupations. Finally he decided to broach the question of marriage; he told me that people were very anxious for him to take a wife, and that he had to found a dynasty . . . I was trembling at the thought that he would mention [his mistress] Miss Howard, I had so little thought of Mlle de Montijo. The Emperor could not disguise his vexation at the refusal from the Princesse de Wasa. I told him at once that

there was no need to hurry, that he had only been Emperor for six weeks [*sic*], that he had a *maîtresse en titre*, whom he had not dismissed. 'I know all that,' he answered, 'but I need to make a decision, and I should like to find a beautiful princess with whom I could fall in love.' He said no more to me; I suspected that he had a plan which he didn't want to discuss. It was then that the thought of Mlle de Montijo came to my mind. I dismissed it . . . I didn't think he was capable of a rash act which put him in a false position in the eyes of Europe. By not marrying a princess, he was making a blunder.[5]

* * *

On the evening of Saturday, 29 January 1854, the civil marriage between the Emperor and Eugénie de Montijo was celebrated at the Tuileries.

Princess Mathilde records in her *Souvenirs*: 'That evening, the future Empress made her first official appearance in public. She looked charming and distinguished, with her pink dress and her set of pearls. As she suspected the hostility to her marriage, she was very troubled. She took my hand, and did not want to leave me. When she reached the Salle des Maréchaux and had to precede me, her emotion was plain; she went to sit on the chair intended for her, beside the Emperor's, both of them sat on a dais by the garden windows.' M. Fould officiated, as Minister of State, and he had the register before him on a table, a register which was burnt during the Commune of 1871. More than once [added Primoli] the Empress reminded us, with a melancholy smile, that Fate pursued her unrelentingly: not only had fire reduced to ashes the palaces she had inhabited, the Tuileries, Saint-Cloud and Biarritz, but fire had also destroyed the traces of the most solemn events in her life: her marriage contract and her son's birth certificate . . .

After the ceremony, the sovereigns, followed by the whole assembly, went into the *salle des fêtes*, where the orchestra of the Opéra played a cantata composed for the occasion, with words by Arsène Houssaye and music by Auber. The Emperor could not conceal his impatience, and soon dismissed his guests.

Once he was alone with his family, he withdrew to change out of his uniform, but a few minutes later he returned in evening dress, and got into a carriage with his wife and his mother-in-law, to go and have supper at the Élysée.

* * *

Next day, Sunday, 30 January, at half-past eleven, the Emperor, his

10

family and the great dignitaries of state assembled at the Tuileries, to await the bride. Two carriages, escorted by a picket of carabineers, had been to the Élysée to fetch the Empress and her mother, who were keeping the company waiting. The most patient man in Europe, as Mérimée called him, could not conceal his impatience. 'At noon, the cannon at the Invalides roared out their joyful salvoes, the trumpets sounded, the drums beat a salute: it was the moment when the Empress arrived at the palais des Tuileries, through the gates of the pavillon de Flore. She dismounted from her carriage at the pavillon de l'Horloge, at the door of which she found the Great Chamberlain, the Master of the Horse, four chamberlains, and the orderly officers on duty. Prince Napoleon and Princess Mathilde awaited her at the foot of the grand staircase; Napoleon III came out of the Emperor's room to greet the Empress, led her into the room, and, taking her hand, appeared on the balcony with her. They were greeted with immense acclamation.'

Husband and wife then entered a carriage drawn by eight horses, preceded by the Fuglemen's band and by a squadron of dragoons. Two marshals acted as equerries, and made their horses caracole on either side of the carriage. The Emperor was radiant with happiness.

The Empress was as white as the terry velvet of her dress, the lace of her veil, and the orange-blossom round the edge of her diamond tiara. 'All the blood had left my face,' she told me, when she recalled that distant day, 'my waxen pallor could not please a nation which only likes bright colours.' All the same, the memory of that vision was unforgettable for those who found themselves on the route of the procession from the Tuileries to Notre-Dame down the rue de Rivoli, 'which had just been finished, and looked like a triumphal way.'

When she got out of the carriage at the portal of Notre-Dame, to the sound of all the bells of Paris, the Empress saw that the square was thronged with an enthusiastic crowd which was trying in vain to catch sight of her face through her veils . . . With a gracious thought, a gracious gesture, she turned round, faced the public, and thanked her future subjects with a touching smile, a slight inclination of her swan-like neck, and the curtsey which was soon to be famous. She had conquered the people. Then she took the arm of the Emperor, who was waiting at the door with the Archbishop of Paris and the chapter of Notre-Dame, who had come in procession to greet the bride and bridegroom. The Emperor, hand in hand with the Empress, made his entrance into the cathedral under a red velvet canopy lined with white satin, to the sound of a wedding march: the music from *Le Prophète*. This profane choice was condemned by the devout, who would have preferred religious music. It would have been more in harmony with the reverent conduct of the pale bride. 'She conquered me at Notre-Dame,' wrote the Duchesse de Dino, who is not always benevolent, 'not by her beauty, but by the pious composure of her bearing.' And the Maréchal de Castellane, with his military brusqueness, granted the Sovereign a certificate of good behaviour. 'The Empress,' he told his daughter, 'bore herself with dignity and great composure, she behaved very correctly during the Mass; she was pale, moved, and very beautiful.'

A happy omen for the future, if from the first moment she had adapted herself so well to the rôle of Sovereign!

There was another omen which was not, alas, so favourable, and was sooner or later to be fulfilled. As they passed under the arch of the pavillon de l'Horloge, the imperial crown in gilded bronze which surmounted the bridal carriage had come loose and fallen off and been smashed. The identical accident had happened to the identical carriage after the wedding of Marie-Louise. They attempted to conceal what had happened, but the Empress learned of it, and her joy was overshadowed. She tried, all the same, to disguise her anxiety so as not to worry the Emperor; and he himself continued to smile, so as not to alarm his wife. And so, from the first day, they both began to play their brilliant, tragic parts.

After the nuptial benediction, the Archbishop of Paris and the chapter accompanied the bride and bridegroom, in procession, under the canopy, as far as the portal, to the sound of *Urbs beata* by Lesueur; then the carriage procession followed the quais to the Tuileries gardens, where there were deputations of workmen and young girls. The imperial carriage drove round the place du Carrousel. Their Majesties reviewed the troops assembled there to cheer them.

The Emperor, proud of his radiant conquest, presented the Empress to the crowd from the two balconies of the Salle des Maréchaux, one of which looked over the courtyard, the other over the garden. He was greeted by wild acclamations.

Here is a personal note on the day which I have found in Princess Mathilde's *Souvenirs*: 'We came back from Notre-Dame to the Tuileries, there were embraces and congratulations, and then the Empress went to change her clothes to go to Saint-Cloud, where she was to stay privately with her husband; she came back very animated, dressed in ruby velvet with furs . . . We saw her climb into a carriage . . . which took her to her new residence. The ladies-in-waiting and household followed. We all went home, tired and sad at heart; we felt that we were losing the Emperor.'

* * *

However, the young bride imagined that at Saint-Cloud she would at last be able to enjoy a few hours of privacy with her husband . . . What were her surprise and disappointment when, on the very entrance steps, and in the great salons, she found an inquisitive crowd awaiting the Imperial couple! The kind-hearted Emperor had felt unable to dismiss the functionaries and residents of the palace, whom he had always allowed to come and sit at his table when he moved to Saint-Cloud!

During the interminable evening which followed the meal, he soon repented of his indulgence. Time went by; the guests had no idea of departing, and Napoleon III and, indeed, the Empress Eugénie, did not dare dismiss them. At last, in exasperation, the amorous husband approached his wife, and, pulling at his moustache, he murmured to her: 'Send them away!' And the young bride, who had not yet entered into her new rôle, did not know how to give the signal for the general departure. At her husband's repeated insistence – and for all his legendary patience, he was threatening to make a scene – she whispered to him: 'Make your way to the door; I'll follow you.' He hurried out of the salon, without even turning to take farewell of his guests, and she followed him; but at the door of the private apartments, as she had done that morning outside the portal of Notre-Dame, she turned round to face the importunate, dismissed them with a touching smile and a gracious bow, leaving them under the spell of that circular curtsey which everyone could think was personally intended for him. Then she disappeared after her husband.

And so it was that Napoleon and Eugénie withdrew, and retired to the bridal chamber.[6]

3

In 1853, when Joseph Primoli was two – and the Second Empire was in its infancy – the Primolis understandably left Rome and settled in Paris. In 1855 they had a second son, Napoleon; in 1858 a third son, Louis, known as Loulou to his family. Joseph, too, received a nickname; it was based on the initial of his Italian Christian-name. Giuseppe Primoli became known as Gégé. The name was to adorn the social life of Paris and Rome for the better part of seventy years.

Gégé was naturally given a Parisian education. He was sent, in time, to the fashionable Collège Rollin; and there, in the 1860s, he began to keep a diary. He gave an intimate impression of his great-aunt (he called her his aunt), Princess Mathilde, and of her country house at Saint-Gratien. The setting was familiar to most of the celebrities of the age. At the end of his life he was still to recall, in affectionate detail, those idyllic summers in the 1860s on the shores of Lake Enghien.

I was then at college . . . Towards the end of July, the prison gates opened at last, and I saw a wonderful apotheosis, the kind that I admired at the end of the pantomines which I was taken to when I'd earned my leave.

This fantastic décor was lit by a joyful summer sun.

In a shady valley there lay a lake, on which a group of snowy swans disported themselves; between an avenue of centennial trees – the remains of an old estate which had been divided up – and green fields stretching out as far as the distant hills, there rose an enchanted palace.

The building which, in my prisoner's dreams, appeared to me like a fairytale palace, was really a big white house with green shutters; a blue china frieze with a Greek key pattern ran round the sides, a virginia creeper covered the brick walls and fell down from the roof again in capricious festoons which were turning gold in the first rays of autumn . . .

What above all helped to transform this bourgeois house into an enchanted palace, was the fairy who lived there.

Although she was over forty – if fairies actually have an age like mere mortal women – she seemed to me very beautiful still . . . Her imposing appearance was softened by the kindly smile which lit up her face when a friend arrived, and cast a shadow over it when he departed . . . And, as the poet said when he celebrated the purity of her classical features:

> César y mit la majesté
> Et Vénus le sourire rose . . .[1]

* * *

1864

26 July

At half-past four on Saturday we left for St Gratien. Mr Sainte-Beuve to dinner as usual . . .

The day before yesterday there was a literary dinner at Saint-Gratien, Mr Sainte-Beuve, E. Augier, E. de Girardin . . .[2]

The literary dinners were notably distinguished. Sainte-Beuve was the pre-eminent literary critic of the day, and Princess Mathilde's adviser in matters of patronage. Émile de Girardin, the founder of *La Presse*, the future owner of *La Liberté*, had recognized that attendance at Saint-Gratien and the rue de Courcelles was a social necessity for the ambitious. As for Émile Augier, the princess enjoyed his sensible moral dramas, and found him both endearing and undemanding: 'There is something frank and solid about him, his wit is ever present and very responsive, he is full of bourgeois good sense . . . He is lazy by nature. Perhaps this is wise, because he doesn't want to outlive his celebrity. He has produced a good deal, and knows where to stop. He is a good friend, without ambition.'[3] He was followed to Saint-Gratien, now, by Théophile Gautier, and by Paul de Musset, the poet's brother. As Primoli reported:

On the 12th, Aunt Mathilde had several writers to dinner, among them Mr E. de Girardin, Mr Gautier, Mr Giraud of the Institut [Charles-Barthélemy Giraud, the jurist], &c. After dinner came Mr and Mme Paul de Musset, this lady had a very nice way with her, she brought Aunt Mathilde a charming little frog in a glass jar . . .[4]

On the evening of the 14th, Aunt Mathilde had her park re-opened to the public, and gave a splendid firework display in it.

15 August . . . In the evening we went for a delightful excursion on the lake . . .

16 August. We bathed at nine o'clock in the morning, it was good fun. Aunt Mathilde has bought a sort of bathing-machine which stays on the surface of the water, and can be directed wherever you want . . .[5]

* * *

Not everyone was so enchanted. In October, dining at Saint-Gratien, the Goncourts were much offended by Pietro Primoli, by his coarseness and outrageous jokes. They were not alone in finding him offensive. The Princess herself reproached him, though she did so, tactfully, in Italian, and Eugène Giraud, the artist, who taught her painting, invented the verb *primoliser*, 'to say something risky'.[6] It was a trait which Gégé was to inherit – along with an affection for practical jokes, some of them distinctly unkind. That trait had not developed yet. The diary for 1864 continues to reflect a naïve adolescent of thirteen.

Sunday, 13 November

At four o'clock I went to tea at my dear Aunt Mathilde's [in the rue de Courcelles, in Paris]. I saw those dear ladies [her dogs]. We had christened them at Saint-Gratien: Miss (the favourite) is the Vicomtesse de Saint-Gratien, Lot is Charlotte de Catinat, Chine is Blanche du Louvre. In other words: Miss has the title of Vicomtesse de Saint-Gratien because she and Saint-Gratien are Aunt Mathilde's two favourite things . . . Chine is called Blanche because her fur is white. She belongs to the Comte de Nieuwer-kerke, director of the Louvre, and she therefore has her master's name.[7]

So Gégé – 'our Gégé' – continued to frequent the rue de Courcelles and Saint-Gratien, and to act in charades, with the Emperor's son, the Prince Imperial, for the pleasure of his great-aunt Mathilde.[8] His father continued to earn the antipathy of the Goncourts. In August 1865 the diarists stayed again at Saint-Gratien, and again recorded their aversion to 'the gross Count Primoli'. 'An enormous man,' they noted, 'he puffs like a seal, and murders the French language, he's always jabbering something malicious ... He hates and despises France. Every morning he picks out something from the papers which is disagreeable for the Napoleons, the Princess, her friends ...' Everyone, added the Goncourts, 'detests him here.'[9]

Years later, after his father's death, Gégé attempted to redress the balance:

I must write something about my Father. He devoted himself so exclusively to his family that his relations owe it to him to make his nature and character generally appreciated. It is sad to write about a vivacious man who is dead. Sainte-Beuve told him that he ought to write an heroi-comic poem in the style of *Le Lutrin* [by Boileau]. The Prince Imperial declared that he was the wittiest man he had known. Father refused to work, as he said his Italian was not good enough, it had been spoilt by too long a stay in Paris. His true language was Latin. I have some occasional verses of his and three notebooks, bound in green, inscribed to his fiancée. His religion was sincere and deep ... He never failed to go to Mass, and always observed the days of fasting and abstinence. He never took a cab, and said that only debtors went by carriage, to escape their creditors.[10]

It was a lame attempt to do justice to an undistinguished man. It remains the only tribute to him among the Primoli Papers.

4

In 1867, at the height of the Second Empire, the Exposition Universelle was held in Paris. Most of the sovereigns of Europe came to visit it, as the guests of Napoleon III. William I of Prussia arrived with Count Bismarck, who, it is thought, made his private assessment of the French army, and already dreamed of the Franco-Prussian War and the German Empire. Alexander II of Russia also came to Paris this summer. Years later, Primoli recorded the Russian visit. He had been sixteen at the time, but no doubt he had often discussed events with the Empress when he came to write his account of them.

On 1 June 1867, invited by the Emperor of the French to visit the Great Exhibition, the Tsar of Russia arrived in Paris with his sons and a numerous suite, among whom, it was noticed, was Prince Gortchakoff. Napoleon III went to meet his guest at the station, and he avoided making him ride down the boulevard de Sébastopol: the name would have reminded him, painfully, that he was among his victors. The memory of the Crimean War was fading into the distance. Between France, however, which seems to have a mission to protect the oppressed – even at her own expense – and the Russian Eagle, which did not seem inclined to release its prey, there rose the shadow of afflicted Poland. For Polish exiles, Paris had become the safest asylum from persecution. Tony Robert Fleury had just exhibited his masterpiece, *Les Massacres de Varsovie*, which had been the main attraction of the last Salon. The illustrated papers had reproduced it with commentaries on the tragedy, rousing general indignation and pity.

When the two Emperors crossed the city in an open carriage, they were therefore greeted by crowds which were inquisitive rather than sympathetic. There were even a few murmurs as the sovereigns passed by, but still discreet enough not to be heard by the autocrat to whom they were addressed. This hostility was soon more openly displayed. The following morning, at the Palais de Justice, M. Floquet welcomed the Tsar with the provocative greeting: 'Long live Poland, Sir!' And that evening, on the way to the Opéra, the imperial berlin which was carrying the Empress Eugénie and Princess Mathilde at the back, and the two Emperors on the front seat, was passing the Bazar des voyages when the same seditious cry rose from the crowds: 'Long live Poland!' As the carriage was lit up inside, the Empress looked at the Tsar. He wanted to appear impassible, but, from his pallor, she knew that he had struggled to suppress a surge of anger. Anyone who had dared to utter such a cry in Russia would soon have been deported to Siberia . . .

If there was such a show of hostility everywhere against the Tsar, against whom the French nation had no personal grievance, how were they going to greet the King of Prussia on the morrow of [the battle of] Sadowa, which the most perceptive considered, not without foresight, as the prelude to disaster for France? . . .

French diplomats had therefore alleged that there were problems of protocol; and finally, with great difficulty, they had ensured that the two sovereigns did not arrive in Paris together, as they had intended to do. M. de Bismarck's only concession had been to put four days between the two arrivals. Alexander had come first, on 1 June, William had followed on the 5th, and on the 6th there was to be the grand review at Longchamp.

As it was thought that the King of Prussia would be more exposed to public hostility than the Tsar of Russia, the Empress, trusting in French gallantry to women, asked to have William in her carriage, and they both arrived safely at the racecourse. On the way back from the review, two incidents occurred, one of them comic, the other tragic, the latter better known than the former, and yet the trivial news item which belonged to the gossip-columns helped to prevent an event which – had it succeeded – would have changed the course of history.

That day, the equerry on duty with the Empress was the Marquis de X—, who was caracoling by the carriage door and attracting everyone's attention. In fact, if you had looked at him closely, you would have found something strange in the way he made his horse pirouette . . . Absorbed in his dreams of equitation, he had forgotten the itinerary which had been laid down for the procession, and he had made the Empress's carriage follow the route which had been chosen for the Emperor . . .

This providential error helped to keep the assassin's bullet from

19

its victim. The assassin, who had been precisely informed of the Sovereign's route, found himself mistaken in his calculations. He had posted himself on the hillock to the right of the cascade in front of which Alexander and Napoleon were to pass. Thanks to the negligence of the equerry, he found himself a long way from his target. As soon as he saw the procession approaching in the distance, he had to run across the field to get to it and to reach the hillock on the left. This delay allowed Firmin Raimbaut to put his horse between the Tsar and the bullet which was destined for him, and so it diverted the bullet and enabled the police to arrest the [would-be] assassin.

As for the Empress, the only inconvenience of this confusion was a carriage block; an obstruction stopped the imperial daumont in the midst of the crowds. The Empress looked round with her most gracious smile, and William gave his most affectionate and most grandfatherly salute to disarm the hostile public and to rouse their sympathy. The crowds appeared to be conquered by this engaging old man and this pretty woman. A quite unforeseen occurrence – which was not to the Empress's taste – was more effective than the smiles and salutes, and finally put the idle crowds into a good humour.

Just by the imperial barouche, in a little yellow victoria, sat a demi-mondaine. She was having great trouble in keeping a little ratter with gleaming eyes on her lap . . . The equerry, who was caracoling between the two carriages, was seized by some unaccountable whim, and began to bark at the little mongrel, which stood up and barked furiously back . . . A duet began between the man and the animal, the crowd joined in, and laughed, and excited one against the other. The Empress, horribly embarrassed, tried in vain to call her equerry to order . . . Unable to do so, she ordered the postilion to hurry, and, while the outrider struggled to make his way through the crowd, amid the laughter of the spectators, the man continued to bark and the dog to howl . . . Then, carried away by his horse, the wretched equerry escorted the barouche, declaiming lines from *Ruy Blas* . . . He had gone mad, and next day he was put into a strait-jacket. In his moments of calm he was taken to the Bois de Boulogne, and nothing was more painful for the Empress than to meet her former servant, who did not acknowledge her greeting, since he did not recognize her . . .

* * *

In the meanwhile, the procession had finally reached the Tuileries. The Empress had just gone back into her boudoir when she saw the Emperor at the door. He came up to her in his placid way, with

20

his customary smile; his attitude of indifference was in such contrast to his words that he seemed to be talking of someone else's adventure. The Empress was stupefied by this contrast, and at first she did not understand.

'They have just fired at the Tsar,' he said . . .

'At the Tsar? . . . So they fired at you?'

'Yes, and I said to him, "Sire, we have been under fire together, but neither of us has been scratched."'

'They fired at him, then – but you ran the same danger . . . and you are unmoved? . . . This time, you've had the ungrateful and dangerous part that I have when we go out together. "They have fired at the Emperor," people say, but they never add – "and at the Empress!" They forget that I run the risk of being wounded just as much as you – and they even deprive me of the glory, the danger I have run! . . . Come on, tell me . . .'

And with imperturbable composure, as if he had described a play which he had been watching from the stalls, as a mere theatregoer, the Emperor described the scene at the cascade: the presence of mind of the equerry Raimbaut, the poor horse which had received the bullet destined for the Tsar, and the Tsar bending in anguish over his sons, taking their hands, pressing them, asking them in Russian if they were hurt . . .

'But it's terrible!' cried the Empress, revolted both as a Sovereign and as the descendant of those hidalgos for whom a guest was someone sacred . . . Her indignation was increased by the Emperor's calm, which exasperated her.

'I must go at once to get news of him, I must assure myself that he wasn't touched . . .'

Despite the assurances she was given, and the objections which they tried to make, she didn't listen to anyone, she rushed down to the courtyard, climbed into the dun-coloured brougham which was parked day and night outside the grille, and she had herself driven to the Élysée.

In a state of great emotion, she went upstairs, and, without even having herself announced, she entered the Tsar's study. She found Alexander a prey to a feverish agitation which surprised her all the more by its contrast to the calm of Napoleon III.

No doubt by reaction, having made a superhuman effort to control himself in public, he was giving way to his natural feelings. He was pacing nervously up and down and talking of returning at once to Russia.

Despite her wish to be rid of such a dangerous guest, the Empress felt she ought to show him that he could not cut his visit short without appearing to run away in the face of threats from the anarchists ... The attempted assassination would serve as a lesson: it would prevent other attempts, and mean that the police precautions would be redoubled. The official programme was not yet over, it must be carried out to the end. There were only another two days: a fête that evening, given by the Préfet de la Seine, and an excursion next day to Fontainebleau.

The Tsar allowed himself to be convinced. He agreed to appear at the grand ball at the Hôtel de Ville that evening.

This so-called festivity particularly alarmed the Emperor and Empress, and concerned the police; for, in these dangerous circumstances, the doors would be open wide to countless guests, and would make supervision very difficult.

Napoleon III had no fears at all for himself. He was a fatalist, and he believed in his star, which, until now, had always protected him. He trusted not so much in his police as in the piercing eyes of his wife, which discovered conspirators in the crowd. More than once, with the mere suggestion of her steely eyes, she had paralysed the assassin's arm; in a number of trials, certain people who had been arrested had confessed that they had felt themselves to be discovered when the Empress's clear gaze had focused on them, and that they had not dared to fire their revolvers.

And so, as they entered the ballroom, the Emperor advised the Empress to keep watch on their guest. 'Have no fear,' she answered, 'I shall be his shield.'

She graciously took Alexander's arm. He was more moved than he cared to appear. Then, apparently pressing against him, like a coquette, she rested her elbow, closely, on her escort's back, and enveloped him like a living shield to guard his heart against any treacherous stab from a dagger.

All these precautions remained unnecessary; the ball passed without incident. The attempt on his life had aroused the general indignation, and had given the Tsar a new popularity. People acclaimed him for his courage, and they anticipated magnanimity towards the assassin of eighteen who seemed, now, only a desperate patriot.

Confidence was being restored.

* * *

Only twenty-four hours before the departure!

The last day was spent in the country. Far away from the metropolis, people would breathe a purer air, the strain would be eased. As they left the streets behind, drew closer to nature, they would be safer from the wickedness of men ...

As they got out of the train, on the platform at Fontainebleau

22

station, while the two Sovereigns were talking to each other – no doubt relieved by the prospect of the imminent departure – the Prefect came up to the Empress, and whispered to her that they had discovered an enormous plot to kill the Tsar. All the conspirators had been arrested – except for one dangerous anarchist, who had managed to escape. He had left for Fontaine-bleau, declaring that he would succeed where Berezowski had failed. The Tsar must therefore be shut up all day in the château, where surveillance would be easier, and, whatever happened, he must be prevented from walking in the forest where they had planned to exercise the hounds, and to have a picnic . . .

The Empress was terrified, and she wanted to tell the Emperor about her fears at once, and to agree about the precautions which must be taken; but she could not speak to him, he was so absorbed in his guest, and she was determined, above all, not to alarm Alexander, since she knew how nervous he was. She therefore had to resign herself in silence, and to keep her anguish to herself. They had to get to the château as soon as possible. She climbed into one of the *chars-à-bancs* which were waiting for the guests, she made the Tsar sit beside her, and asked Napoleon to sit on his other side. Alexander found himself wedged between the two Sovereigns who hedged him in like a bodyguard. Anyone who struck the guest would have had to strike the hosts.

The journey passed without incident. They reached the palace, and the Empress, who had been in anguish on the journey, felt a little reassured. But she had still been unable to confide in the Emperor, who had planned a ride in the forest. When he got out of the carriage, Napoleon asked her why she was so silent and so agitated. She took advantage of a moment when the Tsar was talking to his son to tell her husband, quickly, about the advice from the Prefect of Police, and to repeat that, whatever happened, Alexander must not be allowed to leave the palace during the day. They must therefore contrive to entertain him within the four walls . . . They had *déjeuner*, they prolonged the meal as long as possible, but what was to happen after that? . . . How could they keep the Tsar, how could they prevent him from going out? How could they occupy him? Amuse him for twelve hours? . . .

The Empress began by offering to take her guest on an exhaustive tour of the palace. She escorted him from cellar to attic, displayed her wit and erudition, and told him piquant anecdotes about every room. She talked about Queen Christina of Sweden and Monaldeschi, Louis XIV, Napoleon I; she showed him the table on which the abdication had been signed, she called all the Sovereigns to her aid, she quoted the historic sayings – and even

23

the apocryphal ones. She summoned up her personal recollections; she showed him the most important pieces in the Chinese museum, the golden vases from the Temple of Heaven, she identified the ladies in Winterhalter's *Decameron* . . .

In fact she was the charmer that she could be, when she chose . . .

But the Tsar reproached himself for tiring her, and he suggested a walk in the park. She maintained that it was too hot . . . He asked several times for the promised programme to be carried out. He very much wanted to see the forest, and watch the hounds being exercised . . .

They told him that the paths had become impassable because of the recent rain. As he insisted, they had to warn Count Schouvaloff of the danger which threatened his master, if he took a walk in the forest, and they finally stayed imprisoned in the palace until the Russians caught the train for St Petersburg.

Thank heavens! No doubt a sigh of relief escaped the Emperor and Empress on the departure of such a dangerous guest . . .

Apart from some satisfaction to vanity – acquired at the cost of much trouble and anguish – this visit, from which they expected a Franco-Russian alliance, produced the diametrically opposite effect. Bismarck and Gortchakoff reached an understanding behind Rouher's back, uncle and nephew drew closer together and allied themselves against the democratic Government of France.

The Berezowski affair did the rest. For a moment they had dreamed of turning the attempted assassination to the advantage of the good cause. The assassin would naturally have been condemned to death. Alexander would then have intervened and asked for his reprieve, which would, naturally, have been granted to him. This magnanimity would doubtless have restored some Polish sympathy to the autocrat.

Instead of this excellently ordered *combinazione*, the jury decided that there were extenuating circumstances, and they therefore deprived the Tsar of the occasion to make a noble gesture. Alexander was doubly angry at the indulgence of French justice, and the regrettable impression which he took away from his visit to France may have helped to prevent his intervention to help Napoleon III in 1870.

And Mme Adam, in her *Memoirs*, which are often prophecies – published after they have come true – declares that the Duc Decazes had seen the hand of Bismarck in Berezowski's attempt at assassination.[1]

5

In the summer of 1867, Gégé Primoli returned to Saint-Gratien. He claimed that his notes had hardly been altered when he eventually published them.

1 August

This morning I lay in wait for Théo[phile Gautier] in the park, where he was taking his daily walk before *déjeuner*.

At the turn of a path, I saw him appear. Like his Capitaine Fracasse, he was wearing a broad-brimmed grey felt hat. He had adorned it with a swan's feather, which he had doubtless found by the lake. He advanced slowly, solemnly, leaning on a gold-topped cane; he might have been the Jupiter of Olympus down from his pedestal.

He did not avoid me, an intruder; he invited me to walk with him. He seemed to take pleasure in dazzling the adolescent, whose eyes he felt fixed on his own with unconcealed admiration, and he deigned to talk to him as an equal.

According to his habit, especially in the country, Gautier had brought with him the seed of a sonnet which, in a sleepless hour last night, had burgeoned in his mind. His first poetic salutation was of course addressed to the lady of the house *quae nobis haec otia fecit*. When I disturbed his solitude, he was finishing the first quatrain; at my request, in the heat of inspiration, he recited it with boyish enthusiasm:

> Hôte pour quelques jours de votre beau domaine,
> Voyant le gai soleil qui dore le matin
> Et perce d'un rayon les feuilles de satin,
> Je descends dans le parc et tout seul m'y promène.

He did not pause in his slow, majestic walk to continue his

25

sonnet. New images, he said, would present themselves at the moment when he thought about them least.

In fact, at the edge of the wood he caught a rhyme that had escaped him in his room, because – impeccable in his occasional verses as he was in his great poems – he wanted it to be perfect, with consonance of stress, and to conform with the strictest rules of prosody; otherwise, he rejected it like a parasitic, useless word. He always went from rhyme to idea. From time to time one of those rare, familiar rhymes sang in his memory and recalled him to his task without interrupting his conversation. So it was that he divided himself and made one watch the flowering of his poem. At last the noonday sun pierced the clouds and, in its rays, like some marvellous flower, the sonnet half opened its petals and soon blossomed.

We continued to wander on in silence, or, rather, to circle slowly in a restricted space, without the poet's seeming to dream of the work that he was sculpting within himself . . . The improvisation flowed on, silently, like a subterranean stream, and, when we reached the point of departure, the four lines had described our marking time and the second quatrain had been finished:

> On pense aller bien loin, mais tout sentier ramène,
> – Quand il vous a montré le village lointain, –
> À travers prés et bois, par un contour certain,
> Au portique où César a mis l'aigle romaine . . .

The bell for *déjeuner* interrupted our walk and summoned us back to the château. Théo saw the Princess in the distance, coming down the steps to meet us. He was put on his mettle, and, as he followed the path which led us back to her, he improvised the final tercets. He greeted her with them in his grave, harmonious voice, as he approached her and kissed the hand which she held out to him with her welcoming grace.

> À la blanche villa, votre temple d'été,
> Où, lasse du fardeau de la divinité,
> Vous daignez n'être plus que la bonne princesse.

> Ainsi fait mon esprit trompé dans ses détours:
> Il croit poursuivre un rêve interrompu sans cesse
> Et devant votre image il se trouve toujours.[1]

3 August

As we were strolling in the park, we reached a pinewood. Under a canopy of sombre branches interlacing over the azure sky, there

26

stood a few little columns of black and white marble; each of them bore a date and a name: Phil, Soc, Miss, Ronflot . . .

It was the cemetery of the Princess's dogs.

Gautier, that charmer of cats, could not of course feel excessive sympathy for their traditional enemies. Only the previous evening, he had made his profession of faith. He had been vexed by the Princess's indifference. Instead of listening to his own gallant conversation, she was absorbed by her little pack of dogs, abandoning her hands to their kisses. He feigned a gesture of comic jealousy and, to the great scandal of the assembled company, he declared his aversion for the canine race. 'Yes, I hate dogs,' he said, boldly, 'because they always take the place of a human being. They monopolize caresses which could make men happy.'

The sight of their tombs roused gentler feelings. He wanted to address his salutation to the ghosts of these faithful 'four-footed hearts', as the blind painter Anastasi used to call them – which had been so tenderly cherished by their mistress. He also wanted to excuse his hostile tirade of the previous day, and answer the profane who smiled at this posthumous cult. So he improvised this epitaph which I noted down:

> Avec raison, sous cet ombrage,
> On a fait des tombeaux aux chiens,
> Car s'ils n'avaient parfois la rage,
> Ils vaudraient mieux que des chrétiens.[2]

4 August

A walk in the park. Théo talked to me about education which, according to him, has three keys to open the mind of youth: the key of reading, the key of drawing and the key of music. The first key teaches us to understand, the second to see and the third to feel . . . 'It is a mistake,' he said, 'for the university curriculum to demand Latin verses and exclude French ones, which are excellent gymnastics for the mind: they teach one to write good prose, to concentrate one's thoughts, to polish one's style, to find transitions.' The love of *rimes riches* has preserved him, so he maintains, from bad taste and from banalities. 'One of the most characteristic features of nineteenth-century literature,' so he went on, 'is that all the great poets have written equally well in prose: Hugo, Musset, Lamartine, Vigny. On the other hand, there are essentially poetic natures which have never managed to lay a good verse: Jean-Jacques, the precursor of Romanticism; Chateaubriand, all impregnated with poetry, justly considered to be the father of the

27

generation of 1830; Mme Sand, whose novels are sometimes prose-poems. Balzac tried to embark on an epic poem, and fortunately stopped at the first line, which remains famous:

Ô Inca, ô roi infortuné et malheureux! . . .

Each of them, as Banville said of the bad verse of Scribe, seems to have received the gift of not rhyming.'[3]

6 August

This morning Théo saw how eagerly I drank in his words, and he paused. He looked me in the eyes and said that, at my age, it was impossible that I had not 'wooed the Muse,' as people put it during the Restoration. He understood from my embarrassment that he had guessed right, and ordered me to recite to him then and there.

The previous week I had celebrated my fifteenth year [Primoli had actually been sixteen in May] in one of those enthusiastic odes which, in the heady days of adolescence, rise from the heart to the lips without concern for rhythm and rhyme. Blushing deeply, and half choking with emotion, I murmured the insipid stanzas which the good Princess, in her affection for me, had been pleased to send to her intellectual mentor.

Sainte-Beuve, for he it was, tried to please his imperial correspondent. He answered in phrases which were certainly more poetic than my vapid lucubrations. I haven't the least illusion as to why I earned the excessively kind judgement of the critic who, on this one occasion, turned courtier, but I cannot refrain from quoting it, not so much for the vague compliments which it contains for me as for the exquisite way in which it is expressed.

I have read these charming lines which embody the fragrance and, as it were, the rapture of the springtime of life. The sap flows from the young tree in bloom. There is a lively sense of harmony. All that remains is to find a subject for this youthful and still aimless poetry. These subjects appear of their own accord. I congratulate the nice young man whose talent is taking wing.

I was touched to the heart, not so much by this undeserved praise, as by the severity of Théo. He seemed to take me seriously, and he did not spare me his observations on the poverty of my rhymes and the carelessness of my prosody. I felt especially flattered when, in the heat of his criticism, the faultless writer forgot himself and used the intimate form of address. This familiarity from master to disciple made me prouder than a Spanish grandee *tutoyé* by his king: I felt I had been consecrated as a poet!

My childish pride knew no bounds when, on his return to the château, Théophile Gautier addressed this impromptu madrigal to my young mother. In her natural blindness she took it literally:

> Votre fils fait des vers: à cette fantaisie,
> Chacun, en l'admirant, se récrie étonné:
> Quoi de plus naturel que de la Poésie,
> Comme un fruit d'une fleur, un poète soit né?

. . . Alas [added Primoli, years later], I have far from realized the master's prediction. I have had to come down a good many pegs since then.[4]

* * *

Meanwhile, on 1 September 1867, the *collégien* continued his diary.

Saint-Gratien. That is the name of Princess Mathilde's country house, where I have been staying for several days. It is an hour from Paris, and ten minutes from Enghien . . . At either end of the house is a large room almost entirely glazed in . . . One is the dining-room and the other is the studio. Over these two wings are two large terraces, one of them next to the Princess's room, with a view over the lake . . . It is all surrounded by vivid, sweet-smelling flowers. On every side there are varied and delightful views, and, in front of the verandah, the great trees part to reveal a vast meadow which stretches as far as the eye can see. Baskets of fragrant flowers are strung out here and there, and blue porcelain vases filled with red geraniums. Occasionally, a clump of pines or plane-trees breaks the monotony of the meadow. The horizon is boundless; at the back of the picture, one vaguely catches a glimpse of the fields, the white roofs of the village on the slopes of the hills. In the foreground, on the right, is the lake which reflects the sunlight. On the left are impenetrable clumps of trees; and, here and there, the daylight pierces through the foliage.

At 7 o'clock, the château stirs, the green shutters open, the valets sweep and dust; the gardeners water the shrubs, and change the flowers in the rooms. At 11 o'clock they ring the first bell for *déjeuner*, at 11.15 they ring the second, and all the guests assemble on the verandah from which they pass into the dining-room. After *déjeuner* they go back to the salons, smoke, and read the papers, and chat until about 1 o'clock. Then the Princess goes to work in her studio, you are free to follow her or to go back to your room. Usually you go out in a carriage at 4 o'clock, get out at some beauty spot, and walk for an hour and a half; then you pick up the carriage in another village. There are countless walks in the neighbourhood, the roads are picturesque, and for the most part they are carriageable, but the Princess never tires of walking. At half past six we come back to dress, because we dine at 7 o'clock; there are always a few people coming from Paris . . .

After dinner we go back to the salons. The men smoke and the women work and chat. We play cards or lotto, we read the papers until 11.30 when we part company . . .[5]

On 31 August Mr Taine came to dine here to take his leave, he's going to join his sister in the country . . .

Mr Taine is not much more than 38 [he was thirty-nine] but he wants to seem older; he is quite tall and rather thin but he doesn't hold himself well; his head is a real German head, pale and fair, his expression is gentle and intelligent, his face is interesting and aristocratic, his blue eyes are full of kindness as well as fire, but unfortunately, in spite of the blue spectacles he wears, they are squinting. He possesses the charm of speech to such a degree that one hardly notices this slight infirmity. He was very witty – perhaps too witty; I think he listens to his own conversation. When you hear him it's like deciphering a manuscript: first he says something clever, in an unstudied form; then comes the correction, he repeats the same idea, but more clearly; gradually the idea emerges into broad daylight . . .

His greatest pleasure, so he says, is to go and shut himself up in an old monastery, and there continually re-read his two favourite poems: *Iphigénie en Tauride*, by Goethe, and a romance in verse by Miss B. Browning [*sic*], *Aurora Leigh*.

As for French poets, the only one he knows and appreciates is Musset. Hugo is a giant, grandiose when he is not absurd; Lamartine is also a giant, but more edulcorated; as for M. Gautier, he attaches so much importance to harmony, even to the detriment of good sense, that he is merely a musician. [M. Taine] goes so far as to find only one line in Racine, one of the most insignificant: 'La fille de Minos et de Pasiphaë.'[6]

Aunt Mathilde has just taken refuge in her room so as not to see a boring man who, though he is banned, has made his appearance in the salon. The M[arquis] Strozzi . . . is nearly 60, and for the past 35 years, since he first knew her, he has believed himself to be in love with Princess Mathilde . . .

30

He has proposed marriage six times to the lady of his dreams, and, having been refused six times, he threw himself, in despair, into the Arno, from which he was pulled out safe and sound though no doubt rather wet.[7]

We have had Théophile Gautier here for a fortnight. He's certainly the most agreeable man I have ever met. He has all the qualities of the great genius without his arrogance . . . I've heard him talk clothes with women, and turn philosophers into poets. He is a master of the art of conversation, and – while he sometimes delights in toying with the fan of paradox, which he does with incredible dexterity – he expresses sound new ideas in poetic and original forms . . .

But wit is the least of his qualities; he has feeling and excessive delicacy . . . How does this almost wild exterior hide a susceptibility which even the heroine of a novel doesn't possess? He has a fine head, and I think he still keeps some claim to masculine beauty . . . His hair is still hanging down his neck, but a few threads of silver mingle with the jet locks; his eyes are still dark, but the fire has gone out in them as it does in the eyes of a vanquished lion . . .

During his stay at Saint-Gratien, he was finishing a report on nineteenth-century poetry for the Académie . . . [He] assured us that there were many gifted poets today, especially one called Leconte de Lisle . . . Then he read us a little comedy called *Pierrot posthume ou Le Tricorne enchanté* in which he claimed to have given a faultless imitation of Molière . . . I love hearing Théo read: he sits on the carpet, cross-legged, in the oriental style. He read all sorts of things, mostly poetry, including *Tristesse d'Olympio*, which he says is Victor Hugo's masterpiece.[8]

Undated [2 October?]

Théo talked to me this morning about his admiration for *Renée Mauperin*, the engaging novel which the Goncourts have dedicated to him.

The two brothers were the first novelists [he said] who dared to paint the young girl of today as she really is – *les demoiselles* Benoiton are caricatures. However well brought up a young girl or a young woman may be today, one cannot prevent her from breathing the everyday air. She always has a father, a brother or a husband who spends a large part of his life with courtesans, or simply at the club; and he unconsciously brings home something indefinable which he passes on to his sister or his wife: a young girl is corrupted by her father! And then she sees them in

31

the street and brushes against them in the crowd: lorettes with made-up faces, gold-dust in their hair, and trailing flounces down their backs, saying come hither, inviting passers-by . . .

Naturally, a purist like myself is particularly struck by the intrusion of slang into the most exclusive salons. When something annoys the Princess, she dares to say: 'What a bore!' If Mme de Maintenon had surprised that observation on the lips of the Duchesse de Bourgogne, she would have fainted. . . The Empress herself, however impeccable she may be, however inaccessible to the noise of the outside world in her ivory tower, does not escape the contagion. One day, when she had decorated her boudoir at the Tuileries, she actually said to me: 'I'm furnished at last!' 'Is Your Majesty furnished,' I replied, slightly surprised, 'in rosewood or mahogany?' And then you mustn't think that there's a great difference between the salons of the *haute bicherie* and the Princess's *hôtel*. At Mme de P[aïva]'s and at other courtesans', one meets the same guests, Sainte-Beuve, Renan, Taine, Saint-Victor, the Goncourts, etc. There are the same scents by Houbigant and Lubin, the same dresses by Worth or Laferrière. Each of them wants to believe that the other is ill-washed, ill-dressed. But one of them wants above all to appear the great lady, because she isn't that by birth, and the grace of the other consists in making one forget her rank. None of this means – as some people claim – that we are today witnessing a great decline in morals: far from it! Read the memoirs of the eighteenth century, and you will see with what shameless unawareness the most honoured noblemen of the time – from the Régence to the Revolution – boast of crimes which today would send them straight to penal servitude . . .[9]

Théophile Gautier is over fifty [Primoli continued], but his aesthetic sense has survived his youth, and it sometimes gives him the illusion that he could still declaim the triumphant couplet which he wrote in his twentieth year:

> Je suis jeune, le sang dans mes veines abonde,
> Mes cheveux sont de jaïs et mes regards de feu . . .

The Princess wanted to moderate his enthusiasm, and, à propos of Mme Sand, who has cloistered herself at Nohant, she said to him:

'There comes a time when one must abandon external pretentions, and the mind must take the place of everything . . .'

'Forgive me, Princess,' he replied, 'writers and actors are ten years younger than the vulgar bourgeois. One can fall in love with them through the characters which they create or represent. If a young girl read my verse, conceived an irresistible passion for the poet, and came to cónfess it to him, what would you do in his place?'

'I should make her understand her folly, and I should not abuse it.'

'Oh, Princess, how little you know about men and poets! . . . To show this reserve that you suggest, one would have to be a saint or a dotard.'

'No, you would just have to be a gentleman.'

'Well, perhaps you're right: the misfortune with most men is that they forget to treat women as the children which they really are – the children which they never cease to be.'

* * *

There was one unlikely admirer, whom Théo certainly did not expect, and that was Count Bismarck. There was a young woman at Saint-Gratien who collected the autographs of famous people. She sent her album to the Minister, who had accompanied his Sovereign to the Exhibition of 1867. In the train that took him back to Prussia, the messenger handed Bismarck the precious little book. Leafing through it, he was struck by the clear and minuscule writing, which covered two or three pages. It was the famous poem, *Les Vieux de la Vieille*, which describes the march-past of the ghosts of the [Imperial Guard on their] disastrous retreat from Russia:

> Si leurs mains tremblent, c'est sans doute
> Du froid de la Bérésina,
> Et s'ils boitent, c'est que la route
> Est longue du Caire à Wilna.
>
> S'ils sont perclus, c'est qu'à la guerre
> Les drapeaux étaient leurs seuls draps,
> Et si leur manche ne va guère,
> C'est qu'un boulet a pris leur bras.

The future Prince read the poem; then he added, in a corner of the page: 'Pregnies Station, 14 June 1867. Von Bismarck regretted that he had not written this.'

Did he simply regret that he had not written this tragic ode, or did he really regret that he had not yet provoked another retreat from Russia, which he was already ruminating in his bloodthirsty dreams? Did he see the festive Bengal lights of 1867 illuminate the blaze of 1870?[10]

* * *

[October 1867]

. . . This morning, at *déjeuner*, the châtelaine was talking about an article which she had just read in her paper. It had made her very angry. A so-called critic had violently attacked a young artist whose beginnings she had encouraged. The good Princess was justly proud: at the private view of the Salons she had bought the first pictures which had been exhibited by young people who had since become more or less famous. She had found a certain satisfaction in showing the first Bonnat, the first Detaille, the first Roybet, the first Zamacoïs, the first Jacquet in her gallery of modern pictures; and often, when they became fashionable, these artists had lost some of their original qualities.

Gautier, with his usual kindness, attempted to defend his colleague. According to him, he had tried to do his work as honestly as he could. The Princess rebuked him violently:

'I have a horror of these human failures,' she said, becoming heated. 'They cannot hold a brush themselves, and they adorn themselves with the splendid title of art critics to attack the people who know much more about it than they do. By what right do these pretentious fools allow themselves to judge artists?'

'This reproach doesn't touch me,' answered Gautier, impertubably calm, 'because *anch'io son pittore!*'

'Yes, you're a painter, but you paint with your pen . . . It isn't the same thing . . .'

'Oh, no, Princess, I began by being an art student. I used to go to Rioult's studio – I was his best pupil. It was half a century ago.'

'Oh, that's too long ago, you must have forgotten everything.'

'I have regretted all my life that I abandoned my first calling . . . Since then, all I've done is to make transpositions of art.' . . .

* * *

In fact, the 'perfect magician of French literature', as Baudelaire christened him, loved only poetry, his natural language . . .

It was of course his princess who inspired him, and all his verses turned towards her as the sunflowers turn towards the sun . . .

'Do you remember,' asked one of her guests, 'do you remember the charm and wit with which he sang of your endearing grace? When an ingenious thought, a witticism fell from your lips, he gathered them up at once like so many jewels . . . And, if he

34

praised your sweet relationship, that bond he described so charmingly as *amitié voluptueuse*, if he extolled the particular elegance of your dress, you said at once, delighted by his perfect cadenced prose: "Come, Gautier, a sonnet!" The poet who proclaimed himself your own, the old lion who became a Newfoundland dog at your feet, did not keep you waiting.'[11]

6

Gégé Primoli was not the only diarist in his family. His aunt, Julie Bonaparte, the Marquise de Roccagiovine, kept a voluminous journal entitled 'Notes et souvenirs'. She also filled numerous exercise-books with extracts from her reading, portraits of relatives, and notes on politics and literature. Sainte-Beuve had begged her to lend him one of her notebooks, no doubt hoping (as Gégé was to surmise)

> that he might find some anecdote in it to add spice to one of his *Lundis*. Flattered in her self-esteem as an author, she hastened to send him the little book he wanted; but, in her hurry to satisfy the critic, she sent him the first of her notebooks that came to hand. She forgot that it contained an invidious page about Sainte-Beuve, the author of *Volupté*, in which she described his unedifying domestic life. Alas, instead of smiling at this blunder, Sainte-Beuve divulged it in his most cutting style, and filled the poor feckless woman with despair. When Napoleon III was told of his cousin's error, he simply said with his usual phlegm: 'How can one conceivably write down what one thinks of people?'[1]

It was not the end of her misfortunes. On 16 June 1868, Sainte-Beuve told Princess Mathilde about Princess Julie's blunder.[2] On 28 June, Princess Mathilde announced to Sainte-Beuve: 'Apparently she went to the Collège [Rollin] to tell Joseph about her adventure. He . . . made her tear up a page which was no less flattering for Flaubert.'[3] It was strange that Princess Julie chose to tell a nephew of seventeen, but Gégé was already a good listener, especially to confessions. He already used his persuasive powers.

In the autumn of 1868, the shrewd, inquisitive *collégien*

returned once again to Saint-Gratien. He was well aware of the crisis in the life of its châtelaine. Since 1846, when her marriage to Demidoff had ended, Princess Mathilde had been the mistress of the Comte de Nieuwerkerke. He had been an ambitious lover, well aware of his Bonaparte connection. Through her influence, he had become Surintendant des Beaux-Arts, a Senator, and a member of the Institut de France; he had amassed a constellation of sinecures and decorations. He had also proved himself notoriously unfaithful; and now, when she was forty-eight, the long liaison had ended. Primoli recorded events.

Wednesday, 14 October 1868

I spent a month at Saint-Gratien, the month of September. The Princess was not as happy as usual, but I still enjoyed myself with her . . .

As I say, my aunt was sadder this year: she feels she's growing old, and she finds herself alone. How unhappy they are, the women who are obliged to leave their husbands!

M is in this situation . . . For twenty years [in fact twenty-three years] she has been, so to speak, morality itself in her immorality. She has sacrificed everything to the man she loves. Her brother and father have quarrelled with her; misfortune has brought them together and reconciled them.

As long as she was young, beautiful, attractive, and, above all, influential, she was adored, surrounded by admirers, almost happy . . . One day she became aware that her hair was turning grey, and that her circle of friends had curiously shrunk . . .

She has sacrificed everything to the man she loves: her honour, her friends, and her beliefs, and now that he has had every advancement which she could procure him, he is turning from her.[4]

[Undated]

I spent Sunday at Saint-Gratien with my aunt Mathilde . . .

Oh, I do love her, because when I think about her the tears come into my eyes and a strange tremor runs through my body . . . My ideal is composed of her and my mother . . . When I read, it is always the two of them who assume the likeness of the heroine . . . That is my dearest dream, the one in which I cradle myself before I go to sleep.

If she had only had a passable husband, I am sure that M would

37

have been the most virtuous of all women . . . No, it had to be as it is, the other was impossible, for then perfection would have dwelt on earth, God would have been jealous, He would have called Her back to Him.

This is how I imagine the enchantresses of Antiquity and the Saints of Christianity to have been . . .

And yet how happy her loving soul, her loyal heart would easily have been if she could have leant nobly on a husband's arm and given her other hand to a child! Oh, a child! . . . A child of hers! How she would have kissed it, adored it, spoilt it! . . . She wouldn't have had the time to love anyone else! . . . When she sinks into these unhappy dreams, the tears must surely come into her eyes . . . She has come to have a horror of marriage and husbands, she says she wouldn't want to have children . . .

Really, if she were younger, and I were older, I should think I was in love with her . . .

What fools, what utter fools they are, the people who think that love consists in material advantages!

I only want to know it as late as possible, and I have vowed to myself to remain a virgin until I am in love, really in love with a woman . . .

What's the use of falling in love? I'm so happy as I am: I love my mother so![5]

[Autumn]

I have been with Mother to Worth's. He is the great couturier in fashion. He charges sixteen hundred francs for a simple little costume! Ladies arrange to meet at Worth's, and they talk politics there as they sip tea. At Worth's, the faubourg Saint-Germain sits between two kept women, and the world of officialdom meets the faubourg Saint-Germain. Perhaps M. Worth doesn't even realize what he is doing, but . . . he is reconciling all political parties, and mingling all social classes. An artistically rumpled bit of fabric has achieved what wit has been unable to contrive.

And so M. Worth gives delightful *matinées*. I don't only mean on his first floor in the rue de la Paix, where all the young men look like embassy attachés with their English accents, curled hair, pearl tie-pins and turquoise rings . . .; I don't only mean the apartment which exhales some atmosphere of degraded aristocracy, some heady fragrance of elegance, wealth, and forbidden fruit . . . Besides this apartment, I may add, M. Worth has a country house at Suresnes, and the noble faubourg aspires to the honour of being received there. This villa, it appears, is full of marvels of every kind. People go there in *séries*, as they do to Compiègne.[6]

On Saturday, 12 September, from the rue de Lille, Prosper Mérimée asked the Princess: 'Will Your Imperial Highness allow me to bring her my head, like St Denis, at about two o'clock on Monday?'[7] The date was apparently changed, for Primoli gave a different account of events. He recorded in his diary how Mérimée sat to the Imperial artist.

Prosper Mérimée [His Literary Majesty] wrote to the Princess that he would like to see her painting a watercolour. She answered at once; she invited him to *déjeuner* next day at Saint-Gratien, and said that she would then sketch his portrait.

And so he arrived by the 10 o'clock train – I might have said the hearse, because he looked exactly like a stuffed corpse. His movements are slow, and when he moves you seem to hear the creaking of bones . . . His sparse hair is completely white, and brushed up over his ears. He has a huge, creased forehead, ending in two bushes of black eyebrow; the brows which shook Olympus could not have been more terrible, and they are the most notable features of his face. As for his glance, it is lacklustre, only his smile keeps its youthful, mocking expression.

If it were not for the size, which was either too large or too small, the watercolour would have been quite successful. As for the model, I have never seen him pose worse than he did during the sitting. At the beginning I gave him a packet of twelve cigarettes, and two hours later he had smoked them all. And so my poor asphyxiated aunt was obliged to quit her easel, to go out and leave the rest for next day.[8]

Wednesday [undated]

The Comte de Nieuwerkerke, whom my aunt loves so much, is the absolute model of a French gentleman. He is handsome, proud, a man of taste, but excessively touchy and self-centred: he has all the pettinesses of grandeur.[9]

[Undated]

You don't know what St Gratien means to her: this park made up of patches of vineyards and fields which she has stitched together, this park where she has sown the grass and marked out the paths with her own hand. Every tree reminds her of a moment in her life. And so she wanders round there for days on end, among her gardeners, stirring memories with every step and contemplating hopes which have yet to bloom. It was there, for fifteen years, that she scattered her happiness around her. Is it not there, and there alone, that she should find contentment once again?[10]

28 December

I went to Princess Mathilde's [in Paris] . . . I found her alone in her delightful studio, among her dogs and flowers and pictures. She stretched out on a chaise longue, and I sat on the floor, and we talked for nearly two hours.

She told me that the previous evening she had had a visit from Olozaga, the first lover of Isabella the Catholic, and the present Ambassador from the Spanish Republic. He told her ignoble things about the former Court in Madrid.[11]

*　*　*

She herself had a Court. As Primoli was later to recall:

With the natural timidity which this assembly imposed on me, . . . I used to slip behind a palm-tree where I hid myself, and, in my corner I became intoxicated with these discussions, which were sometimes aesthetic, sometimes gallant, rarely political, in which they vied in wit and eloquence, all these different people who, half a century later, have disappeared and become ancestors.

There were Sainte-Beuve, Renan, Taine, the Goncourts, Saint-Victor, Rivière, Octave Feuillet, Flaubert, Mérimée, Émile Augier, Alexandre Dumas *fils*, Popelin, Caro, Coppée, Lavoix, Heredia . . . There were musicians: Gounod, Sauzay, Saint-Saëns . . . There were scientists: Pasteur, Claude Bernard, Blanchard, Berthelot, Joseph Bertrand, Adolphe Franck, Dieulafoy . . . There were artists: Hébert, Baudry, Carpeaux, Chaplain, Gérôme, the Girauds, Dupré, Boulanger, Bonnat, Detaille, Amaury Duval, Fromentin . . .

And then there were the unexpected visits of sovereigns who were passing through Paris: the Queens of the Netherlands, Spain and Portugal. One fine day the Shah of Persia disembarked at the little harbour on Lake Enghien; his appearance would deserve a page to itself. Another day it was Abd-el-Kader, who had always been grateful to Napoleon III for freeing him from prison on his accession to the throne. When the Emir was first received by the Emperor, he greeted him in his picturesque language and said to him: 'My eyes had long been jealous of my ears.' And, on the fall of the Empire, he wrote to the Empress Eugénie: 'Only the sun and moon have an eclipse.'

At Saint-Gratien, while Carpeaux was quietly sketching him, the Emir wrote in an album a line of Arabic which the interpreter

40

translated like this: 'My heart tells me that it is you who make me suffer; I shall sacrifice my soul for you, whether you know it or not. ABD-EL-KADER.'

* * *

But of all these illustrious personages, the most eloquent, the wittiest, the most dazzling, the most original, the one who had the art of giving himself entirely in conversation, and opening horizons for his listeners with a magic word, was Théophile Gautier.

I transcribe this sketch of him which the Princess drew herself. One will recognize a touch which is feminine rather than literary: 'He was a man of middle height with a broad, long torso and short legs; he had the head of a southerner, a monocle to correct his short sight; he wore his hair long, curling on his neck, a relic of the Romantic of 1830. His expression was kind, though a little sleepy, his glance calm, without vivacity, like his gestures and his whole demeanour. In private he often sat on the floor, cross-legged, a cigar between his lips: you might have mistaken him for an oriental.'

It is in fact in this posture that I myself remember him at Saint-Gratien. I see him again at the feet of the Princess, gathering up the lines of poetry which seemed to be born under her magic glance, and making them into sonnets. 'Do you know,' Jules de Goncourt said to him one day, 'that with your half-closed eyes and your fine curly beard you make me think of Homer?' 'Oh,' replied Théo, 'at most a sad Anacreon!' Anacreon or Homer, everyone was dazzled by this magician of words . . .

More than once, I tried to note his improvisations in verse and prose, but the pencil soon dropped from my fingers, I was so bemused, and I could only delight in what he said. With his inexhaustible verve he constantly began anew, and, when I was going to fix a word, another one arose which made me forget the one I had wanted to catch.

Only the artistic style of the Goncourts in their *Journal*, the accuracy of Bergerat in his *Entretiens*, can give a remote idea of Théo's conversation, and even they cannot render the charm of his deep voice which – as the Princess rightly observed – 'gave his words the appearance of singularly original axioms'. Nor can they recall the charm of the simple, harmonious gestures which accompanied and completed his words. People have managed to catch a few sparks of this dazzling, winged speech; but, trying in my turn to catch them in my clumsy hands, I should be afraid of finding only dust on my fingertips.[12]

41

7

1869

Edmond de Goncourt is nine years older than Jules, and yet I have never seen more perfect and more extraordinary harmony. One of them wears the watch and the other carries the purse. When you talk to them separately, they will ask you the same questions and give you the same answers, without any previous consultation.

I only once knew them to disagree, and that was when one of them had to be decorated. The elder brother wanted it to be the younger brother. He was the one, he said, who wrote the most and showed the greatest wit. The younger brother wanted the elder to be decorated, saying that he had more good sense – and that he was older. This consideration prevailed. They were then at Trouville (August 1867). Mother wrote to congratulate Edmond; when he answered, he signed the letter alone but ended it: 'Your most grateful *friends Edmond* de Goncourt.'[1]

On 16 March came the Prince Imperial's birthday. Princess Mathilde, 'the most faithful and the most devoted of aunts,'[2] gave him a bicycle. The primitive, cumbersome machine is now in the Museo Napoleonico in Rome. Primoli recorded:

17 March

The Prince Imperial was thirteen yesterday. He celebrated by giving a dinner for twenty, to which he invited my brothers and me. I was on his right . . . There were toasts of every sort: to the Emperor, the Empress, the French Army, the Imperial Navy, the *garde mobile*. No one was forgotten, not even Michaux, the inventor of the velocipede, to whom the Prince gave an honourable mention.[3]

22 April

My aunt Mathilde told me that C[arpeaux, the sculptor] came to stay with her for a while at Saint-Gratien to do her bust, and that during the day he used to go and drink and gamble at the local inn with the coachmen and valets. She had had to ask Giraud to ask him to stop because it was strange to see him served at dinner in the evening by those with whom he'd clinked glasses in the morning.[4]

*   *   *

On 29 April, at a soirée at her *hôtel*, attended by the Emperor and Empress and *le Tout-Paris*, Princess Mathilde regaled her guests with a performance of *Le Passant*. This brief poetic drama – recently given at the Odéon – made the name of its author, the young François Coppée, and established both the actresses who took part in it: Agar and the youthful Sarah Bernhardt. Years later, Primoli recalled the scene in the rue de Courcelles:

> On the evening of 29 April 1869, the french windows of the salon were thrown open, and trains of satin and of velvet, lace and lamé gauze unfurled on the thick carpet. It was like Boccaccio's *Decameron* transported from Florence to Paris.
>
> Beside the statue in silvered bronze, *le petit Chanteur florentin*, by Paul Dubois, there stood a Florentine minstrel in flesh and blood, his hair escaping in glossy golden curls from his feathered cap. He was tuning his mandoline; he was waiting for Silvia's cue to spring on to the stage, where the sombre Agar, with her tragic countenance, was cursing love in harmonious poetry, her caressing tone belying her bitter words.
>
> While the blonde Zanetto, standing in the wings, hummed the song which was soon to be famous, the song which Massenet later set to music:
>
> Mignonne, voici l'avril . . .,

the reporter Marcellin pushed aside the shrubs, observed the room, and took this note for *La Vie Parisienne*: 'Here, in the wings, I am facing the audience . . . There, in the middle of the front row, are Their Majesties, showing exemplary benevolence and attention. What is the Emperor dreaming of, head bowed, and eyes half-closed? One cannot tell, but the Empress, absorbed, is watching the smallest gestures of the actress, the slightest shades of meaning in her performance, . . . her big eyes shining, open wide beneath her arched eyebrows, seeing everything.' . . .

The Emperor was so struck by Agar's classical beauty and noble attitudes that, as a result of this performance, he had her received by the Théâtre-Français where, soon afterwards, she gave the first performance of her poet's second play, *Les Deux Douleurs*, and brilliantly took the regal rôles in the repertoire.

As for the Empress, she was charmed by the golden voice of the blonde débutante. She did not only tell her how she admired her, she invited her to the Tuileries to repeat this pretty poem in dialogue for 'her little boy'. In her memoirs, Sarah Bernhardt gave an account of that private *soirée* in which one sees all the sweetness of the poor child who was to have such a tragic destiny . . .

This lunar play, as Théophile Gautier christened it, was the last ray of poetry which lit up the melancholy evening of the Second Empire.

* * *

On this occasion, once again, Gautier had been the kindly intermediary between a young poet and the Princess. One fine day, the modest clerk at the Ministère de la Guerre, living in humble rooms in Montmartre with his mother and elder sister, was dumbfounded by the arrival of the great Théo.

The master had been delegated by the Emperor's cousin to call on the author of *Le Passant*, which had delighted her, and to ask him to let her have his play performed for a sympathetic audience in the rue de Courcelles. All intellectual and official Paris attended this visual and intellectual festival, which was a notable event in the social annals of the time. Only one person failed to come. François Coppée had ordered his first tail coat for the occasion. But, alas, his delicate health seemed to be threatened by tuberculosis, and it obliged him to quit the mists of the Seine to warm himself in the sun of the South . . .

From the depths of his exile he sent a grateful sonnet to the good fairy who had befriended him, the Princess who never ceased to envelop him with maternal affection.

The evening's entertainment ended with a recitation of Hugo's ode: *Le Retour des cendres de Napoléon*, and with Gautier's poetic version of a passage of prose which Napoleon III – then a prisoner at Ham – had written on the return of the Emperor's body from St Helena.

44

These last stanzas [Primoli continued] were declaimed to general enthusiasm; then Their Majesties rose, and the audience dispersed through the salons.

The Sovereigns seemed enchanted not to feel themselves enclosed in the four walls of the Tuileries, not to restrict themselves to their official relationships. On this neutral ground, they could at last meet people who rarely came to Court, people with whom they could enjoy an ordinary conversation. The Emperor hid the emotion which he had felt at the recollection of his youth, and stopped to talk to the artist Eugène Giraud, who was standing respectfully as he passed, and he seemed to be amused by the broad stories which the joyful Bohemian was no doubt telling him. Indeed, he conversed with him long enough to intrigue the other guests. One of them, more inquisitive than the rest, did not resist the pleasure of enquiring what had been said. He whispered to the witty artist, who was strutting round happily after his Imperial tête-à-tête: 'What was the Emperor saying which seemed so interesting to both of you?' Giraud assumed an air of gravity and discretion, and murmured: 'Do you want to know? His Majesty was asking me for money.'

As for the Empress, she took leave of the guests at the door of the great salon, making her celebrated all-embracing curtsey, the great art of which was to make every person present say: 'She smiled at me!' Then she went to the boudoir which had been set aside for her, so that she could give her private audiences.

In the midst of a group of tail-coated men, towering over them with his great height, the Sovereign recognized Alexandre Dumas *fils*. He had been presented to her twenty years earlier, at the time of the 'Spanish marriages' at Seville, to which his father had been invited by the Duc de Montpensier; but he rarely went to the Tuileries. She had him summoned by a chamberlain; he came up at once, and bowed low. The Empress gave him her hand to kiss, and made him sit down beside her.

'Why,' she enquired, point-blank, as she toyed with her fan, 'why do you always extol the women of the demi-monde to the detriment of honest women?'

'Is it the woman of the world who is speaking to the dramatist? In that case, all I need to do is to offer her my humblest apologies. Or is it the Empress of the French who is questioning Alexandre Dumas? In that case, I shall answer . . .'

'That's how I mean it!' she interrupted, smiling. 'With your name and talent, your experience, authority and character, you could do a great service to your country and to the government, which would be only too happy to use your exceptional

45

abilities . . .'

'There is only one position I aspire to . . .'

'Which?'

'Oh, a place I couldn't get . . .'

'And why?'

'Because the post has not been created . . .'

'Tell me, anyway.'

'I should consent to be a Prefect . . .'

'In which *département*?'

'Oh, not so far away: Prefect of Morals! And if Your Majesty were to have me appointed this evening, the Government would throw me out tomorrow, because tonight I should send about ten of the smartest women in Paris to Saint-Lazare.'

'One can't have a serious conversation with you!'

* * *

Théophile Gautier was relieved that his *tour de force* had been a brilliant success; and, with the same smile, he received congratulations on his poem and condolences on his failure that morning at the Académie.

The Princess had been much more concerned with his candidature than he was himself, and she had brought to bear all the influence which she thought herself entitled to use. She had counted on a success, and she had hoped that this evening would be a twofold triumph for her poet.

During the day – according to her habit when she was interested in a candidate – she had gone to the Institut, where she had waited – generally with the permanent secretary – for the result of the ballot. This time, since she was late, she stayed in the courtyard . . . When she learned of Auguste Barbier's success and Gautier's failure, she could not contain herself, and every time an Academician passed her and she suspected that he had been hostile to her protégé, she relieved her anger by muttering an epithet which was hardly academic. Then she climbed into her brougham and had herself driven to Neuilly, where her poet lived, so that they could both unburden themselves. Her exasperation knew no bounds when she found herself faced with Théo's imperturbable calm. He welcomed her with a grateful smile, and he tried to soothe her. She believed in the immortality of the Académie; he had not believed that the Académie would make him immortal. And so he had only stood to please her, and he remained more or less indifferent to his failure.

'If at least they had elected one of our friends!' continued the Princess. 'But to reject you for an unknown man whose only claim to glory is the infamous diatribe which he spat at my uncle: this election is unworthy of the Académie-Française!'

'Forgive me, Princess, Auguste Barbier was very wrong to attack the Emperor, but he is not unknown, he is a poet, and the Académie has done itself honour in electing him.'

The Emperor's niece was speechless with indignation, and she could only answer angrily:

'If you think that, you've just got what you deserve . . . I will see you this evening, anyway!'

And she went back to the rue de Courcelles to superintend the preparations for her fête.[5]

* * *

Thursday, 26 August 1869

I spent Saturday at Saint-Gratien with Théophile Gautier, the Goncourt brothers and François Coppée . . . [Coppée] is twenty-six, but to judge by his beardless face and his timid manners you wouldn't think that he was more than twenty. He looked like Sardou and Bonaparte . . .

The Goncourts have come to Saint-Gratien for a few days, at last. The younger one is very ill with a liver complaint . . . When Edmond sees him in pain, he looks more ill than the invalid, and Jules controls himself so as not to alarm Edmond. No mother would show more concern for her child . . . After dinner they both played billiards, and then Mother sent Baby to bed with a poultice on the stomach. But I think that this very intimacy is the cause of the illness.[6]

* * *

That autumn, Théophile Gautier went to Egypt to attend the opening of the Suez Canal.[7] It was not an entirely successful voyage. Soon after he embarked on the *Mœris* at Marseilles, he slipped, dislocated his shoulder and broke his arm. In October he found himself at Shepheards Hotel in Cairo. He was incapacitated, homesick and forlorn as he awaited the opening ceremony, which was to be performed by the Empress Eugénie. As he explained to Princess Mathilde, his depression was suddenly lightened.

47

Princess,

Your letter, ornamented with an address, a model of imperial calligraphy, has reached me safely in Cairo, and I need not tell Your Highness what joy it has given me . . .

Yesterday I was in my room, and rather miserable, finding that time was long as one often does on one's travels, when the door opened and there appeared a charming youth, fresh and pink-cheeked, wearing a blue veil like a young Englishwoman. He smiled and called me by name. It was the poet of Saint-Gratien: the delightful Primoli in person. This meeting in Cairo has given me the liveliest pleasure. We see one another several times a day and we make excursions together. He will tell you better than I can of our visit to the Virgin's Tree, and our visit to the ruins of Heliopolis which were remarkable for their complete absence. The fortnight that remains before the opening of the Isthmus would have been long, but it will seem short in this pleasant company.[8]

I should have liked [continued Primoli] to describe our pilgrimage to the Virgin's Tree, so called because, they say, it gave shelter to the Holy Family . . .

Despite the sacredness of its purpose, this sunlit expedition might have ended for me in a dark dungeon. As we were passing through a cotton plantation which was shining in the sun, Théo had a fancy to see one of the snowy tufts at close quarters. With the impulsiveness of my sixteen years [he was in fact eighteen], and my ardent zeal to fulfil the master's desire, I leapt out of the carriage, plunged regardless into the enclosure, and uprooted one of the fleecy flowers.

As I went back to my companions, brandishing my trophy, I felt an iron hand fall roughly on my shoulder, and arrest my joyful errand. It was a furious custodian, who wanted to take me to the police station for stealing . . . It took the powerful authority of Théo pasha to make the Arab loose his hold and to give me back my liberty. He assumed his Olympian air, and threatened with the wrath of the Khedive this reckless man who had dared to touch a guest of the Viceroy – a sacred personage! But it was not these fine words which had most effect. The argument which loosened the sbirro's fingers and made him hold out his hand was the golden coin I slipped to him in exchange for the silver sprig, which I presented to the poet.[9]

* * *

Cairo, November 1869

The other morning, at the request of Théophile Gautier, we expressed a wish to see an almehs' dance. When evening came, our dragoman informed us that everything had been prepared for one of those oriental fêtes which foreigners are so fond of. We went down to Esbekieh Square, and, at the door of the hotel, we found a regiment of asses, already caparisoned and waiting for us. The engaging donkeys, grey, white and black, had been baptized, by their masters, with names as far-fetched as they were unexpected: Rigolboche was kicking beside Pharaoh, and Moses licked the fur of Gazelle.

We climbed astride our mounts and set off, preceded by young Saïs clad in gauze shirts. Their sleeves, split to the shoulders, floated behind them, held up by the wind, and seemed to set angels' wings upon their backs ... Beside us walked the donkey-drivers, armed with their sticks, and the troop was escorted by the protecting cavas, wearing sabres in their belts and rifles slung across their shoulders.

The great Sheik of this caravan, composed of disparate elements, was naturally Théophile Gautier. Wearing the oriental tarboosh, he sat solemnly enthroned on his red morocco saddle which was set on a multicoloured carpet; the little grey ass which bore him seemed to be aware of its mission: it slowly advanced its slender legs, one after the other, and set down its hooves with caution on the paving, as if it were afraid of a jerk which might hurt the injured man.

Only the luminous crescent rising in the blue sky lit up our way through the sombre alleyways which took us to the bounds of old Cairo.

At a whistle blast from the guides, the caravan stopped in front of a low double door, the two halves of which, encrusted with iron ornaments, swung back on their hinges as we approached. It was an Arab house; the moucharabies, lit up inside, revealed a glimpse, through the lace of their arabesques, of female figures which were watching us.

In China, one would have given this hospitable abode the poetic name of *flowerbasket*, but, in Cairo, it had to be given a more European name because it was frequented by Westerners.

A fellah introduced us. She was draped in a long blue robe

49

which was slit over the breast and fell over her bare feet which were heavy with rings. She lifted a Caramanian door-curtain, and we found ourselves in a square patio, with red and white marble flagstones, and its walls covered with Persian tiles. At the far end of the courtyard a stream of limpid water was flowing from an antique mask into a big granite basin.

From the door through which we entered, we seemed to see a confused vision of a flock of snowy swans around the fountain . . . As we went on, we distinguished, through clouds of silvered muslin, stretched out on the flagstones, the forms of women who were concealing themselves beneath their veils. These were the almehs, who were waiting for us before they performed their dances.

But when we had settled on the raised divan which stood against the walls, they refused, in terror, to undress. At first we thought it was an attempt at extortion, and we offered to double the sum which had been agreed. They stubbornly refused to yield to our prayers – until they were threatened by the old harridans who were with them . . .

The interpreter explained the reason for this hesitation: they were afraid of the evil eyes of 'these dogs of Christians', which could have afflicted them with some mysterious malady. The most suspect – who would have thought it? – was the inoffensive Théo, whose fierce monocle inspired them with insurmountable terror. When the monocle was dropped, they decided to drop their clothes.

The graceful gestures which accompanied their undressing revealed their different characters. One, in her vivacity, cast aside all her veils pell-mell, laughing fit to burst. Another, solemn, grave and sad, recalled the draped statue of Modesty; finally, with melancholy resignation, she decided to remove her veils one by one, and they seemed to part with difficulty from her youthful body . . .

Soon they all appeared in their golden nakedness; only their breasts remained adorned with Mussulman amulets which were exactly like Neapolitan scapulars.

The dances had scarcely begun when once again they were suspended: the incriminated monocle had been replaced by a lorgnette. Moved over their naked bodies with the curiosity of the myopic, it made them tremble with apprehension . . .

They stopped, in terror, falling over one another. They reminded one of the terrorized Niobides protecting themselves against the arrows of Diana and Apollo.

The boldest among them approached the poet and tried to take away his lorgnette, which he refused to give her. She grew annoyed by this refusal, which was aggravated by the master's impassibility; he did not caress her as the other spectators did. She tried in vain to provoke him, and manoeuvred so sharply that she knocked against the arm which was in a sling . . .

The pain was so acute that it brought a moan of agony from the injured man . . . Startled by this unexpected groan, she stopped in utter confusion, like a naughty child, afraid of being punished. The interpreter then intervened, and explained to the culprit that this solemn personage was a magician from the West. As he crossed the sea to accomplish his pilgrimage to the city of the caliphs, he had been the victim of a *mal occhio*: he had fallen on the bridge of the ship, and he had dislocated his shoulder. When she knocked against him a moment ago, she had re-opened his wound [*sic*] and delayed his recovery.

As she stood before the injured man – and the man whom she herself had injured – there was a sudden change. In the dancer there awoke the nurse who sleeps in the heart of every woman; her pretty face, which had been so happy, grew sombre and passed from sadness to compassion.

As she could not express herself in French, she spoke through her great dark eyes, which gazed in sympathy at the victim of the *jettatura*. She translated her feelings by gestures which were so gracious, so innocent, so sincere, that she must have reminded the poet of his divine Grisi in *La Péri* or in *Sacountala*. She bowed over the injured hand without touching it, refreshed it with her breath, she scarcely dared brush against it with her lips: it was the dumbshow of a dream . . . Then she put her fingers on her eyes as if to show her tears of regret, while she implored his pardon with an irresistible smile.

The poet did not lose his Olympian solemnity. Like an officiating pontiff, he gravely took the girl's hand in his own free hand, and carried it to his lips with as much respect as he did for his princess.

At this homage, to which she was hardly accustomed in her own country, where women are treated like beasts of burden, the young girl suddenly drew herself up, a smile of triumph half-opened her rosy lips, and she allowed herself to be adored.

Then she lay down on the step of the divan where the poet sat cross-legged, in Turkish style. She rested her head on the invalid's lap, and gave him her little hand with the nails painted like pearly shells. She stayed with him, as if she were taking him under her protection – or as if she were putting herself under his. Throughout the spectacle, Théo held the little almeh under his spell, and

51

this time it was not his double rhymes which had made a conquest.[10]

Soon afterwards, however, he had another literary triumph. When the Empress arrived on *L'Aigle* to open the Suez Canal, and he boarded the imperial yacht to pay homage, 'what should the illustrious traveller be reading,' noted Primoli, 'but *Le Roman de la momie*, which seemed to her the most perfect of travel books. "You must have stayed a long while in this country," she said to him, "to have been so impregnated by its atmosphere, and shown us its people with such exactitude." "I had never been to Egypt, but I had seen it," he answered, with such assurance that the Empress did not insist: she knew that she was talking to a visionary and a poet.'[11]

* * *

Primoli himself returned from Cairo to Paris. Soon after his return he visited his aunt, Princess Julie, at the handsome Hôtel Montholon, in the rue de Grenelle. In her drawing-room, which was hung with white satin, she brought together men of the most diverse political opinions (among them Prince Napoleon and Thiers), and writers of the utmost distinction (among them Mérimée and Flaubert). The Archbishop of Paris, Monseigneur Darboy, might be found there in conversation with Père Hyacinthe, and Lord Lyons, the British Ambassador, with the Chevalier Nigra, the Italian Minister.[12]

Women were in the minority, but, as Primoli observed, there was sometimes

an unexpected visitor who seemed to jar in this austere setting with her shrill voice and exotic accent. This was Princess Metternich. The witty Austrian, who liked contrasts, did not disdain – between two social functions – to make an appearance in this *salon* which was more serious than her own. Either she took a mischievous pleasure in shocking dowagers, or else she found a certain satisfaction in showing them that, in spite of her loud behaviour, and thanks to her gift of assimilation, she could sing a philosophical couplet as easily as a smutty song.

I remember that, one December Wednesday in 1869, Renan and Caro were absorbed in an argument about the idea of God, when the double doors of the white salon burst open, and the butler announced: 'Her Highness the Austrian Ambassadress!' Everyone rose to their feet, the Princess burst in like a whirlwind, and, casting a smile of satisfaction round the dazed assembly, she fell into a chair, closed her eyes, and cried: 'I've done it!'

Everyone looked at each other, and wondered what diplomatic alliance the Ambassadress was about to reveal: she who knew the secrets of the gods. It was just a question of the resumption of marital relations between the *jolie laide* and her husband – whose infidelities had been denounced by the popular Press. The skilful Princess had harnessed him to her chariot again. 'I've done it!' was a somewhat informal way of announcing the future birth of her third child – after an interval of twelve years.[13]

8

In February 1870, Primoli began the seventh volume of his diary. 'I shan't be content to be something,' he wrote. 'I want to be somebody. Personally, I prefer a rose to a rosette. It smells sweeter, and it suggests fewer intrigues: at most an intrigue of the heart.'[1]

He had a disarming indifference to worldly success. He had no need for decorations, no ambition for power. Influence and social status were his, nonetheless, because he chanced to be a Bonaparte. On 1 February he was first invited to the family dinner at the Tuileries. It seemed to him an elegant comedy. 'Princess Mathilde appeared. Her frank and noble simplicity contrasted with the rest, she seemed to me like a good page of Molière which had gone astray in a play by Marivaux.'[2] He noted a snatch of conversation:

Empress: I should take much more interest in a man who had crossed Africa than I should in a man who wrote poetry!
Princess Mathilde: Well, I shouldn't!
Empress: We are the two extremes. You're the town mouse and I'm the country mouse. I'm the carrier pigeon, and you're the homing dove.[3]

In these closing months of the Second Empire, the eager diarist continued to visit the rue de Courcelles.

2 March

The last time [the Goncourts] went to dine with Princess Mathilde, there was the most heartrending scene. During the evening, Jules went up to my aunt. She paused in her tapestry work, and looked

54

up at him. Then he bent down, and kissed her forehead, and tittered like a fool. Speechless and motionless, the poor woman made no protest. She pretended not to have noticed anything, but she found it hard to restrain her tears . . . Edmond stood in a corner, weeping. After that evening, he did not bring his brother to the rue de Courcelles again.[4]

Jules de Goncourt was suffering from venereal disease, and it had affected his mind. He died, insane, on 20 June, at the age of thirty-nine. 'I am sick at heart when I think of your grief,' the Princess wrote to Edmond. 'I am really distressed by the thought of your solitude, of your life cut in two . . .'[5]

It was not the only death to touch her. On 29 April, Anatole Demidoff had died, also – it appeared – of his old venereal disease. Next day she told Primoli how, a week before his death, Demidoff 'had bought the bust of his wife by Carpeaux, and had put it in his mistress's salon.'[6] She talked, too, about Nieuwerkerke:

After twenty years she loved Nieuwerkerke as she had done on the first day, but his love for her decreased with every new favour he received. At the end of last year, . . . he had decided to get rid of her. And then there had been scenes which the gossip columns related in veiled words . . .

My Aunt A[ugusta] asked her why she was sad. 'For ten years, now, Nieuwerkerke has only been a friend. For some time he has created quite ridiculous scenes of jealousy with me, and I know that all he wants is a pretext to leave. He loves someone else.' . . .

'Until now,' she said, 'I've lived for one person; now I am going to live for everyone . . . I have gaiety on my lips, and death in my soul.' . . .

A few days before the death of Prince Demidoff [Primoli continued], I went with my aunt to the Porte-Saint-Martin, where she wanted to see *Mathilde* by Eugène Sue. This drama had been written at the time of her marriage, and the author had had Prince Demidoff in mind when he created Lugarto. Isn't it strange that it's during a revival of this play that its hero dies in Paris?

I also went to the Gymnase with my aunt the other day to see Sardou's new play, *Fernande*, which is teeming with allusions to her present situation. My poor Princess saw herself in the part, she called [the Marquis] des Arcis infamous and cowardly, . . . she wept, she sobbed. In the end she had such a headache that, in spite of her interest in the play, she was obliged to leave in the third act. It was really heartrending.[7]

What a good, wise man he is, Gustave Flaubert!

Some of his sayings engrave themselves in the mind . . . The other evening I caught a phrase or two in flight, but, as soon as one fixes them on paper, the gold-dust which covers them disappears. 'There is nothing worse than chaste men and unchaste women. Do not trust chaste men . . . Cynics are chaste: Rabelais . . . Don't confuse the timid with the chaste.'

He adds this distinction for himself. He wrote delicately in [Mother's] album: 'Women will never understand how timid men are!' Two more thoughts to finish with: 'The Critic is the Tenth Muse and goodness is the Fourth Grace.' 'The man who never speaks ill of women does not love them, since the deepest way of loving something is to suffer from it.' There, it seems to me, is the explanation of *Madame Bovary*.[8]

* * *

On 15 July 1870, thanks to the machinations of Bismarck, Napoleon III declared war on Prussia. The Franco-Prussian War was to be brief and disastrous. The Emperor, who was a sick man, without experience of war, set out to command the French army. On 3 September, the news reached Paris that he had surrendered at Sedan. On 4 September, the fall of the Empire and of the Bonaparte dynasty was decreed, and the French Republic was proclaimed. The Emperor went into captivity at Wilhelmshohe; the Empress and her son escaped to England. Primoli recorded the fortunes of Princess Mathilde.

Brussels, 8–15 September

Brussels is a suburb of Paris, usually peopled by provincials and French exiles. Up to a certain point one can copy the city, but not the Parisians. For the moment, yesterday's exiles have gone home again, and the official world of the Empire has taken refuge in Brussels.[9]

Mons, 12 September

One of my deepest regrets when I left France was that I did not really know the fate of my beloved Aunt Mathilde, and one of the reasons which drew me to Belgium was the hope that I should find her there . . .

And so I was greatly surprised and delighted when I learned that she was at Mons, an hour from Brussels. I hastened to send a telegram to the Hôtel de la Couronne, addressed to [the Princess's lady-in-waiting] Mme de Galbois . . . She replied at once, with an invitation to *déjeuner* next day. I went there with Mother. At the hotel, we were shown into a little dining-room on the ground floor, where I found Eugène, my aunt's old and faithful butler. We couldn't look at each other without weeping. A few moments later, Alexandrine [Princess Mathilde's lady's-maid] came in to say that *Madame* would like to see Mr Joseph. She found it hard to say Madame instead of Her Highness. My heart was throbbing with emotion, ready to burst, as I went up to Room 21, on the second floor. All I saw at first was my dear aunt, who had just been dressed in deep mourning. She threw herself into my arms, and for a few moments she rested her head against my shoulder. We couldn't look at one another, we were crying so! . . .

She had foreseen it all! Even at the time of the fanatical enthusiasm for Émile Ollivier, she had not wanted to have his government, she had known that liberalism would bring the end of the Empire. She had openly disapproved of the war and of the Prince Imperial's departure for the army. As for her brother, she said she would not speak to him again, his behaviour had been so infamous. 'At least,' she said, 'I can say that I enjoyed my good fortune. My poor Saint-Gratien! It must be ransacked by the Prussians! My furniture, which I collected piece by piece! My beautiful bedroom, and my terrace! . . .' And, with a vivid recollection of those marvels of taste, I looked at this miserable hotel room, with its narrow white bed. She did not even have her own sheets, just a single pillowcase trimmed with lace. On a small table was *The Christian Day*; on another, larger, table, where no doubt she usually dined, a few books (*La Robe de Nessus*, by [Amédée] Achard – *L'Ensorcelée*, by Barbey d'Aurevilly), a little porphyry box with some matches, some letters, a pincushion in the shape of an imperial crown, which was sewn with pearls. On a washstand, next to a crude Delftware basin, stood a half-open dressing-case. The contents, made of gold and marked with her cypher, were spread out on a walnut dressing-table. A jewel-case was wrapped up and hidden in the folds of a shawl. I was very moved to see this flotsam of memories and grandeur beside these common things. My poor aunt had been accustomed to all the refinements of luxury. 'And to think,' she sighed, 'that we have to escape as if we'd committed crimes!' . . .

And then she told me about her sad departure. She had left Paris on the evening of the 3rd on the insistence of her friends. She was accompanied by the Baronne de Galbois, her reader [*sic*], by M. Eugène Giraud, her old [art-]master and devoted friend, by her butler, his wife and his mother. My poor aunt has no parents, or husband, or children. She is alone. I offered myself, [I'd be] only too happy to sacrifice my life to her service, but she did not want me. A good friend of mine, the Marquis Nicolas de Faletans, saw her on to the train, and took advantage of his uniform as an officer in the Garde Mobile to be of service to her. In the midst of all these sad events, the brave young man is madly in love, and he is waiting for the end of the war in order to get married, if he doesn't die in the struggle. As soon as he learned from the papers of the alleged arrest of the Princess at Alexandre Dumas *fils'*, at Puys, he had rushed to the republican Prefect of Police, M. de Kératry, secured a safe conduct for my aunt, and left for Dieppe, where he learned of his error. My aunt had, in fact, stopped at Rouen. She expected to spend the night there before she reached Dieppe, where Dumas had promised to find her a lodging. At midnight, someone came to say that a gentleman wanted to speak to her urgently: it was Alexandre Dumas *fils*. He came to tell her that the republic had been proclaimed, and to advise her to turn back at once towards Belgium. Some packing-cases had been seized at Dieppe, and were thought to be hers, and this error might put people on the alert. So she crossed the frontier with only a trunk of linen between her, her lady-in-waiting and her *femme de chambre* [*sic*], and she stopped at the first Belgian town she came to: at Mons. She had no trouble with the French authorities, since she had a Belgian passport, and a Dutch one which her cousin the Queen of the Netherlands had had sent to her. The pictures had been rolled up and were still in Paris, some of her jewels had been sent to the bank in London, and the other things had stayed at Saint-Gratien, exposed to the Prussians, and in the *hôtel* in the rue de Courcelles where the Republic had affixed their seals. And so there was not a word of truth in the infamous libel about the 73 trunks she was taking with her. And a cry escaped from her heart, so noble and so generous: 'They treat me like a thief! And I gave 100,000 francs a year to the poor, I never boasted of it, but if they look at my accounts, that's what they'll find . . .'

I tried to persuade her to come to Italy, but I could not tear her away from the frontiers of France.[10]

* * *

He himself went to Italy. As he remembered, thirty years later:

In September 1870 a double revolution broke out in my two

countries . . . On one side I left France in collapse. I watched in anguish as the country of my dreams was vanquished, my family were exiled, my mother wept. And then, on 21 September, I arrived in a country full of joyful celebration. I entered a Verona which was all bedecked with flags, banners were floating from every balcony, there were illuminations at night: they were celebrating the entry of the Italian troops into Rome. Unity had been achieved at last, a nation had been born, the future was radiant for the young. And, despite myself, my mourning for the nation which I had left in blood and tears prevented me from rejoicing in the awakening of this noble land which, after all, was my own. I spent a long, sad winter in the country – *l'année terrible* – living through the grievous rumours which came to me from the letters of friends who remained behind, friends whose suffering I could only share from a distance.[11]

Some of the letters came from Princess Mathilde.

It is a fearful torment, unexampled in history [she wrote from Mons on 14 September]. I have had an answer from *him* [Napoleon III], as cold as if he were still at the Tuileries. He doesn't want me to visit him, since he has told the Empress to stay in England. If my country were saved, I could easily reconcile myself to all the rest . . . I couldn't live here – it is so sombre, sad and monotonous . . .'[12]

On 12 October she wrote again:

I should like to wait here in Brussels for the end of the Siege of Paris . . . If Rome were not so far away I should go and join you there, but over there one is rather lost. I went to spend a few days with Queen Sophie [of the Netherlands]. She received me more affectionately than ever. She has a heart of gold. The climate is terrible there; there were fogs already; no sunlight, and the soul grows sadder still when the light is absent from the Heavens.[13]

'I saw only France in mourning [Primoli repeated]. I could not look at the dawn of Italy which was rising. The misfortune of my life comes from the fact that I have always turned towards the past. Instead of looking behind me, I should have looked ahead.'[14] The Franco-Prussian War and the fall of the Second Empire ended the first phase of his life. For seventeen years, since his family had followed their Imperial fortunes, he had made his home in Paris. Now, at the age of nineteen, he returned to the city where he had been born. The most Roman of Parisians was to become the most Parisian Roman of them all.

Two

1

The Roman Bonapartes were 'a quite numerous clan.'[1] There were, wrote Comte Paul Vasili in 1887,

> the four granddaughters of Lucien, and two grandsons: Cardinal Bonaparte and Prince Charles . . . They are allied to Prince Ruspoli and Prince Gabrielli, to Count Primoli and Count Campello, and to the Marquis Roccagiovine.
>
> This branch of the Bonapartes lives in isolation, refusing to accept a situation inferior to the one which the Second Empire had re-created for it . . . It would have been very difficult for the four sisters not to group themselves around the present head of the family, who is a cardinal: especially for Princess [Augusta] Gabrielli, who is entirely given up to devotion and to inexhaustible good works. Cardinal Bonaparte . . . is entirely occupied by his salvation and by his prayers. Prince Charles Bonaparte, who married a Princess Ruspoli, lives in a noble style, but without ostentation . . . He has remained very French at heart.[2]

So, too, had Gégé Primoli. He had been born in Rome, and he was drawn to it, now, by the presence of his family; he was inevitably moved by its history. Yet he had spent all his sentient life in Paris; it was Paris which spoke to his heart and would always speak to his intellect. It was at the Collège Rollin that he had taken the degree of *bachelier en droit*. It was at the rue de Courcelles and at Saint-Gratien that he had met some of the foremost spirits of the age. Paris was always to remain his necessary spiritual home; and he left it, now, with a sense of exile. He changed the setting of his life with profound regret. 'I shall only have footholds everywhere,' he lamented.[3]

He suffered all the more as he felt his exile was unnecessary.

63

It seemed to him that the war which had brought the overwhelming defeat of France, and the fall of his family from their imperial splendour, could so easily have been avoided. Queen Sophie of the Netherlands was, he thought,

> more Bonapartist than the Bonapartes. A few years before the disastrous campaign of 1870 she wrote to the Emperor and sent him some salutary warnings and predicted what, alas! has now come to pass. These remarkable letters were found at the Tuileries after 4 September, and they were shamefully published, at the risk of starting a conflict between Holland and Prussia.[4]

* * *

In May 1871, when the war had ended and the Commune had been overthrown, Princess Mathilde returned to Saint-Gratien, and to a new *hôtel* in Paris: 18, rue de Berry. In 1872 she leased no. 20, rue de Berry, and in 1879 she finally bought it.

> All you need [wrote Vincent Benedetti, the former French Ambassador to Berlin], is the courage to look at things without weakening; you come from a family which has never failed in this. Remember that, at every moment of the day, and you will have the strength to endure and to resist . . . The only thing I fear for you is your own grief, which undermines body and spirit; and you are the only one who can fight against this. Do it for your friends, for you really owe them something, and they will be very grateful to you.[5]

Primoli soon resumed his rôle as the *enfant terrible* of her household, in the new Republican world. Ferdinand Bac reported that

> Primoli greatly entertained the Princess, and, when she called him *intolerable*, it meant that she particularly delighted in his gaiety, in the drollery which he had shown, the witticism he had thrown out in the hope that it would encourage others. He had been the page, at first, and something of the jester . . . He had become, with time, the inseparable familiar: obliging, attentive, happily bringing back the gossip of Court [*sic*] and town . . .
> The Princess said, laughing, that in Rome, because of a certain unction in his voice and attitudes, the *Reds* called him '*figlio di prete* . . .', but that he must be related to a cardinal. Sometimes she accused him, jokingly, of serving God and Mammon, when he

came back from the Empress's [at Chislehurst] and emptied on to the table the store of tales and anecdotes which he had gathered there. She never asked him what they had said about her own household. She preferred not to know. [She and the Empress] had lived for so long on a policy of silence, and of letters when occasion demanded.

Primoli had a very keen sense of social notability, of the honours that were due, and of those whom it was useful and prestigious to frequent. The *salon* of Princess Mathilde had given him a world which he had not known at his parents' in Rome, or at the Tuileries. It had flattered his taste for literature (he had a delightful gift for it himself, not so much as a writer of prose, but as a poet). But his nonchalance, his *active indolence*, his *sterile activity*, had finally forbidden him to exert himself. Inspiration came to him at the moment when he least expected it, suddenly appeared on the sheet of paper, and immediately evaporated.

His curiosity, which he was determined to conceal, revealed itself in an assiduity which was never importunate, but closely followed his aunt's great protégés. He knew how to listen to them, talk to them, and, above all, how to laugh with them. The Princess was amused by his repartee and by his jokes. But she did not ask for his help in exchanges which demanded too much depth of thought, although he could appreciate all the refinements of the intellect. He was generous and parsimonious, faithful, hospitable and somewhat capricious. He was sensitive to everything, and he was frivolous. Anxious and confident, audacious and a coward. People liked him and they avoided him. 'He isn't good,' said the Princess, 'but he is full of generous feelings.'

This respectable collection of paradoxes attracted her, and she set this figure in the middle of her chessboard, to play him against the rest. She gave herself the pleasure of having a wit in her household who could contend with them without loss of face. It was not a question of beating them. She did not ask so much of him. But he filled to perfection the dual rôle of intermediary between the poet and the patrician, and of liaison officer between Paris and Rome.[6]

He was in Paris in the autumn of 1872, and he was there to bid farewell to one of the best-loved figures of the past. Théophile Gautier had not recovered from the rigours of the siege, and he was dying of a heart condition. Ernest Hébert, now director of the École Française de Rome, had given Primoli a letter for *le grand Théo*. Primoli delivered it on 21

65

October; two days later, Gautier died. On 24 October, Primoli told Hébert:

It is I, alas, who will answer the letter which you entrusted to me for poor Théo. Perhaps you gave him his last pleasure: he received your missive two days before he died, because I was determined to give it to him myself and I couldn't go to Neuilly earlier.

You yourself frequented and loved the house in the happy days when the master gave it life with his poetic, mischievous verve, the days when his two grown-up daughters filled it with the charm of their youth and beauty ... The house remains unchanged, except that the war and the siege have of course left their devastating traces.

I crossed the salon on the ground floor. It was hung with a red material on which there still stood out the souvenirs of artist friends, from a study by Ingres for his *Homer*, and a padishah by Delacroix, to nymphs by Puvis [de Chavannes] and an Italian peasant from your *Malaria*. On the piano stood an open score of *Tannhäuser* – and this in the house of the man whom they accused of blaspheming music! They showed me up a small, winding staircase to the master's room. It was absolute chaos. I should like to describe it to you, but I can't remember anything; when I recall the importance which Théo attached to the colour of a hanging, which doesn't generally strike the eyes of an ordinary visitor, I feel that he would certainly not have set me among the privileged beings for whom 'the visible world exists ...' Yet, perhaps, this time he would have forgiven me, because I saw nothing but him. ...

He was there, in the middle of the room, sitting painfully in a big armchair that he had not left for a fortnight. His stiff body was swathed in his capacious blue flannel robe, the sort of nocturnal uniform of the guests at Saint-Gratien. He was wearing a red knitted cap; the tassel drooping down on his curling hair gave it the appearance of a tarboosh, and recalled our journey to Egypt, where we had all adopted the oriental fez. His waxen complexion, his sagging cheeks, his unkempt beard, his half-closed eyes gave him the look of a Christ in agony.

One bloodless hand rested sadly against his heart and the other, on the arm of the chair, held a cigar which was half extinguished. The swelling of his legs, which constantly increased, paralysed the lower part of his body. As I entered he came out of his torpor, recognized me and smiled ...

He must in a flash have recalled the fine days at Saint-Gratien, the radiant sun of Cairo ... Perhaps, confusedly, he remembered our pilgrimage to the Virgin's Tree, when I had jumped from the carriage in a cotton field, to pick him the flower he wanted, and had been arrested by one of His Highness the Khedive's officials . . . For a moment he seemed happy to see me again and to forget his illness . . . He wanted to be agreeable, and he even tried to joke a little . . .

On the back of his chair leant his pretty daughter Estelle, whom he had nicknamed Monstre Vert. I believe that you have done her portrait.

In a corner of the room were his two old sisters, Zoé and Lili: one of them, paralysed, shivering in a woollen wrap; the other sitting on a low divan with a big white cat at her feet and a black cat in her arms. They tried to look unconcerned, but I saw their tears shining: they felt that he was lost.

When I mentioned you and handed him your letter, his expressionless face lit up . . . He opened the envelope with difficulty, turned the letter in all directions like a child who cannot read; he was astonished not to see, and at once accused the digitalin of troubling his sight. I told him your writing was difficult to decipher. When his daughter asked him what you had written, he gave her the unfolded page and said to her: 'The best thing is to read it.' The conversation lagged, and the silence was only broken by vague words. The enchanting conversationalist whom I had known, or, rather, the enchanter whose winged and coloured words had borne us to distant or fantastic lands, like a magician's wand, sought painfully for the words that would not always come. He attributed this difficulty, too, to the digitalin . . .

He had feared death all his life, and he did not want to see himself dying . . .

Little by little, I saw sleep fall upon him, and I had the impression that I watched the beginning of his agony . . . I looked upon him with grief, and I rose silently to leave the room . . .

His cigar fell, and he opened his eyes. Then, seeing I was near him: 'You mustn't think I'm asleep,' he said, smiling. 'You must punch my head and wake me . . . But it's a month now since I've been to bed.'

'As you don't go to bed,' I answered, 'it is only natural that you should feel drowsy now, and I'm going to let you sleep.'

'So I must sleep?' he asked, with the resignation of a child.

'Yes. Before I leave for Rome, I'll come back to see you and take your messages for Hébert.'

'Good-bye, then!'

'Good-bye till next time,' I said, and turned to hide my grief.

I took the hand which he held out to me as if to keep me, but I disengaged myself gently and went away, unable to hide my emotion any longer. It was the first time I had seen someone dying.[7]

* * *

Gautier remained, to Primoli, the best-loved man of letters who had adorned Princess Mathilde's in her imperial days; he had been his literary mentor, and, as an old man, Primoli would still recall his legendary charm, the brilliance of his conversation. Yet, within a few weeks of Gautier's death, Primoli encountered another of his aunt's protégés: a notable dramatist who was to be almost a father to him. On 29 November, for the first time, he met Dumas *fils*. Primoli expressed his ardent admiration for the author of *La Dame aux camélias* and *Le Demi-Monde*. Dumas was delighted by his enthusiasm and sensibility. Twenty-seven years his senior, he saw him as a son. Soon after their first meeting, he sent him a book inscribed: 'To Joseph Primoli, a son whom I should like to have, and love as if I had him.'[8]

2

When Napoleon III was released from Wilhelmshohe, he joined his wife and son at Camden Place, at Chislehurst, in Kent. His exile did not last for long. On 9 January 1873, Franceschini Pietri, private secretary to the Empress, sent a telegram to Princess Mathilde: 'I deeply regret to inform you that the Emperor died this morning.'[1] 'Had a great regard for the Emperor,' wrote Queen Victoria in her journal, 'who was so amiable and kind, and had borne his terrible misfortunes with such meekness, dignity and patience.'[2]

Primoli was less concerned with imperial dignity. That year he wrote *Caprice de Prince*: a fictionalized account of the Emperor's amorous exploits.

> The other evening, when I had shared a frugal supper with the Duchesse [d'Asti], I led her, as usual, to the fireside in her boudoir . . . There I began to read aloud from the *Journal des Débats* . . . They announced from Chislehurst the death of Napoleon III. When the Duchess heard this news, she shuddered, and cried: 'Poor dear Emperor! He was so noble and so good! . . .'[3]
>
> Then she recalled, how, long ago, she had resisted the advances of Napoleon III.
>
> When I got home [continued Primoli], I hastened to make a note of this confession, so that, some years hence, my friends could share the impression which it had made upon me. It does not contain any sensational intrigue, and it may seem of rather slight historical importance, but a simple memory, honestly recalled, seems to me more interesting than some marvellous account which has sprung from the novelist's imagination.[4]

The observation was typical of Primoli. He always enjoyed paradox and double bluff.

* * *

69

The Emperor was buried in the little Roman Catholic church of St Mary at Chislehurst, until the mausoleum was built at Farnborough. The Empress lived on at Camden Place, withdrawn from the world. In 1874 her retirement was dramatically disturbed. Queen Victoria's second son, the Duke of Edinburgh, had recently married the Grand Duchess Marie, daughter of Alexander II of Russia; in May the Tsar paid a visit to England as Queen Victoria's guest. As Primoli recorded:

Napoleon III had been dead for a few months [*sic*], his widow was living in deep retirement at Chislehurst, and the Prince Imperial was finishing his studies at the military college [the Royal Military Academy] at Woolwich.

Alexander had the Empress Eugénie informed that he would like to visit the Prince Imperial at Chislehurst. The Empress was still bitter about the fatal Russian indecision in 1870, when a gesture from the Tsar might have prevented the German invasion. She answered that her son was boarding at the Military Academy, and that the rules did not allow her to ask for leave for him.

Alexander recalled how anxiously she had hastened to the Élysée, after the attempted assassination by Berezowski. He remembered, too, how, at the Hôtel de Ville and at Fontainebleau, the imperial couple had protected him like a living shield against the daggers of the assassins. He answered that, if she consented to see him, he would go late the following day to present his respects to her.

She agreed; and next day, at the time arranged, the Tsar arrived at Camden Place . . .

The Empress dreaded this meeting, because it would stir up the recollections of happier days, and she was afraid that she might not be able to control her emotion. However, she struggled hard to control herself, and she went to greet the illustrious visitor at the door of her villa [*sic*]. When the two survivors of the festivities of 1867 found themselves in one another's presence, the fairytale memories arose and then dissolved – and they were both overcome by poignant anguish. Instead of the Sovereign radiant with beauty and power whom he had left three years earlier [*sic*], the Tsar found a widow who was deposed, exiled and grown old . . . And she who had welcomed the all-powerful Sovereign to her Empire saw the appearance, in her retreat, of the man who, with a gesture – so she believed – could have prevented her misfortunes and, above all, the misfortune of France . . .

Such was the emotion for both of them, their invincible regret, that for a few moments they stood, facing one another, gazing into each other's tear-filled eyes, unable to say a word . . .

Finally, after a long silence full of regrets, perhaps of remorse, the Tsar took the Empress's hand, clasped it tenderly, and bore it to his lips: 'Ah, Madame!' he murmured. 'If we had another chance!'

'Too late, Sire,' she answered, not without involuntary bitterness at destiny . . .

* * *

Next day, the Tsar was to attend a grand review at Aldershot. Before he went to the parade-ground, he had accepted an invitation to luncheon from General Symons [Major-General Sir Lintorn Simmons, Lieutenant-Governor of the Royal Military Academy] . . .

By a . . . providential chance, the company of cadets which was mounting guard that day was the Prince Imperial's company. The Tsar was told that this young soldier presenting arms to him was the son of Napoleon III, and he could not refrain from addressing a few words to him . . . Soon afterwards, Lieutenant Louis-Napoleon was told that, with the permission of General Symons [sic], His Majesty the Tsar of Russia invited him to luncheon . . .

Towards the end of the meal, Lieutenant Louis-Napoleon found himself on tenterhooks, torn between imperial etiquette and his military duty: he and his regiment were to precede the Tsar and to salute him on the parade-ground, and he did not dare to leave the table.

The young officer exchanged desperate glances with his general, who made him a sign to go . . . Finally, he ventured to ask the Tsar for permission to join his brother-soldiers, so that he could appear on the parade-ground on the Tsar of Russia's arrival . . .

'Oh no,' replied Alexander, smiling, 'I won't give you permission to precede me. If your general has no objection, I'd like you to come to the parade-ground with me, and we'll review the march-past together.' And so it was that the son of Napoleon III reviewed the British Army beside the son of the Tsar who had been defeated at Sebastopol.

This act of courtesy to the young French Prince was performed, perhaps, in spite of the Ambassador of the Republic, who did not dare to make too loud a protest. It had its effect on the situation of the exile. Alexander was the first to raise him *coram populo* from the station to which modesty and dignity confined him. Gradually the young Prince was to gain the consideration which he deserved for his personal merits and the respectful sympathy he inspired.

And he deserved the praise which Queen Victoria one day gave his mother. 'You and your son,' the old Sovereign told her, 'have never caused me any trouble.'

Alas, the only trouble which the young hero was to cause England was his death.[5]

3

In the mid 1870s, the Primolis' palace was one of the two or three centres in Rome for cosmopolitan society. Albert Besnard, who succeeded Hébert at the Villa Médicis, remembered: 'Very worldly, very elegant, the Countess Primoli received in her little palazzo dell'Orso, near the Tiber, which sometimes overflowed its banks and flooded over the threshold.'[1]

Gégé Primoli still lived with his parents. Apart from a brief period of military service, he was ineluctably caught up in this unremitting social life. At the age of twenty-three, he already saw its consuming nature, and wanted to escape, to be self-contained. An idealist, as ever, he had also come to believe that he was in love.

Rome, 15 November 1874

I must fight against the social current, frequently examine my conscience. Live with myself.

I begin to believe that I really love. Yesterday I should have said: I hope so, today I say: I'm afraid so. I am already retreating before the love which I have longed for so ardently. Would it be true that it only brings grief, bitterness and despair? I am discontented with myself and therefore discontented with everyone. I am not satiated, but I am unassuaged. All my physical, emotional and intellectual faculties have tended towards one single object which could not be enough to satisfy them. Possession itself would not satisfy me. My heart, oppressed until today, is overflowing on every side: youth, beliefs, illusions, hopes, they all want to burst out, and perhaps the heart that I have chosen is not deep enough to receive this superabundance of youth. Perhaps, in her,

73

everything is on the surface and not in depth. Is the horizon I seem to see only the effect of a mirage? . . .

However it may be, the more I become aware of her faults, the less distant I feel, and the nearer to her. I had set her so high in my esteem that the discovery of the pettinesses which bring her down to earth flatters my self-love, and shows me that I am less unworthy of her. Yesterday I did not see her faults, today I see them, but I love them.[2]

The object of his love was, needless to say, a married woman: Teresa Marescotti, who, six years earlier, had married Ignazio Boncompagni, Prince de Venosa. Primoli's feelings remained unspoken; but, in his diaries, he was often to embroider on the theme of his love for the woman whom he called Formosa. Such behaviour was characteristic of him. His sentimental life was always superficial. As he said himself, he had uncertainty of soul, he lacked determination and energy. Perhaps, in fact, he was incapable of feeling passion, or lasting love. Primoli's love for Formosa remained, predictably, in his mind: a subject for cogitation and, perhaps, for dreams. Finally it turned into solid friendship.

In the meanwhile he continued, sadly, to analyse himself.

Rome, 30 November

I am ill-satisfied with the beginning of this notebook. It is dull, tame and insignificant. I ask myself: what is the use of collecting so many banalities? It is my life which is colourless, and this notebook is the mirror which reflects it. It serves at least to show me my dull idleness and to make me blush at myself. My day is not filled, but it is occupied. I can do more and I am worth more. I want to change my way of life. I want to go out rather less and reflect rather more. This morning is devoted to business: solicitor, advocates, errands for Papa, etc.; after *déjeuner*, instead of going out, I decide to go up to my room and write my novel *Un Prince romain*. The plan is done. There is an abundance of material, ideas are coming. It only remains to write. From two to four at my table. At five o'clock, go and pay a visit, have a good chat, so necessary to prevent ideas from rusting.[3]

The chat continued, and the ideas rusted. He had three ideas for novels: *Un Prince romain*, *Le Père du Prince* and *Le Mari de la Reine*; but no trace of *Un Prince romain* exists among his papers, and none of these novels seems to have been finished.

Primoli missed the brilliance, the intellectual vigour, the pace of Paris. He missed the company of his Parisian friends. He found Rome inadequate; he felt cut off not only from his past, but from the present which he would have chosen. He was already lost in a kind of *dolce far niente*, or, rather, in a kind of sluggish indifference to life. In 1876, just after his twenty-fifth birthday, he wrote, with middle-aged despondency:

I am becoming dismally indifferent to everything that happens around me. Nothing interests me enough for me to take an active part in it, I can only be a spectator. If I could identify myself with something, grow impassioned about someone! My life has been broken in two. There is a clear dividing line which separates the indifferent Future from the lamented Past. If I were only afraid of something! But there is nothing which is worth the trouble of being concerned with it, of being disturbed. I have attained classical serenity. Is it really serenity, since it contains regret?

One should write a novel, and paint that nostalgia for Paris which overcomes the man who has lived there and has left it for ever. Those who are most to be pitied are the ones who are absent, the ones who have neither the prestige nor the martyrdom of the exile to console them. Far from this intellectual and literary movement, one is dead before one dies. There is a heartrending book to be written . . .

I have little real sensibility and much literary feeling. If facts and characters are to impress me, they must pass through Art. I weep more easily at the account of an event that I do at the event itself. I am indirectly in touch with Nature.

My greatest pleasure is to read an article which makes me meditate, pencil in hand, occasionally noting the thoughts and images and memories called up by a word, a poem, a double-meaning. Incomparable conversation! Everything can be serious and a subject of study, everything is frivolous and itself a recreation, that depends on one's disposition and on the importance one attaches to the thing: Paul de Kock has made me think and Plato has made me laugh.[4]

4

He lived, now, in Italy, but his thoughts were frequently in France and, especially, at the rue de Berry and Saint-Gratien. He was kept abreast of events by Princess Mathilde and by her new lover, the enameller and poet Claudius Popelin. The old order, alas, was passing. Late in 1876 came the death of Gustave Chaix d'Est-Ange, who had been *procureur impérial*, a Councillor of State and Senator during the Second Empire. On 20 December, Popelin reported:

> We have had the funeral of the good & witty Chaix d'Est-Ange . . . The Princess was much affected by this tragedy; she had dined with him, a week earlier, with Queen Sophie, & he had since come and spent an hour at the rue de Berry, and talked with the charm which was peculiar to him. Your aunt attended the funeral service.[1]

Since the fall of the Second Empire, the Princess had learned how much the affection and loyalty of others depended on political success, and on the vicissitudes of power. Émile de Girardin, the Press magnate, had once assured her of his respectful adoration; he was now urging a rapprochement between France and Germany, and – so Popelin told Primoli – 'the poor dotard . . . was disgustingly offensive about the Empire.'[2]

Primoli's devotion to the Princess did not waver; after his mother, she remained first in his thoughts and his affections. However, he continued to keep a delicate balance between Princess and Empress. He not only stayed with the Empress in her English exile; this year he also escorted her to Spain.

In 1877, when I accompanied the Empress to Spain, she told me that [in 1846], at the celebration of the Spanish Marriages, she had met the two Dumas: the father dazzling with his endless verve; the son, tall and handsome, with curly fair hair, timid, saying little and observing much. On the eve of their departure, Doña Eugenia had received some anonymous verses. She easily discovered their author, although she had not noticed the impression which she had made on the future author of *La Dame aux camélias*.

I wrote to Alexandre Dumas *fils* [continued Primoli] to ask him if he remembered that 'youthful transgression' which had not been reprinted in his first volume of poems. Here is his answer:

Paris, 8 April 1877

I too remember the verses which Her Majesty is good enough to recall, here they are:

> Salut, ma sœur, je fus cueillie
> Dans les jardins de l'Alhambra
> Par quelqu'un que ta main oublie,
> Mais dont ton cœur se souviendra,
> Et qui me charge de t'apprendre
> Qu'un jour, si Grenade est à vendre,
> C'est pour toi qu'il l'achètera.

Since we are talking of memories, here is a rather amusing detail. I had seen Mlle de Montijo at the marriage celebrations, and I had found her to be what indeed she was, that is to say the most beautiful and the most gracious woman one could imagine.

I had told my father so – I kept nothing from him, especially that sort of thing. One day he said to me: 'Would you like us to stay in Madrid? . . .' 'What should we do here?' I asked. 'I should work,' he answered, 'and you would pay court to Mlle de Montijo, and marry her.'

If the Empress had remembered this old admirer rather sooner, this admirer who was not an utter fool and had nothing to ask of her, if she had done him the honour of talking to him sometimes, as she did one day, or rather one evening at Princess Mathilde's, who knows if this admirer would not have told her about a lot of things? Perhaps he would have given her some of that disinterested advice which the greatest people in the world sometimes need to follow. It is so easy to govern this country, when one is in power, and it was so easy for Napoleon III! Unfortunately neither of them had spent their childhood in Paris. They didn't understand the Frenchman, how to endear themselves to him. Today the cause is lost, irrevocably lost . . .

You are going to make a very interesting journey, and I should dearly like to come with you. How many memories the Empress will rediscover on Spanish soil and conjure up before you! What a strange destiny this charming woman will have had, and how many reflexions must have conflicted in the past seven years in that head, in which it seemed that only happy and joyful thoughts should arise! . . .

ALEXANDRE DUMAS

He was quite right [continued Primoli] when he spoke of the memories which Spain would stir in the Empress's heart.[3]

And here, one suspects, the diarist's imagination took possession of him. Not for the first time, fact gave place to vivid fiction.

During that same visit to Ronda, Her Majesty told me [Primoli went on] about her ride of forty days in Andalusia, when she was escaping the band of Carlists led by the famous Pimentero. I asked the Empress for the exact date of this adventure. 'How do I know?' she answered. 'In Spain, these revolutions followed one another so fast that you counted them by the month. So it must have been during the July insurrection . . .'

The young Comtesse de Teba (as she then was), with her sister, her brother-in-law, her cousins the Alcanices [Alcanisez], and a few friends, had been hunting on the Duke of Alba's estate. In vain they had been warned that insurgents were hiding in the neighbourhood. Instead of diverting the huntsmen from their plans, the attraction of danger doubled their pleasure, and the fear of finding the roads already searched by the police even hastened their departure.

After the first day, the joyful band stopped at the castle of Romanille to rest there overnight. Overcome by tiredness and by the heat, they were all fast asleep when, at about two o'clock in the morning, they were woken by a knock at the door and pebbles thrown at the windows . . .

Two guards came to warn them that Pimentero, attracted by the prospect of splendid loot, and by the gathering of such illustrious people, had assembled his men to capture the cavaliers and amazons to whom, moreover, he would pay all the honour due to them, as he prized them very highly and would demand a ransom worthy of their excellence.

Pimentero was camping with his band in the neighbouring

forest, and at dawn he would begin to besiege the castle. If they were not disposed to give up their arms and provisions to him, and perhaps their lives, there was no time to lose.

They all leapt from their beds and got dressed in a trice, and in darkness, so as not to put him on his guard. The Duke and his friends went down to the stables to saddle the horses, while the young women packed the cases and secured them on the mules' backs with leather straps.

A secret door, leading into the forest, was half opened, and the whole troop, still half asleep, set out in silence – *per amicia silentia lunæ* – trusting in the speed of the horses and the darkness of the night to escape the bandits who were sporting Carlist cockades.

All day long, they crossed woods and mountains, and never paused for breath. Only when evening fell did they reach a village where they hoped to spend the night, but the inhabitants had recently been disarmed by a police regulation, and they refused to receive these compromising guests. 'You would draw the insurgents down on us,' they answered in terror. 'We take no sides in politics, but we want peace. Go and rest somewhere else . . .'

And the dizzying ride continued across Andalusia. They were young and bold and in love: even the privations became amusements. When the heat grew excessive, they stopped for refreshment, and at night they slept in the open, wrapped up in the traditional capes; the mules' big *bardelle* served as pillows; everyone kept watch in turn, and at dawn they set off again, across country.

* * *

One evening, instead of riding first, as usual, Doña Eugenia, the boldest of the band, rode painfully at the end of the file; she had not wanted to admit that she was defeated, and, at a distance, she followed the joyful band, who had crossed the forest without worrying about her. Exhausted with tiredness, she had dozed off on her saddle, and she had let go of the reins . . . The horse no longer felt controlled, and stopped, and, at this slight movement, the sleeping amazon slipped down on to the moss, still asleep. The poor animal was as exhausted as its mistress, whom it saw stretched out on the ground. It brushed against her, as if to ask if she was hurt, and, feeling that she was motionless, it stretched out beside her . . .

After a few hours of deep sleep, the young girl was woken by a moonbeam shining on her eyelids; she opened her eyes. For a moment she was dazed, then she came to her senses, sat up, and found herself on the ground beside her horse. She understood

79

what had happened; and, with a certain anxiety, she called out. No one answered . . . She had been abandoned by her companions.

A moment of surprise was followed by a fit of anger; she leapt on her horse and returned to the main road, where she followed the traces of the cavalcade. Finally she rediscovered her friends, who had pitched their tent on the edge of the forest . . . She burst out, and understandably reproached them for their indifference . . . But what was her astonishment when she found that, instead of being greeted by her guilty companions with the confusion that their behaviour should have inspired, she was greeted with uncontrollable bursts of laughter . . . which redoubled whenever a new arrival caught sight of her. Her bewilderment only increased the comedy of the situation.

'What is so ridiculous about me?' she wondered. She was unable to understand the hilarity she caused.

'Just look at yourself!' said her sister.

And, since she had no mirror, the young girl bent over the stream, beside which the caravan had camped . . .

'Is this monster me?' she murmured, as the clear stream reflected her image. 'It's impossible!'

Her pretty face was disfigured by erysipelas, which she had contracted while she was sleeping in the open air, her face uncovered; the mist and dew had completed the work of the night, and made her cheeks bloom like a field of poppies lit up by two luminous cornflowers.

* * *

The comic interlude was scarcely over when the drama began again; the bandits were drawing ever nearer the hunters, who had now become the hunted. The joyful band were no longer as joyful as they had been when they set out, either because they felt tired, or because they understood the approach of danger. The different villages through which they passed always refused to shelter them, and obliged them to resume their desperate ride . . . Even hunger began to make itself felt; they became thieves themselves, and more than once they stole a turkey or two and attached them to the saddle, where the tossing and shaking of the gallop turned the birds black as crows.

After several days of desperate rides, the fugitives' relations, who had been afraid, and then exasperated, were moved by anxiety; but they didn't know how to reach them; and, if they were to bring them home by force or by persuasion, they would either have to pay a substantial ransom or to receive a packet containing an ear or a nose, according to the traditional habit of well-trained bandits.

One morning, pursuers and pursued learned that they had spent the night in the same wood, a few feet away from each other . . . There was no more time to lose. They had to think seriously about defence, because the attack was imminent and the munitions were exhausted. They didn't know where to revictual themselves; the peasants were still afraid to compromise themselves by providing arms against the terrible Pimentero. They suspected that an old servant of the Casa Montijo had kept his loaded rifles; they despatched his favourite, the beautiful Doña Eugenia, to bribe him; but he absolutely refused to hand over his treasure.

'It's true,' he finally confessed, 'I've kept three bullets.'

'Who are you keeping them for?' she asked.

'For you and your sister.'

'Then give them to me.'

'Oh, that's not what I mean.'

'And what do you mean?'

'If you were ever on the point of being taken by these bandits, I should kill you both, rather than let you fall into their hands alive.'

'Oh no!' cried the young woman. She was doubtless more alarmed by the threatening defence of the over-ardent guardian than she would have been by the attacks of the gallant bandit.

'And you would feel no remorse for your double murder?'

'I shouldn't have time for that, because I'd use the third bullet to blow my brains out.'

The zeal of the fierce servant revealed the gravity of the situation, and the joyful band decided to put an end to the perilous escapade. This hunt, which had begun as a pleasure, was threatening to end in tragedy.

They felt so oppressed that they now despaired of reaching the Portuguese frontier, and they resigned themselves to entering Burgos, in spite of the risk of being imprisoned there by Pimentero's bandits. But, contrary to all expectation, the fugitives found the city fortified and armed for resistance. The gates closed behind them, and the rebels, who were now at bay, remained outside and had finally to abandon their pursuit.

Some time later, when they were still hunting for Pimentero in the mountains of Andalusia, the great chief made his appearance in Madrid. He calmly rang the bell at the gate of the Palacio de Liria, and had himself announced to the Duke of Alba. As soon as he was admitted into the presence of the grandee, the bandit asked if he might present his respects to the valiant steeds which had been able to outstrip his mules, for all their fabled speed.

The Duke gallantly did him the honours of his stables, and did not think for a moment of denouncing to the police the man who had pursued him for forty days and forty nights. But the alcade on the watch had thought that he had seen Pimentero enter the Duke of Alba's, and he asked him to hand the bandit over. The Duke warned the brigand, so that he could hide, and told the agent he must have been mistaken. He could not however refuse the police permission to search the palace, and it was inspected from the cellars to the attics.

The police even opened the door of the dressing-room where the Duke was putting on his shoes. 'Come in, gentlemen,' he said, 'and have a good look in my boots . . .' In fact, the valet was arranging his master's shoes on a console-table, on which there stood a huge grotesque Chinese figure with a big belly; . . . but the Duke, who felt reassured, could not escape a pang when he heard a resounding snore emerge from the china paunch . . .

Fortunately, the police commissioner was deaf, or feigned to be, and he shut the dressing-room door with profuse apologies and salutations.

*   *   *

This time, again, the leader of the insurgents could escape; but, some months later, when [Eugénie de Montijo] finally left Spain to go to France, where such a brilliant and tragic destiny awaited her, she passed through Burgos . . . There she saw that they were erecting a scaffold in the middle of the square; she made enquiries, and she was told that they were going to execute the notorious Pimentero. Betrayed, perhaps, by his own men, he had finally been caught . . .

If the execution had been postponed to the following year, the proud Spanish woman, . . . who had become the Empress of the French, would have demanded and obtained a pardon for Hernani, in memory of the romantic emotions which he had inspired in Doña Sol.[4]

The Primoli family, *c.* 1875. Charlotte Primoli with her sons, Joseph (left), Napoleon and Louis.

'A fairytale palace': Saint-Gratien, so often and so fondly described by Primoli.
Princess Mathilde stands in the foreground.

Claudius Popelin in a donkey-carriage at Saint-Gratien. This photograph shows him in the early
years of his liaison with Princess Mathilde.

Princess Mathilde and Popelin at Saint-Gratien, 20 July 1888. Marie Abbatucci appears on the right in the first photograph; but 'the one which gives me the best impression of reality,' wrote Primoli, 'is the one of the invalid leaning on the Princess, and followed by a dog [*sic*]. You see the couple from behind, but you would know them anywhere, and they touch the heart like a glimpse of Philemon and Baucis.'

Nurses and children in
the gardens of the
Palais-Royal, 1888.

Mothers and children
in a public garden: a
Renoir-like impression
of life in Paris, *c.* 1889.

Princess Mathilde at the wedding of her niece, Marie-Laetitia, to the Duke of Aosta. Turin, 11 September 1888. She is attended by Comte Vincent Benedetti (the former French Ambassador to Berlin), by his daughter-in-law, and by (centre) Mme de Galbois.

'The perfect oarsman.' Maupassant with Geneviève Straus (the daughter of Halévy and the widow of Bizet) and Colette Lippmann (the daughter of Dumas *fils*). A photograph taken at Triel in June 1889.

The Empress Eugénie
entering the chapel at
Farnborough Hill, built
in memory of her
husband and son.
A photograph taken late
in July, 1889.

Farnborough Hill, late July 1889. The Empress at prayer.

Edgar Degas leaving a
public lavatory in Paris,
25 July 1889.

Edmond de Goncourt on his doorstep at Auteuil, June 1889.

Thomas Edison (centre) with his wife on the fifth floor of the Eiffel Tower, August 1889.

5

Now, in the summer of 1877, Primoli and the Empress returned from Spain to England. As Bac had observed, Gégé Primoli was sometimes accused of serving God and Mammon: of cultivating both Empress and Princess. He was confidant, escort and Court jester to them both, and to both of them he served as adopted son; yet, between the two, there was no choice: no doubt whose company he preferred. On 16 July, from Camden Place, he wrote to Popelin: 'I dream of my dear St Gratien where even the bad weather seems like sunshine. And so I'm afraid that as soon as I'm on the shores of Lake Enghien, I shan't be able to tear myself away . . .'[1] Saint-Gratien, answered Popelin, 'is a haven I don't need to praise to you. The place is greener than ever: green enough, if I may say so, to make Ireland blush . . . Mme de Galbois has an inflammation which does not exactly model her face according to the canon of Praxiteles . . . We are like those nations with a boring history, very happy.'[2]

Saint-Gratien and its châtelaine, its devoted guests, remained with Primoli. That autumn, he received a copy of Flaubert's latest book. 'I recently had a very nice letter from M. Joseph Primoli, thanking me for *Trois Contes*,' Flaubert announced to Princess Mathilde. 'What a pity he lives in Rome! He ought to live with us in Paris.'[3] From Paris, the obliging Popelin continued to send news of the rue de Berry. On 31 January 1878, he reported to Gégé: 'Dumas dined yesterday with the Princess. It was the return of a prodigal son . . . I thought for a moment that Flaubert was going to knock the table over, he almost came to blows with Dumas over *le père* Hugo. Happily the Divinities which protect the hearth intervened, & all's well that ends well.'[4]

* * *

Early in 1879, as he approached his twenty-third birthday, the Prince Imperial grew tired of his aimless life; he determined to go to South Africa and fight in the Zulu War. His mother tried to dissuade him; the Duke of Cambridge, then Commander-in-Chief of the British Army, refused the Prince Imperial's request. But there was nothing, now, that the Prince could do for his own country, and he wanted to show his gratitude to Queen Victoria and to England. The Empress finally overcame her natural repugnance and went herself to intercede with the Duke of Cambridge. The Duke agreed that the Prince might go to South Africa as an ordinary traveller; on his arrival, he could be attached to the general staff in some innocuous capacity. Queen Victoria reluctantly gave her consent. From Camden Place, the Empress wrote to Princess Mathilde:

> My dear Cousin,
>   My son has asked me to tell you that he has decided to go to the Cape with the British Army. You will read [in the papers] about the reasons which have led him to make this decision. I can only tell you what he asked me to tell you, because he is very anxious that you shouldn't learn it from the Press. I hope that Providence will bring him back safe and sound.[5]

On 1 June, the Prince Imperial was killed by Zulu warriors at Ulundi.

This devastating death plunged Princess Mathilde into a despair which she had not known since her exile; it revived her old, deep-seated antipathy to the Empress. In a state of shock, she accused her of causing her son's death by her own intransigence.

> Every day I have had more details about the Prince's death and about his last wishes [this to Primoli on 4 July]. There are a great many comments on these, and they do not always do honour to the Empress, whose conduct is beginning to be known . . . She killed him, just as she killed his father. He couldn't live with her any more. She drove him to go to the war. He left at the end of his

strength and courage! It's horrible! She is an unnatural wife and mother![6]

The letter was presumably sent to Camden Place, where Primoli was staying with the Empress. On 22 July, in a letter to the novelist Octave Feuillet, he gave his account of events.

. . . On the news of the catastrophe, I left Rome for Chislehurst, where the poor Empress is suffering absolute martyrdom. The month which passed between the death and the arrival of the body was a long agony for her, and she remains unconsoled. Every ship that came from the Cape brought her letters from the son who was no more; they had been happy letters when they were written, they were dismal when they were read. For a long time she kept them unopened. Only yesterday, she had a pencilled letter which her son had written her before he mounted his horse on 1 June. And the night before the funeral! She spent the whole night praying and weeping beside the coffin. I can still hear the sound of the last kisses which she laid on the pall at dawn, as she ended her mournful vigil. And next day, when they bore her son away, you can understand what she must have felt at the sound of the funeral marches and the gun salutes which echoed so grievously in her heart.

In the morning, when she went into the Prince's study, she saw the saddle which had been torn in her son's last struggle, and had caused his death. This eloquent testimony brought the final scene before her eyes in all its horror, and she fell back in a faint. All these painful blows are going to follow one another, now, and keep her in a state of nervous over-excitement, and they will make her pass through fits of weeping; but I am less afraid of them than of the state of prostration which will follow. The moment will come when she is more serene, and sees her sad life before her, broken for ever; at that moment she will plumb the very depths of grief.[7]

6

Primoli left the disconsolate Empress, and went to stay with Princess Mathilde. On 15 September, at Saint-Gratien, he turned once again to his diary:

Gustave Flaubert and Edmond de Goncourt have come here for a week. It is here that I knew them both, some seventeen years ago, and it is in the same salon, hung with the same green chintz, patterned with bunches of flowers, that I hear them talking . . . They have not changed at all except that Flaubert has developed a paunch and that Goncourt has grown grey. I was forgetting that little Goncourt, as we called that half of the Goncourts, has disappeared, and Big Brother has managed, by working, to fill the void which had opened beside him.

At our request, Flaubert read us two chapters of *Salammbô* (the Snake and the tent). Nothing can really give an exact idea of Flaubert reading, declaiming, chanting his works, for anyone who has not heard him do so. It's like Frédérick Lemaître performing in a boulevard drama . . . Words fall from his lips with the sound of a cascade falling through his body. He seemed to be the barbarian Mathô whose story he was reading . . .

My aunt told me that last year he wanted to stay with her after everyone else had gone to bed . . . She was waiting to see what he would do when, after a moment, he clasped his stomach with both hands and ran, because he had colic . . .[1]

After Flaubert's death, Primoli felt obliged to revise the legend of the interview.

This anecdote amused us for a long while [he wrote], because the Princess did not fail to repeat it; but it ceased to make us smile when Flaubert died. The medical revelations of treacherous friends

86

told us of the infirmity which poor Flaubert had spent his life concealing from us. He had been overcome, no doubt, with absolute terror that his emotion might bring on an attack, and he chose to seem timid and ridiculous rather than reveal himself epileptic.[2]

Flaubert's private audience with the Princess remained too promising an episode to be dismissed in two or three lines. Years later, Primoli changed the date of the event, added many details, and gave a heightened account of the tête-à-tête in his preface to Flaubert's *Lettres inédites à la Princesse Mathilde*.

It is a September evening in 186–, at the château of Saint-Gratien. On the ground floor, in the long gallery hung with green chintz, patterned with full-blown, multicoloured flowers, three large bay windows open on to the verandah celebrated by Théophile Gautier; from the verandah, five or six stone steps lead down to a lawn which stretches as far as the eye can see under the starry sky.

To the left of the entrance door are two unfolded screens, one with bands of tapestry, red poppies embroidered on a gold ground, the other with seven glass panels. They form a little boudoir in the corner of the big room, and reveal the châtelaine's love of intimacy.

In the middle of this *buen retiro* is a round table, covered with a cashmere shawl, around which several people are sitting. On the table, a lamp in yellow Chinese porcelain, surmounted by a big shade, lights up the illustrated papers, the reviews, the albums, the books which have recently been presented. At the edge of the table [is] a lacquer tray, with countless feminine trinkets spread out on it: a fan, a phial, an enamel *bonbonnière*, a pair of gold scissors, a jasper paperknife, a microscopic clock, a mirror, a scent-spray, a bunch of violets in a silver vase – and, behind this scented tray-basket, sitting on a small sofa, is the Princess.

She is *décolletée*, in a burnous of white crêpe de Chine; round her neck, a row of big black pearls. Her wavy hair with auburn lights is parted in two smooth bandeaux, carefully brought down on the temples and held over the ears by two little tortoiseshell combs edged with pearls.

Her agile fingers are working at a band of green tapestry which is fixed to the table by a big pin; she is embroidering variegated carnations of every colour, as the fancy moves her.

Beside her, up against her – under her arm, huddled in a woollen shawl, shivering, with its tongue out – is a little black ratter, ill with old age; on her lap, a white fox-terrier; and, under the table, there are the muffled snarls of other dogs which are fighting over the basket . . .

'Come on, Phil and Mouche, you're unbearable! You've both got your own baskets. Be quiet, or . . .'

She scolds them, and she does her best to make her voice sound terrible, but in it one senses a caress, and woe betide the over-zealous courtier who thought he could take her at her word and carry out the mistress's threat!

The two opponents don't calm down, they rush out of their baskets; the fox-terrier leaps off its mistress's lap, even old Miss gives a groan . . .

The whole small pack, unleashed, are barking round a kind of giant who has just risen noisily from his chair and thrown a book down on the table . . . He is a Gallic colossus with broad shoulders, a powerful build, a florid face, a thick drooping moustache, and kind, bright, goggle eyes . . .

He mops his brow, his gleaming pate, his fine hair which curls at the ends and flows over his collar . . . He seems to be emerging from a terrible struggle which has broken him: one thinks of Jacob's battle with an invisible angel. This mysterious victory earns him the congratulations of the audience and provokes the barking of the yapping pack at his feet . . .

He is red, he is purple – 'a cherry in brandy fallen in the fire', Théo used to say. It is Gustave Flaubert.

He has just read aloud, declaimed, some passages from *Salammbô*: the serpent scene, the meeting of Hamilcar's daughter and Mathô.

It is Mathô himself, or, rather, it is Frédérick Lemaître, performing a Romantic drama. Neither this great actor, nor an actor imitating him, could give an idea of Flaubert reading, vociferating, singing his work. His sea-green eyes flash forth, beneath his black eyebrows; his moustache is bristling. His chest is swelling, his hand is trembling, and the book which he is holding seems to be moved by some ocean wave . . .

And he reads, in his bellowing, sonorous voice which rocks you, as Goncourt says, in a sound like a purr of bronze. And when he emerges from one of these readings, he seems to be coming round from an attack . . .

Never has he been more content, his satisfaction bursts forth from every pore: 'It's true,' he says, 'I even dazzled myself by the way I recited the last chapter . . .' And, on the urgent insistence of the group of admirers, he obligingly repeats the famous phrase:

Les Mercenaires crurent voir au haut d'un caroubier quelque-chose d'extraordinaire: une tête de lion se dressait au-dessus des feuilles.

Then, at the thundering voice, the artist's mimicry, one seemed to see Flaubert's head turn into a lion's head, with a mane which seemed to float over his neck. Even the dogs were seized with fear. They redoubled their howling and vociferation, as if they wanted to give chase to this invisible animal which had appeared to them . . .

The audience goes into the smoking-room; Flaubert remains alone with the Princess.

'Come on,' she says to him, 'calm yourself . . . Don't make my dogs bark . . . What's the good of getting yourself into such a state? . . . You'll make yourself ill. Look after yourself . . . Oh, men! What creatures they are! Couldn't you read like anybody else? . . . Phil! Mouche! Soc! Chine! Be quiet! You're unbearable . . . And you were howling, too, they thought you were scolding me, the poor little things! . . . Back to your baskets, mesdemoiselles! . . . And you, Flaubert, come over here, just be sensible . . . In heaven's name, how hot can you get?'

And, with her fine lace handkerchief, the good Princess wipes the face of her old friend, who has allowed himself to sit beside her . . .

Touched by this maternal care, the good giant takes the pretty hand and holds it to his lips . . .

'Be sensible and don't do it again. I shall get someone more reasonable to read me the rest of your book, since it gets you into such a state.'

'But I calm myself for you, Princess, I moderate my voice in your honour. When I am alone at night, at Croisset, in my *gueuloir*, I shout very much louder . . .'

'That must be splendid!'

'The other night, when I tried the effect of my last chapter, my voice made the steel pens reverberate in the bronze goblet: I thought that a vein had burst in my chest; I stopped, I expected to bring up a stream of blood . . .'

'You're mad! You're going to kill yourself with your profession.'

'It's my profession.'

'And a fine one it is!'

'Work is also the best way to get through life . . . If it weren't for that, what should I live for?'

'That's nice of you! For the people who love you.'

'Oh? . . . You, of course . . . You're good . . . to everybody, . . . but you're good to too many people!'

'You might as well reproach me for being trivial.'

'No, but you belong to everyone . . . You reign in the middle of a Court . . . One can never have you all to oneself . . . It's unbearable, and I'd have so much to say to you,' he added, sighing.

'You've never asked me for a private meeting.'

'I haven't dared.'

'Then dare!'

'Well, I beg Your Highness for a private audience.'

'Whenever you like.'

'One evening . . .'

'This evening?'

'This evening.'

'Yes, of course.'

'And where?'

'Here, in this salon.'

'With all these people?'

'No, alone . . . It's very simple: at eleven, I dismiss my guests as usual; you pretend to retire as well, and, a few minutes later, you come back. You will find me alone, and ready to listen.'

At half-past ten, a valet comes to announce that the little château omnibus is ready to take the guests to the station at Sannois. The regular Wednesday visitors rise at once to take their leave of the Princess, and to kiss her hand: Sainte-Beuve, Renan, Taine, Lavoix, Edmond and Jules de Goncourt . . .

When they have left, the conversation flags. The men unfold newspapers; the women, who are tired from their walk in the forest of Montmorency, stifle a few yawns; Flaubert has grown silent, and he is fidgeting on his chair . . .

* * *

Eleven o'clock strikes at last on the Louis XVI clock over the door. The Princess rolls up her band of tapestry, and fixes it with her needle. Then she puts it into her gilt wicker workbasket and rises to her feet.

Affable and smiling, she dismisses her guests, giving the men her hand to kiss, embracing the women and wishing everyone good night.

Then the company goes out through the main door, with Flaubert bringing up the rear. The Princess, followed by her dogs, makes her way to a little spiral staircase, hung with green chintz, which leads to her room . . .

Just as the servants are about to remove the lamps from the salon, the Princess reappears on the threshold and, to the butler's

90

great astonishment, she orders them not to put out the lights yet, and to go.

Resigned [to the conversation], she resumes her place on the sofa, by the big round table, and begins her work.

'Now we're going to hear what he has to say that is so interesting!' she thinks, as she unrolls her tapestry. '. . . He really bores me, with his splendid phrases which lead nowhere: it's simply literature, that's all it is! . . .'

The door half-opens. Mathô comes in furtively, more like a timid schoolboy than a conquering hero. With a mistrustful glance round the room, he assures himself that all the guests have gone . . . Then he slips between the armchair and the sofa, and sits down on a buttoned armchair beside the Princess. Silently, he watches her at work – and it is indeed a picture worthy of an artist or a poet: this imperial profile bent over the embroidery under the pink light of the lamp. He gazes at the neck as smooth as a column, and at the pearl which is trembling on the lobe of her ear; he gazes at the famous shoulders, so often celebrated, which emerge from the shot-silver burnous, he gazes at the fairy fingers as they course across the canvas, making the flowers bloom . . .

The Princess feels this burning look as it passes across her neck, her shoulders, and her hand, and . . . she waits . . . There is a long silence, and then, provoked by these eyes which are fixed upon her, she suddenly looks up:

'Well? What have you got to tell me that's so confidential and urgent? We're alone, as you asked, and I'm perfectly ready to listen . . .'

Imagine her surprise when she sees him turn very red and then very pale! The most diverse expressions cross his face: fear, anguish, terror, despair . . . He stammers some incoherent sounds, then he rises precipitately, makes for the door, and runs . . .

She waits for ten minutes, and then she rings. The butler comes back.

'Monsieur Flaubert?'

'He went across the ante-room and ran upstairs.'

'He hasn't appeared again?'

'He seemed so agitated that I followed him. He went straight to his room; he must have gone to bed . . .'

'Ah!' murmurs the Princess, with a slight shrug of the shoulders. 'You can put out the lights.'

She rolls up her tapestry a second time, puts it away in her basket, then rises, and, with the bearing of a goddess, goes across the salon on her way to her room.

'From now on, at least, he will leave me in peace!'

What is the answer to the riddle? It was no doubt given to us by Gustave Flaubert himself. Soon afterwards, he wrote in an album at Saint-Gratien: 'Women will never understand how timid men are.'[3]

And here, again, we catch Primoli embroidering history. Among Flaubert's correspondence is a letter from Flaubert to his niece Caroline Commanville. It is dated only 'Wednesday', but it was presumably written in February 1865. 'Princess Primoli sent me her album on Saturday so that I could put some mighty thoughts into it. I put a thought in, but it wasn't mighty.'[4] One may date the contribution more precisely. In Charlotte Primoli's autograph book is a line from the author of *Salammbô*: 'Les femmes ne sauront jamais combien les hommes sont timides! G^ve Flaubert. 20 février 65.'[5]

7

Meanwhile, in 1879, Primoli returned to his diary.

19 September

Flaubert is revising the proofs of a small edition of *L'Éducation sentimentale* and next spring he is bringing out a sort of philosophic tale in two volumes – Dictionary (Bouvard et Pécuchet).[1]

21 September

Yesterday evening a heated discussion between Goncourt and the Princess about Théo. The Princess, who regretted her lack of literary sense, grew even more impassioned than she intended . . .
   There are two phases in her judgement: in the first she admires only the talents of the people she loves, in the second she frets because she can't appreciate the talents of her friends . . . She is very artistic, but she lacks the sense of the picturesque.[2]

21, evening

Relations have always been strained between Chislehurst and Saint-Gratien. The two women have not ceased to detest each other. Who is to blame? Both of them . . . Mathilde was lost because of her heart, Eugénie escaped because she completely lacked an amorous disposition.[3]

Sunday evening

Talked about Musset with Giraud and M. de Foyes, who knew him . . . He was invited twice to Princess Mathilde's, and on both occasions he was drunk . . . One evening it was at a dinner given in his honour at the rue de Courcelles. They waited for him for an hour, and, when they sat down at table, they saw him emerging from the far end of the salon. He stumbled along, and, catching sight of his empty chair, he fell into it without a word. A sign was made to the servants not to give him any drink, and in fact he didn't eat or drink anything throughout dinner. Then he went upstairs to a bedroom where he sobered down as best he could, but the spell was broken.

Another time, he was going to read his *cantate d'Auguste* [*sic*], and Gounod was playing the piano, when Musset collapsed and fell asleep in the middle of the reading . . . He used to get drunk on a mixture of beer and brandy.[4]

He was not the only guest who had earned contempt. Viollet-le-Duc had decorated Notre-Dame for the Emperor's wedding, he had been the Emperor's architect, and he had restored the Château de Pierrefonds. He had proved, alas, to be time-serving; he had left the Princess's salon after 1870, and he had published hostile comments on the Emperor and the Empire. On 2 October, Primoli recorded: 'The illustrated papers all carry the portrait of Viollet-le-Duc, who died in Lausanne a few days ago . . . I was saying this evening that they would put up a statue on the Château de Pierrefonds – as a weathercock, retorted General Chauchard.'[5]

The Princess herself remained unchanging in her loyalties and affections; but she was now fifty-nine, and, despite the presence of Popelin, she was sadly conscious of her age.

The secret cause of the Princess's animosity against the world is [continued Primoli] that she is growing old. She is nearing her sixties, and yet she seems a woman of forty, and she feels full of life. Her doctor comes every week out of habit, and he's proud of his patient. The other day she said to him: 'The trouble with me is that I have a good appetite and I like to walk and move around . . .' She loves everything she does, and she does everything with gusto . . . She has springtime in her heart. A woman is young as long as she loves, she is beautiful as long as she is loved . . .

Only the head of such a beautiful woman has suffered the brush of [passing] time: the skin is slightly parchment-like, the enamel of the teeth is somewhat impaired, the small nose has perhaps thickened slightly, and . . . the hair which in her first youth had golden, almost auburn tones, like Titians, has turned brown before turning grey . . .[6]

Primoli talked to her, now, about her husband, Anatole Demidoff: 'You couldn't have any idea of the corruption of this cossack, whom she even found in bed one day with another man. This was the Comte de S., who was not only the husband's *mistress* but was wildly in love with the young wife.'[7]

Saint-Gratien. Friday 17 October, 11.30 p.m.

In bed. Here is the day at Saint-Gratien . . .

Until *déjeuner* at 11.30 a.m. you stay in your room unless you prefer to stroll in the park. The second bell finds all the guests assembled on the pretty verandah next to the big salon. On the stroke of 11.30, the Princess appears, holding the morning papers which she has already read, always very well-groomed and elegant, fresh and scented like a flower which has just received its dew and its first ray of sunlight. She usually wears a navy-blue silk dress with white spots, and suede gloves, her auburn hair is looped up on her temples, and swept off her ears, which are adorned with pearl earrings.

The guests bow and kiss the hand which she holds out to them, and she kisses the ladies. She takes someone's arm, and we go in to table. The dining-room is a later addition to the château, and the three large bay-windows open on to the park. Opposite the Princess sits her maid of honour, the Baronne de Galbois; we call the old spinster Dame Pluche, because of her proverbial naïveté.

The menu is very simple. It consists of new-laid eggs from the farm, two meat dishes, vegetables from the kitchen-garden, a cake, stewed fruit, tea and coffee. The centre-piece is Minton china – children carrying flowers and fruit.

The conversation is generally animated. The Princess is [not] domineering, but she has no time for indifference and so she often catches fire . . . She has the art of painting [something] with a stroke in her vivid language like Saint-Simon – her favourite author.

After *déjeuner* we go on to the verandah, where she allows cigars – although she does not smoke herself and she dislikes the smell of tobacco.

The day is spent between walks in the park with the little pack [of dogs], or outings in a carriage in the forest of Montmorency, or boating expeditions on Lake Enghien; but generally there are long sessions in the studio – which was built as a counterpart to the dining-room. She paints her pretty water-colours until darkness falls.

When she can no longer see clearly enough to draw, she leaves her easel for the divan, where she half reclines in the midst of her brood of little dogs, she takes up some knitting and works until the darkness makes the needles drop from her hands. And then, in that half-light which is an aid to recollection, she talks of her youth in Italy, her proposals of marriage, her travels in Russia, the beginnings of the Empire . . .

And so one waits for the arrival of the six o'clock train, which brings the friends who are bringing news from Paris.

At about half-past six the Princess goes upstairs to get dressed. At seven o'clock she reappears in a low-necked dress, with a string a pearls round her neck, a flower or a jewel in her hair, and her smooth shining plaits held back over her ears by little combs edged with pearls.

The men are wearing tails and black cravats.

At 7 o'clock we go into the dining-room.

After dinner – which is generally for ten to twenty people – the men go and smoke in the billiard-room, and the Princess stays and works in the salon, on her little sofa, by the big round table, with the ladies and the non-smokers . . .

At 10 o'clock, the little omnibus takes the guests away; only the inhabitants of the château stay on in the salon, and, while the ladies resume their work, one of the men reads *La Revue des Deux Mondes*, or *La Nouvelle Revue*, or the *Mémoires* of Saint-Simon, the châtelaine's favourite author. Although she has an antipathy for Louis XIV and Mme de Maintenon, she is passionately interested in everything to do with this period. Did she not – stay-at-home though she is – go and visit the Château de Maintenon?

On the stroke of 11 o'clock, she folds up her work and rises to her feet, says good night to the company – there are embraces and kissings of hands – and goes up to her room. At midnight the château is fast asleep – transformed by the wave of a wand into the palace of the Sleeping Beauty. Everyone is asleep but me, the writer of these lines. Good night![8]

21 October

Talked about the artist-poet Ernest Hébert. He is small, and he limps as the result of a fall from his horse which he had during his youth in Italy. His features are fine, his eyes expressive and tender, his long beard and hair, which were very black, are turning grey with time, and look unkempt, and despite this appearance, which is that of an artist of the Jeune France, he has been adored all his life, and he still is today.[9]

8

Hébert remained a devoted admirer, but Flaubert had paid his last autumn visit to Saint-Gratien. He was tired from constant overwork and from financial worries; his health had long been indifferent. On 8 May 1880, very suddenly, he died. His death found the Princess writing an appreciation of him. 'Alas,' she added, 'as I draw this portrait I learn that my poor friend has died. I lack the courage to go on. His faults have vanished. All I can do now is to regret him . . .'[1]

That autumn, Gégé Primoli continued his diary:

NOTES. SAINT-GRATIEN. SEPTEMBER 1880

[Paris.] It seems to me that the air is purer there, more vivifying, in spite of the miasmas and decompositions of the Republic . . .

Friday [–] in Paris. Had *déjeuner* in Gabriel Ferrier's studio . . . There was young Gustave Popelin [son of Claudius]. He is twenty-one, and he has the brightest of futures. He has an annual income of 80,000 livres, and a good deal of talent. His picture [at this year's Salon], *Le Sacrifice à Esculape*, earned him a mention. It was the first that he'd exhibited.[2]

16 September

Goncourt said to me: 'It is extraordinary that the Princess should surround herself with people whose books she cannot bear: Gautier, Flaubert, Me, etc., while one evening I saw her put off dinner to finish reading *La Comtesse de Chalis* by Feydeau, whom she cannot abide.'[3]

That day the Princess discussed Sainte-Beuve.

'He was my friend for twenty-five years, and I was proud of his friendship. He enabled me to do a little good. I felt that I needed to justify my position and my fortune in the eyes of the world . . . I was determined to bring the intelligentsia closer to those in power, Sainte-Beuve used to help me in my task . . . I had met him first in 1841 . . . During the Empire I used to go and spend two hours with him every Sunday, and I used to look forward to my Sunday as if I were meeting a handsome young man . . . On Wednesday he was the soul of my *dîners de bêtes*, as they called them at the Tuileries, . . . the incomparable conductor of the orchestra. He used to give everyone their note.'[4]

21 September

Flaubert despised Mr de Sade as a man and as a stylist, but he could not prevent himself from having a certain admiration for his bourgeois temperament, and he used to call him The Old Man, which is what Goethe calls God.[5]

1 December

Rue de Berry. 'Since I didn't have a palace,' the Princess said to me, 'I wanted to deck out a nest for myself . . .' . . .

The first evening, when I came solemnly down the stairs to escort her to dinner with B, she was in full evening-dress, décolletée, and I was wearing a white tie and tails. We both burst out laughing, and our good humour has continued more or less ever since.[6]

It had been slightly ruffled when Hébert had written to announce his impending marriage to Mlle Gaby d'Uckermann. The Princess painted a fan for her: blue butterflies on pink flowers; but she was feminine enough to regret the marriage of an old admirer – especially to a woman forty years younger than himself.[7]

13 December

Do you know, asked Mme de Beaulaincourt, what Princess Mathilde said to Mme Hébert? 'How could you marry that old fogy?' she asked her. The young German answered: 'Genius has no age.'[8]

'I am a woman of impressions, . . . a smell, . . . a ray of sunlight . . . What do I care about the colour of something uninteresting? Like Goncourt with his Fragonard, Chardin, Watteau? . . . I don't see the need to appreciate the Flemish, they have dull, commonplace natures, I can't like them. My nature is all of a piece, I am an impressionable person . . .'

'I like every dish at a dinner.'

'I can't, I have my preferences.'[9]

* * *

Talked about the Princess with Alex. Dumas. He believes that she has not forgotten Nieuwerkerke. She has, he says, put the image of the second [lover, Claudius Popelin] over that of the first, and it overlaps all round. Has she married Popelin? [Goncourt] would be tempted to believe it, because the denial was so half-hearted. There should have been a public denial. He thinks that it was Popelin who demanded it so as not to expose himself to being dismissed like the other.[10]

* * *

Talked about the Princess with Popelin. She has an established reputation as a woman of superior intelligence and culture. She owes it largely to the intelligent and enlightened entourage whom she has chosen, the friends to whom she has endeared herself. But She is above all a woman of impressions.[11]

* * *

[Primoli, sorting out her books:] 'Thiers: *Histoire de la Révolution française?*' 'In the ante-room.' 'Thiers: *Histoire du Consulat et de l'Empire?*' 'Oh, that one goes in the salon!'[12]

* * *

What dominates in her is the woman, the Frenchwoman . . . It is clearly She who has known the most men of distinction: they have been the ornament of her *salon*, but they have had no influence at all on her tastes: She has remained Herself.[13]

* * *

Str. [Straus, the advocate?] told me that the Princess told me about the break [with Nieuwerkerke] as they were walking in the park at Saint-Gratien.

'Look, it was here. We were walking side by side. They brought us the post, and we started to read our letters. "What news?" "My wife is very ill . . . And look at this, so's Mr Demidoff." "How strange if we became free together, we could get married." "That would be impossible." "Why? Have you been the lover of the Comtesse [Castiglione?]?" "Has she been my mistress? What an insult! She's an honest woman." "What about me?"[14]

* * *

The personal problems in her life had, it seemed, been settled. The political complexities still remained. On 7 May 1881 the Princess assured Primoli: 'Your old aunt is still very spoilt – quite surrounded with friends and often very tired – but I do my best to stand up to everything. Pietri dined with me yesterday evening. *She* has sent me three marble busts, one of them of King Louis which I didn't want, and I don't know what to do with it.'[15]

9

Primoli was more concerned, in 1881, with a princess of the theatre. In January Dumas *fils* wrote to him about his latest play, *La Princesse de Bagdad*.

> The first night [he reported] was stormy. It had brought together all the people whom I bore – to use their word – with my paradoxes, and especially with my honesty. They did not want to accept this princess who, like a king's daughter, marched valiantly into battle, . . . and ended, two days later, as mistress of the battlefield. Every day, the curtain rose on takings of 7,500 francs; there are always fifteen performances fully booked, and many people say . . . it's the best thing the dramatist has done. There's Paris for you . . .
>
> Croizette was absolutely wonderful; besides, she is endowed, by nature, with the character of Lionnette. You ought to find some beautiful, passionate Italian who is the equivalent of our Parisian. What the part needs most of all are a character and a temperament.[1]

It almost seemed that, in this letter, Dumas had a presentiment of the advent of La Duse. On 10 May she made her appearance in the play in Rome; and, next day, a delighted Primoli announced to him:

> Yesterday, at last, *mon cher maître*, I had the triumphant evening which I had been expecting for a long time. *La Princesse de Bagdad* was a triumph all the way. It had been presented to us, more than a month ago, by indifferent actors, but yesterday a young actress imposed it on the most recalcitrant public, and compelled them to bow before your work . . .
>
> If Mademoiselle Croizette had not been endowed with the very

character of Lionnette, I doubt whether she could have performed it much better than Mademoiselle Duse, who understood you as if you had taken the trouble to explain the part yourself, with all its charms and dangers. It was just one long salvo of applause.[2]

'I had already received a telegram from [Ernesto] Rossi,' Dumas answered, 'telling me about the success, but I slightly mistrusted the leading actor of a company which was [known to be] the rival of another. Your letter proves that he spoke the truth, and I am delighted.'[3]

My dear Monsieur Rossi [he continued],
   By the same post as your letter, I received one from my young friend [Primoli]. It announced a triumph for you and for Mademoiselle Duse. Would you be my interpreter to that noble woman of matchless talent – so my friend assures me – that woman whose splendour in the part brought benefit to its author?
   . . . I hear that you are soon arriving in Paris. It would give me great pleasure to shake you by the hand, and, if you are acting in Paris, to come and applaud you.
   Thank you again.
                                   Yours ever,
                                   ALEXANDRE DUMAS[4]

This letter, recorded Primoli, was published in an Italian paper, and it was the consecration of La Duse.[5]

* * *

That winter he himself was once again in Paris, recording the conversation at the rue de Berry.

Tuesday, 5 December 1881

Princess Mathilde much amused us this evening by telling us, Frédéric Masson, Robert de Bonnières and me, about Saint-Beuve's visit to Compiègne (December 1863).
   As soon as he received the invitation, the naïve sceptic rushed to the rue de Courcelles, and, in anguish, he handed me the letter from the Great Chamberlain. 'What should I do, my dear Princess?' 'Accept! You are in the same série as I am, so we'll spend a few days together: you won't be really unhappy!' 'But . . .,' he said, taking off his little black skull-cap. 'Come on, what are your objections?' 'To begin with, I only have two women

102

servants, my housekeeper and my cook. I can't take them with me.' 'Why not? You aren't young any more, people know that you are used to having women to look after you . . . Take one of them: they will think it quite natural.' 'It's impossible!' he sighed. 'But, since you are so indulgent towards me, I should like to make a suggestion to you . . .' 'I'm listening.' 'One of your valets is a former zouave, and he is very kind to me . . . Would you lend him to me for my visit to Compiègne?' 'Is that all it is, my dear Sainte-Beuve? He is at your service.' 'Thank you. Then I'll accept the invitation so that I can spend a few days with you.'

The day of departure came [Princess Mathilde continued]. I entrusted Sainte-Beuve to my zouave. The journey was uneventful, at the château we parted company, and each of us was taken to their apartment. I had hardly begun to settle down when I heard a knock at the door. 'Come in!' It was the zouave. 'What is it?' 'Madame, Mr Sainte-Beuve is so worried that I thought I should warn Your Highness.' 'What's happened to him?' 'Nothing, Madame; it's just that he finds his room is too far from . . . a certain place, and he would like to be nearer, if possible . . .' 'That's all right, here's a note for the Prefect of the Palace, he will settle him in another room. Off you go.'

He'll have some peace and so shall I, at least I hope so. I get dressed for dinner . . . Knock, knock! 'Again?' 'It's me, Madame; Mr Sainte-Beuve must inform Her Highness that he can't appear at dinner . . .' 'Why not?' 'Because his shoes are too big.' 'What do you mean, too big?' 'Yes, his feet are lost in them, he would mislay his shoes on the way.' 'Come on, then,' said my lady's-maid, impatiently, 'bring them to me, I'll put paper and cotton-wool inside them.'

The zouave brought the shoes, Julie stuffed them with cotton-wool and returned them to Sainte-Beuve. When I went into the salon, he didn't see me, he was so absorbed in contemplation of those wretched pumps. 'How big they are, aren't they, Princess? They aren't right; I'm going back to my room.' 'What nonsense! No one will notice anything, I assure you.' 'Oh yes, it's obvious.' 'But it makes the foot look longer, it makes it slimmer . . . It looks good . . .'

After dinner, Sainte-Beuve came up to me and said mysteriously: 'I should like to speak to you.' 'Speak on.' 'Oh, not here, in front of everyone.' 'Then come to my room.'

I went upstairs and he followed me, rather awkwardly, because he was still afraid of losing his shoes. When we were alone: 'Look,' he said, 'this is what I wanted to ask you. Might I go out this evening?' 'But . . . yes, of course.' 'Oh, not for long;

I'll be back in an hour; I have a little visit to pay in the neighbourhood . . .' 'Stay out as long as you like. What stops you going out?' 'But . . . What will the sentry say?' 'Do you think you're in prison?'

That was really what it was: he felt he was in prison and being kept under observation. He wrote to his cook every day, and, since he was afraid that someone might intercept his correspondence, he entrusted his letters to me to ensure that they reached the recipient. One morning, he came to me to confess a new embarrassment: 'My good Princess,' he said, 'I am deeply troubled.'

'Tell me, what's the matter, my dear Sainte-Beuve?' 'This has worried me so much that I couldn't sleep last night. Yesterday Mademoiselle de Heeckeren [the young lady-in-waiting] whispered to me: "Tomorrow morning, give me your arm when we go in to table." ' 'Well?' 'Well, what does that mean?' 'That means that Mademoiselle Heeckeren is an intelligent girl, she wanted to do you an act of courtesy and to benefit from your conversation. That's all.' 'That's all? Are you sure it won't go further?'

He had got it into his head that they wanted to lead him into matrimony, and the idea terrified him. Apart from that, he gets on very well with the zouave, and finally I stopped sending my valet to take my notes to the boulevard Montparnasse, because I learned that in his kindness the Academician made my messenger sit down at his table. This became awkward when he served him at dinner at my *hôtel*.[6]

December 1881 brought the death of Eugène Giraud. He had been the Princess's friend even before her cousin came to power. He had been her art master and, as Primoli observed, 'one of the last classic Bohemians,'[7] a constant entertainment in her *salon*. Now he died, unexpectedly, of a stroke. 'I'm brokenhearted!' the Princess wrote to Primoli on 30 December. 'For thirty-four years we had lived the same life, and he was an essential part of mine . . . Tomorrow I shall go with him to his resting-place.'[8] Next day, at the funeral, Goncourt saw her, 'superb in her grief'.[9] The old guard of the *mercredis* was passing, and he and Dumas *fils* remained the last. She herself knew that she must draw a new generation to the rue de Berry.

It was Goncourt who set about introducing the Daudets to the *salon*. He needed all his diplomacy. Frédéric Masson, the Bonaparte historian, 'never stopped repeating that, if Daudet was received, he would write a novel called *La Princesse Bathilde*, in which the Princess would be disgracefully treated.'[10] His warnings went unheeded. On 7 March 1882, Mme Daudet recorded: 'The other evening, for the first time, we were received at Princess Mathilde's.'[11]

The year which brought *le ménage Daudet* to the rue de Berry also reminded the Princess of a scurrilous guest of long ago. It was now eighteen years since Comte Horace de Viel-Castel had died, embittered, and disgraced for stealing from the Louvre. He had left his mistress the little black books in which, for thirteen years, he had recorded the sins of the Second Empire. She had now found a Swiss publisher for the six volumes of memoirs. Late in 1882 it was announced that the first volume of *Mémoires* had been seized. The *Mémoires* were nonetheless published in 1883. The final volume had hardly appeared before a new edition was in preparation.

10

On the last day of 1882, Léon Gambetta died. He had been instrumental, with Thiers, in founding the Third Republic, and though he had recently retired from politics, there were people who saw his death as a political watershed. Goncourt declared that, if the Prince Imperial were alive, the Republic would have ended within a fortnight.

Prince Napoleon was sixty; but he kept his intense and frustrated longing for power. He felt that the death of Gambetta had given him his chance. On 16 January 1883, he had posters published in which he demanded a plebiscite.

The posters were destroyed, and the Prince was arrested and imprisoned in the Conciergerie. Charles Floquet, the popular radical, seized the occasion to attack the Bourbon and Bonaparte dynasties: he proposed exile for the members of families which had reigned in France. Goncourt, reading the morning papers on 17 January, learned of the arrest and of the debate in the Chamber. That afternoon he called at the rue de Berry. Princess Mathilde made some pretence of serenity, but in her eyes he detected the terror of exile.

He was not the only friend who was anxious about her future. A few days later, Édouard Béhaine, the diplomat, mentioned it to President Grévy. Grévy seemed to have little sympathy for the Princess, and he believed that she was working for the Bonaparte restoration; but he told Béhaine that the Republic would not think of distressing a woman. She could be assured that all would be well. The message gave her some relief, but she was still disturbed. Her disturbance was not lessened by the fact that Popelin had decided to leave for Italy with his son. In 1882 Gustave had won the Premier Grand

Prix de Rome, which entitled him to four years at the Villa Médicis. Gégé Primoli had promised to look after him in Rome.

Before I do anything else, I should like to reassure you about your poor aunt's morale [Popelin told him on 20 January]. Her morale is excellent, as good as it can be considering these unfortunate events. I'm really vexed to be leaving her at a moment like this. But she has a crowd of people round her, & there's a great coming & going, which will help her to bear my absence a little. . .

Can you get me a good Room with a fire? I should be so grateful.[1]

Rome, 28 January 1883

Went to meet Claudius Popelin at the station. His son Gustave – whom I'm very fond of – has won the [Premier] Grand Prix de Rome, and his father has come to settle him at the Villa Médicis and to prolong his farewells. This son is all he has, and he can't bring himself to part from him. Gustave had all the more merit in facing the competition which he won, because he had an annual income of 100,000 livres. I had booked a room for Popelin at the Hôtel de Londres, then he came to the house, Papa kept him to dinner . . .[2]

29 January

Popelin came for *déjeuner*. I took him to Aunt Augusta [Gabrielli's].[3]

2 February

Received a telegram from Princess Mathilde to tell me that on doctors' advice Prince Napoleon has been transferred from the Conciergerie to a nursing-home at Auteuil.[4]

9 February

Met the new French Ambassador to the Holy See, Lefebvre de Béhaine . . . He is the brother-in-law of my excellent friend Frédéric Masson, and the cousin of Edmond de Goncourt.[5]

11 February

The two Popelins to *déjeuner*. Then I took them to the Capitol.[6]

107

Prince Napoleon has been released as the accusation has been thrown out.[7]

Popelin came to *déjeuner*. Then we went to see his son, who isn't well.[8]

At the Villa Médicis, to see young Popelin, who is ill. I hope it won't be serious, but it has begun with inflammation of the bowels.[9]

Popelin left at 2 o'clock. I put him on the train, and then his son came back to the house with me. It's the first time he's left his father, and, not being expansive, like most motherless children, he must suffer twice over.[10]

He also continued to be ill. On 7 March, Goncourt recorded: 'Popelin left at four o'clock for Italy, after a telegram from Gégé, telling him to come and fetch his son, who has Roman fever.'[11]

For Gégé it was a sharp reminder of a recent tragedy. Only the previous year his brother, Napoleon, had died at the age of twenty-seven. Marcello Spaziani said that he died of typhoid fever; the Comtesse Clémentine Hugo, on a visit to Rome, gave another explanation for his death. He was, she wrote, 'the most brilliant of the three [Primoli] sons . . . He had been wading in the marshes, shooting duck all day; despite the fever in his bones [*sic*], he refused to miss Don Giannetto Doria's ball. In those galleries, which are as elegant as they are imposing, he ate sorbet after sorbet to cool the fire which malaria was spreading through his veins. After the ball he took to his bed, and never rose from it again.'[12] Gégé had nursed him. In the early weeks of 1883, he was still oppressed by his brother's death.

My friend Gustave Popelin's illness recalls the cruel anguish of last year. These ups and downs of fever, . . . this poor father to prepare, to warn, to summon, to meet at the station . . .[13]

9 March

Went to meet Popelin at the station with the French Ambassador, Lefebvre de Béhaine. Poor man! . . . He was not weeping, but he was overcome by trembling . . . Poor father! When he went into his son's room, . . . he could see how much he had changed.[14]

28 March

Put Claudius and Gustave Popelin on to the train. I am sure that the native air of Paris will completely restore this unfortunate young man . . . My dear Aunt Mathilde has been in the most cruel anguish because of this illness. Letters and telegrams . . . these last days. She maintains that we have prevented her from coming to Rome, and she reproaches me for having made her give up the journey.[15]

16 April

I am reading *Une Vie* by Maupassant. An enormous talent, as his master Flaubert used to say. But I find this novel full of cynical, harrowing and unnecessary details. Once upon a time, when I had a great store of gaiety and good humour, I could face the most disenchanting books with impunity; but today I find life sad enough in itself without the reproduction of its darkest aspects.[16]

11 June

Bought a new novel by Matilde Serao, *Fantasia*. It is only in literary matters that I still feel a little curiosity – but so little! I bore the book off to the Villa Borghese, I just read a few pages, although the beginning enchanted me and I am in sympathy with the author.[17]

16 June

She has a great deal of talent and I couldn't express my real sympathy to her. She must have thought me the lowest kind of man of the world . . . It's at moments like this that I regret that I haven't shown what I can do. I haven't published anything, I've remained a failure. It's just that there are so few people whom I care to please. But it enrages me to be thought an ordinary man of the world, I am prejudiced against men of the world as soldiers are against civilians. And after all I don't deserve any other appreciation, I can't call myself an artist, since the sole aim of my life is trying to understand instead of trying to express myself.[18]

20 June

An extravagance for me! I had *déjeuner* in town for the first time for a year and four months. Went to the good and simple Baronne de Renzis' to make the acquaintance of Matilde Serao, whose talent I admire enormously . . . She has just published a remarkable novel. I accompanied Mlle Serao to her door, and we talked . . . and talked . . .[19]

25 June

In the evening, to Matilde Serao's. I found her all alone in her study. The writer attracted me and the woman kept me. She has a mixture of Greek and Neapolitan blood. There is languor in her grace and vivacity in her smile. The poetry of grace, and the wit of Pulcinella. I read her two chapters of my novel *Un Prince romain*. She made some well-justified criticisms and urged me to go on, but I'm afraid that she was too kind to say what she really thought. She asked me to visit her again tomorrow to continue.[20]

8 July

I was disturbed all night by some sad news which [my brother] Louis brought me yesterday evening. That sweet Maria de Gallese has been carried off by the little poet Gabriele d'Annunzio. She is eighteen, my Greuze (the day before yesterday I should have written *La Cruche cassée*), she is bright-faced, her head is rather large, but it has an aureole of downy golden hair all round it. A nice smile, wide-open eyes, tenderness and wit . . . For some time her gaiety had been turning into melancholy, she didn't chat any more, she was preoccupied, she didn't laugh any more, she only smiled . . . She had learned that what attracted worshippers to her, and deterred fiancés, was her mother. Her mother was charming and attractive, but as hysterical as the heroine of a Naturalist novel: one met her in vineyards, and in cabs, with poets . . . The poor child must have had a glimpse of many things . . . One day, when she was left at home, she found a very young poet in a corner of her palace. He was a child like herself, whose head had been turned by his early success. He was as handsome as a mediaeval page, Fortunio, le Passant. Had he come for her mother? The young girl took him for herself, entrusted herself to him, and leant upon him. He took her in his arms, still believing life to be

110

fiction, and he seduced her. These children, who have barely thirty-six years between them, are acting recklessly. She found that she was pregnant. How could she confess? For three months she struggled. She hesitated to reveal her fault to her mother, who was the real culprit, or to her father, an impulsive soldier who would perhaps have killed her – her or him . . . At last, not caring any more, she eloped with her poet, they were discovered in a train. The mother, finally alerted to the danger, had her brought back to the palace next day by a police officer. The father still doesn't know anything. Since the fact is public, the mother is going round the clubs, calling on her friends to warn them that her husband doesn't know anything, and that in Heaven's name they mustn't say anything to him. And the poor child is crying, crying alone in her room, or, which is still more painful, bravely smiling at her acquaintances in the Corso, in the Pincio, in her barouche beside her mother, who no longer leaves her!

Some likenesses are fatal, and the picture *La Cruche cassée*, which was evoked by the poor child's blonde appearance, should have made one foresee the catastrophe. A friend of mine may be right to judge the people he sees by their resemblance to others whom he knows.[21]

6 August

To Princess Pallavicini's. She told me the sequel to the sad Gallese story. The Duke retired to the country so as not to see the preparations for the wedding. He received some infamous anonymous letters denouncing his wife for her infidelity and for her complicity in this lamentable marriage. Exasperated, he came to Rome, determined to make a scandalous scene. He threatened to sue his poor wife for adultery, and he was only dissuaded by his sister-in-law and his aunt. He agreed to withdraw his suit on condition that his wife left Rome for ever. She went away, escorted by her brother-in-law; she is the most to be pitied of the three, because she is the most guilty. The poor man, disappointed in his conjugal and paternal happiness, buried himself in the country with his pears and roses. And the couple will hardly be married before they separate.[22]

11 September

Scribbled down a plan for a novel which appeals to me and came to me at dawn between sleep and waking: *Le père du Prince*. I want to show the father, an old man, a liberal of '48, and the son, a violent clerical, brought up in Rome during his father's exile . . .[23]

111

Goncourt, too, was writing a new novel, *Chérie*. Late in September he stayed at Saint-Gratien, and he read some of it to the Princess. He had complained, more than once, that she did not appreciate his work; and she listened to him, now, with a certain lack of sympathy. 'Goncourt is leaving tomorrow,' she told Primoli on 28 September. 'He is writing a book, and he read us several chapters with unremitting feeling. It's the life of a young girl up to the age of twenty-nine – her passions and her loves. It's all descriptions . . . When he reads, he beats time with his left hand to emphasize the balance of the phrases. He is very well – happy and charming, apart from his work.'[24]

* * *

Rome, 1 October

I have written little in recent days [continued Primoli]. These notebooks, which were my distraction as a sick-nurse, have been replaced by a more living distraction. A young actress, a great one, the true interpreter of Dumas' plays, has come to perform in Rome. She has made me go back to the theatre, which I hadn't been to for twenty months, and she has made my heart beat for dramas other than my own domestic dramas . . .[25]

2 October

Received a letter from Dumas, who promises me a part for La Duse –he's busy writing a 'very strange' play, he tells me.[26]

3 October

[Teatro] Valle. Saw La Duse in *Fédora* . . . Visited La Duse in the intervals, she was very nervous, mercurial; she didn't like her part, and yet it was an absolute triumph. After the play she took my arm, but she couldn't speak, she was so nervous.[27]

4 October

Called on La Duse at 5 o'clock. Talked for a long while. Her nature is as exquisite as her talent. Shall I fall in love with her? Well, *tant pis*! I saw *Fédora* again. Took back the copy of *Visite des noces* to La Duse, who was in her dressing-room. She had lent it to me.[28]

Primoli had fallen under the spell of La Duse. She was married to Tebaldo Checchi, but her married state would not have

112

deterred a passionate admirer. Once again, no doubt, Primoli's love remained a theme for reverie. Probably he did not dare to show his feelings for her, and her letters to him are affectionate, but hardly suggest that there had been a declaration of love. Nonetheless he remained enthralled by La Duse and by her past. In the autumn of 1883, he released his emotions in a letter to Dumas *fils*.

8 October

Wrote thirty pages or so about La Duse to Alexandre Dumas. I told him her touching story in every detail.[29]

* * *

This enormous letter was not immediately sent. Late in December, Primoli reduced it to normal proportions. It was, perhaps, part of this letter which he later published in *La Revue de Paris*.

[Rome, 188–]

You ask me, mon cher maître, how it revealed itself, this marvellous talent in which it is hard to discern a school and recognize a system.

It was at Turin, in 1881. Eleonora Duse had just come through a cruel year of physical and emotional ordeals which had kept her away from the stage. Cesare Rossi [sic] trusted in her sensibility, which had no doubt been stirred by recent emotions, and he saw that she was undecided about her future. He offered to keep her for the important leading parts. She was still stunned, but she accepted, although she did not think she could keep her promise, and she signed her prima donna's contract, so she told me, 'as you sign a bill of exchange you are sure you will be unable to honour, knowing that when it falls due you will acquit it by suicide.'

Well, the old actor had been right! Art brought her back into the world; she was consecrated as a great actress overnight.

She has become what she is without going through all the grades and the conventions, simply by a cry from the heart. All she has done has been to study herself and to transpose her life into her parts. She has turned her deficiencies to advantage and replaced art by truth. She cannot recall what no one has taught her, but she remembers what she has suffered. Her talent has been formed like this, from her flesh and blood; it has fed on the utter

113

poverty of her childhood and the trials and hardships of her youth.

An insurmountable reserve prevents her from making confidences in her private life, and so she compensates herself on stage, and she lets her heart overflow: a heart which otherwise would burst. She particularly likes the parts in your plays; she rediscovers herself in them more than she does in any others. That is one of the reasons for her cult for you . . .

At every moment she feels again, she finds herself again, she recollects. These are doubtless not the events which have thrown her life into confusion, but these are the feelings that she has known.

What does she care about the conventions of the theatre? She does not know them. This is how she has felt, and this is how she will speak. Everything is reversed, and changed, and unexpected. You tremble, and you weep with her, and break into applause.[30]

Dumas was enthralled by the working of a woman's heart, and he was always looking for a new dramatic theme. He only regretted that Primoli had not sent him the thirty pages: indeed, it seems that he asked for them, and that Primoli sent them to him.

My dear friend [wrote Dumas, no doubt in 1884],
You were very wrong not to send me that long letter last year. I have just read it with the greatest interest and emotion. I should have known this most fascinating woman even better, and I should have shown my affection for her even more when I had occasion to write to her. In your account there is only this series of banal adventures which are common to most women in the situation in which she found herself; but banalities all at once assume a certain colour when talent and renown are added to them . . . To those who ask why God made grief, one might reply that it is sometimes necessary for the creation of genius . . . Will she come to Paris during her leave? Do tell her to let me know. I shall go and see her as soon as I learn of her arrival. She doesn't speak French, I don't speak Italian, but I am sure we shall understand each other very well . . .[31]

* * *

On 9 October 1883, Primoli continued his diary:

Received a note from La Duse to say that she is playing *La Dame [aux camélias]* on Friday.[32]

114

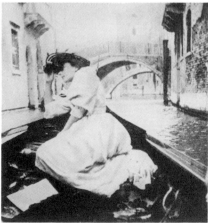

Jean-Louis Forain and his mistress, Jeanne Bosc. This enchanting, almost
cinematic record of a flirtation in a gondola was made by Primoli, in Venice, on
23 August 1889.

The circus comes to Rome: Buffalo Bill
and Annie Oakley, March 1890.

In the snow near Rome: Primoli photographs his waiting carriage.

Self-portrait of Joseph Primoli. He is admiring the distant view of Rome.

The train to Civitavecchia. This photograph shows it crossing the new railway bridge on its way from Rome.

Conversation in Rome. A street scene which records Primoli's skill and humour as a social observer.

26 October

Spent the evening with the Giacosa–Verga–Cecconi trio. [Teatro] Valle. *La Locandiera*. Had supper with La Duse.[33]

30 October

Took Sirène, the little cat, to La Diva. I had had a little collar made for it with its name in diamonds. In the evening – a disappointment – *La femme de Claude*. Supper together (Verga, Giacosa, Cecconi, Schavitch, Minervini, d'Arcais, La Serao, La Duse, her husband and me).[34]

31 October

Spent the morning with La Diva. Went to fetch her by carriage to take her to the station . . .[35]

3 November

Bad-tempered all day. In the evening, the good and witty Matilde Serao came to my room, escorted by [Carlo] Cecconi and [the dramatist Giuseppe] Giacosa. She liked my setting very much, we recited poems and deciphered autographs. A good conversation.[36]

4 November

In the evening Arrigo Boito came to my room: he is one of the strangest and rarest geniuses in existence, because he is both a poet and a musician. Giuseppe Giacosa came too: the sympathetic poet for whom my friendship increases every day, because we have been stamped with the same mark.[37]

10 December

Across the river with Caterina [Primoli's name for Matilde Serao]. Night fell. We got lost as we went deeper into the marshy terrain. There were great shadows round us. We were far away, very far away. She was overcome by fatigue, she was frightened. Only fear could distract her from her old love, she found the traces of it at every step. She was nervous, her voice was trembling, her gaiety was artificial. Towards the hour when night fell, I could find no words to equal the great spectacle unfolding around us. I began to recite *Tristesse d'Olympio*. My love was absorbed in the grandeur of nature. I shall make a short story out of it, she will make a chapter for a novel.[38]

115

In the evening the Fontana di Trevi was illuminated with Bengal lights as Prince Frederick William [of Germany] passed by. The poor *palombelle* nesting in the friezes were woken up with a start, and began to flutter here and there, to fly up in the air and vanish, luminous white specks, in the sombre heights of the heavens. It seemed as if the birds of peace had been put to flight by the Prussian general's golden helmet.[39]

Three

1

Tranquillity was indeed disturbed. On 30 December 1883, less than two years after the death of his son, Pietro Primoli died. He was sixty-three. Gégé returned to his diary.

1884

16 January

The first letters I answered were those of my dear Giacosa, Eleonora Duse, and Verga, whose play *Cavalleria rusticana* has recently been a success.[1]

18 January

In the evening, I was writing in my room, when I heard the *simpatica* voice of Caterina. She did me good. She has such a love of life that she attaches you to it again.[2]

2 March

The reviving Matilde Serao, who seems to be born of a burst of laughter and a ray of sunlight, has created some diversion in my grief. She has been as good as a sister to me, as only my poor mother would have been [*sic*]. Her time is precious, but she has come to waste evenings with me. This morning she brought Luigi Gualdo to *déjeuner* with me. His novella *In ritardo* has made a deep impression on me.[3]

The comments seem strangely literary, even unfeeling, for a son whose father has just died; but Primoli had always been drawn, overwhelmingly, to his mother. He had not simply

119

been dazzled by the brilliance of the Bonapartes, the aura of the Imperial Family. He was unusually close to Charlotte Primoli. Whatever his affection for his father, he had been, and would always be, his mother's son. The double bereavement occasioned the real tragedy of his life – and of hers. Distraught by the death of her son, and of her husband, Charlotte Primoli lost her reason.

That summer, Gégé set out with her for Paris, to consult Dr Esprit Blanche, the specialist in nervous disorders.

10 June

Journey. All is well. Turin at 1.30. La Duse at the station, simple, gentle, good and sad in her grey velvet costume. She wept at her isolation in the midst of the world. She has had unprecedented triumphs at Trieste, Venice, Vicenza and Milan, and she has the dismal sadness of the victor.[4]

18 June

At Saint-Gratien with Louis Ganderax, who writes very remarkable theatrical criticism in the *Revue des 2 mondes* . . . We have the same tastes in literature, we belong to the same generation and we have breathed in the same air.[5]

Paris, 19 June

Alexandre Dumas came from Marly to see me. I found him with Mlle Brandes, a young actress to whom he gave her début in *Diane de Lys*. She is leaving for England with Sarah Bernhardt. He was paternal with me, as usual . . . We talked about La Duse, he will give her a very dramatic play which he is in process of writing.[6]

Throughout the summer, Primoli moved between Saint-Gratien and Paris.

26 August

Went back to Paris with Alexandre Dumas. Spent four hours with him in his study . . . Talked about myself, about my life, which has changed direction, about my getting married. He hardly advises me to do so. If I married, I told him, it would be to seek consolation for my griefs . . . He said: 'If you've quite decided never to marry, don't do it; but if you think that you'll weaken one day, when you can't bear to be alone, then marry at once.' He talked to me like a man and a philosopher.[7]

Dined at Saint-Gratien. The Princess was kind and confiding, and told me about the interview between Popelin and Nieuwerkerke the previous day. She said that if she met [Nieuwerkerke] it would have no effect on her. But I can't believe that one kills one's emotions like that. She told me that he had announced it himself. It had been from him that she had learned, one evening, without reason, without warning, that he had promised to marry a young girl. She didn't understand, she had thought that he was going out of his mind, and she had been to Giraud's with him, to get a witness of this revelation and a proof of reality for what seemed to her to be a dream.[8]

18 September

To the Théâtre-Français, saw Mlle Bartet. I told her that she had the leading part in Dumas' play. Saw Henri Becque, the author of *Les Corbeaux* ... This play made me ill. What happened at the beginning – and what didn't happen at the end. My poor mother! ... She cried so much when she saw this play in her days of happiness. Who would have said that the future destined her to be the heroine – without the happy ending?[9]

8 October

Went to collect [Élémir] Bourges [the novelist] from his apartment, behind Notre-Dame, to take him to Edmond de Goncourt's at Auteuil. Edmond, in clogs, was watering his garden. He was simple and affable. He did Bourges the honours of his drawings and his *japonaiseries* ... Bourges, who had come with a smile on his lips, came away from his visit very sad. He confessed to me that this poor old bachelor had made him desperately unhappy. He is so happy himself with his delightful wife, that with all his heart he pities the people he feels to be alone. I was quite surprised when he said 'that poor old man', meaning Goncourt. Personally I cannot bring myself to consider those I love as *old*. They always seem young to me, and I feel that they should be immortal. I see them through the youthfulness and vivacity of my affection.[10]

30 October

Déjeuner at Popelin's with Princess Mathilde, who is back in Paris.[11]

10 November

Dined at the Princess's with Gustave [Popelin], whom we accompanied to the Gare de Lyon. He was leaving for Rome.[12]

20 November

Learned from the paper of the death of Martino Cafiero, which pained me for Eleonora, who loved him, and of the death of poor Virginia Senni whom Nap. loved so much . . . Virginia Senni dead![13]

On 29 September, Primoli left Paris with his mother. Dr Blanche had been unable to cure her. 'I have a real affection for Primoli,' the Empress wrote to Princess Mathilde. 'One can only admire the care which he and his brother take of their mother.'[14]

Charlotte Primoli withdrew, now, from society; and to some her absence was a mystery. The Comtesse Clémentine Hugo, on a visit to Rome, noted that Gégé and Luigi, 'who are cultivated and very much in the swim everywhere, were receiving guests . . . in the little palazzo in the piazza dell'Orso . . . But why,' she enquired, 'without their mother?'[15] The answer was tragic. Charlotte Primoli was incurably insane; she was to remain so for seventeen years, until her death.

2

Dumas had now finished the 'very dramatic' play which he had written for Eleonora Duse. Late in 1884 he sent a copy of the manuscript to Rome. On 4 January 1885, Primoli reported:

La Duse came to see me yesterday evening, and I read her *Denise*. I was sorry that you weren't there, because the various emotions she went through would have amused and interested and moved you. You can imagine how her heart was beating! The first act charmed her, . . . but she was waiting for her part; the second interested her, but . . . she was still waiting. She didn't say anything, but I understood what she was feeling: great admiration for the play, and regret to see Denise remaining in the wings . . . Half the third act went by, and still no Denise! . . . She didn't know whether to laugh or cry about the splendid part which was escaping her . . .

And then came the scene of the confession, the one round which the play revolves – one of the best you've written – I was sure of the effect. She was breathless, she changed colour, and from her eyes, which were expressionless, the tears fell down her cheeks . . . When I came to the details about the dead child, the details which are so true, she suddenly got up, and held her handkerchief to her mouth. She had to listen to the rest hiding behind the screen.

Then she understood the purity of soul of this Denise who moves, chaste and proud, gentle and silent, through the play. Under her impassible mask one must divine the secret which eats away at her until it finally escapes from her. She never laughs, and she doesn't weep, she sometimes sings, but her accents are so sad that, though she is dry-eyed, she makes her listeners shed tears.

If you had heard the heartfelt feeling with which La Duse called up the exquisite figure of Denise! You would have said that she herself was the heroine. She longed to create the part at once, without even learning it: the part of this ideal living creature which she seemed to have known, and to have lived . . .

P.S. I have just had this from her this morning; it is hardly 9 o'clock, and the reading went on until 2 o'clock. I translate:

> Since yesterday evening, I have kept the melody and fragrance of Denise in my ears and heart. I see this figure, vague, indefinite, full of grief and hope . . . Yesterday evening, when you had gone [*sic*], I wrote two lines to M. Dumas, which I dare not and will not re-read . . . It isn't a letter, it isn't thanks. When I am more serene, I shall write both.
>
> In the meanwhile, since we women should always follow our first instinct, would you forward the enclosed letter to him with a covering note from yourself? At the moment, I shouldn't know what to say and how to thank him . . .
>
> ELEONORA

I am also translating the letter that La Duse had written you, as I know that everything honest interests you.[1]

My dear friend [answered Dumas],

I was moved to tears by your letter and the letter from La Duse. I am very happy to have stirred her so, to have given her this grievous pleasure and a new occasion for success.[2]

For a moment, the prospects were threatened. La Duse was suffering from tuberculosis of the lungs. On 9 January, Primoli wrote again to Dumas *fils*:

Mon cher maître,

I think I told you about the rôle which La Duse dreamed of. It was that of a woman who, after the most cruel ordeals, at the very moment when she thought she had attained happiness, would be borne away by death.

The poor creature has almost seen the actress's dream realized in her own life. The reading of *Denise* the other day, the sight of the manuscript, the certainty of having it soon, had given her one of the liveliest satisfactions to her pride, one of the profoundest delights that has been granted her during her most cruelly chequered life. She was confident, and living with her eyes fixed on the part which she already saw as her own . . . Yesterday, she nearly left for the other world, and she is still not very sure of remaining in this one. She had said goodbye to those around her, not without heartbreak; her eyes were closing, and she opened them by an effort of will, afraid of closing them for the last time . . .

124

She did not want to die, she wanted to be Denise first! . . .

The doctors came, and went away despondent. Indeed, one of them was cynical enough to say that he would come back to certify her death. She heard him, terrified, and found the strength to dismiss him, and she fell back, broken by this cruel emotion. Never had she clung to life as she does today when she has Denise, and she felt her life escaping her . . .

If she recovers, I'm afraid that they will oblige her to act, to act until she drops . . . In a few days she will be on the boards once again, unless she is between four planks, which is still possible. She asked me for Denise's confession to keep her company as soon as she can open her eyes. I wish she'd decide to go and spend a week in the country, to recover, and to study her part.[3]

Marly-le-Roi, 27 January 1885

Mon cher enfant [answered Dumas],

I am sending you a copy of *Denise*, which is published this morning. It is exactly as it was performed . . .[4]

La Duse played Denise in Rome. On Good Friday, Primoli wrote again:

Mon cher maître,

I was waiting to answer you until I had the letter which La Duse wanted to send you herself: a letter which she was to entrust to me. She could not bring herself to write it, because she could not find the words to express her gratitude to you. Besides, she has been absorbed by her unremitting work, and her poor health has been affected by it. *Théodora* was the final blow for her. After the first performance, they had to cancel an act; after the second, they stopped performances. You need the energy of Sarah Bernhardt if you are to endure this overwork. She retired to bed, and hardly rose from it except to leave for South America – from which, it may be, she will return. On the eve of her departure she insisted on giving another performance of *Denise*. It was a triumph from beginning to end.

If there is a reproach to make to her on her interpretation of your last creation, it is that she has identified herself too much with the part. It is no longer Denise, it is herself. In the famous scene of the confession, it was her own child that she was mourning, and her protracted grief, the tears which she could not restrain could finally have wearied the audience if it had not itself been deeply moved . . .

125

She devised a flowing costume, soft and chaste, of some grey material, with long straight folds which mysteriously half open, and seem to hold a secret in their shadows. They fall back all at once, and mould her figure in all its purity, without betraying the shape of her body. When she rose from the piano, and we saw her silhouette, we murmured: 'There's Denise,' and from our first glimpse of her we had the presentiment of a secret; it is both her merit and perhaps her fault.[5]

And, with the understanding which is born of affection, Primoli reflected on the nature and the fascination of La Duse.

Just as the *prime donne*, especially in Italy, look for very showy entrances, so that they can be greeted by applause, so La Duse does all she can to find herself on stage without anyone observing her arrival. She is glad when they haven't seen her, or when they recognize her and murmur: '*That's* all she is!' At the first word from her lips, with a simple gesture, a simple attitude, '*that*' becomes someone; this someone soon becomes everything, and before long nothing else exists on stage or in the theatre.

The fascination which she exercises is due in part to the mobility of her face, which gives the public a spectacle ever varied and constantly changing. Mademoiselle Alma Tadema, the artist's daughter, followed a series of performances, and made some curious observations. 'When you see her play the same part several times,' she said, 'you are struck by certain changes of gesture and intonation, the outward signs of a deeper modification. It is because she does not simply give her past vitality to the character she personifies, and always show it according to her first conception. Every evening she adds her actual vibration. The word *change* is perhaps misleading; it is just a change of shades of meaning: she still presents the same picture, but it is lit up in a different manner according to the day and the hour – and it reflects the colour of her soul.'[6]

3

It was this year, 1885, that Primoli's friend Charles Grandjean – an Inspector-General of Historic Monuments – sent him the latest book by Anatole France: *Le Livre de mon Ami*. Primoli was enchanted by this romanticized autobiography. 'It seems to me,' he noted, 'that instead of making difficulties where there are none, one might extract from my over-numerous notebooks and memoirs one or two volumes in the style of this charming book.'[1] The volumes were, predictably, not to be written; but Anatole France later inscribed a copy of *Le Petit Pierre* 'to the noble representative of France in Italy: to Joseph-Napoleon Primoli, whose life is dedicated to the arts and to friendship.'[2]

Among his friends was Paul Bourget. He came, in time, to Rome, where, under the friendly, watchful eyes of the most Parisian Roman, he gathered material for *Cosmopolis*. This novel of international society was dedicated to Primoli.[3] Attending an evening reception at the Austrian Embassy, Primoli himself was tempted to write a chapter for a similar book. 'One might observe the different ways in which the ladies kiss the cardinals' hands. There is a chapter of Roman life to be written – for Parisians.'[4] There was, indeed; but, yet again, he lacked the determination to write it.

Meanwhile, the spring and summer of 1885 were devoted to his friends. Late in April, from the Hôtel Costanzi, there came a note from Maupassant: 'I arrived in Rome this morning, and I'd be delighted to shake you by the hand. I hope you haven't forgotten our meeting at Princess Mathilde's . . .'[5] Acquaintance blossomed into friendship; and from Naples, early in May, Maupassant assured Primoli: 'You are the kindest of men

127

and the most obliging of Italians. I look forward to coming back and seeing Rome with you.'[6] Primoli at once invited Maupassant to stay with him.

> My dear friend [came the answer, on 15 May],
> . . . I still have another twelve days here [at Catania], and then you will see me back in Rome.
> My heartfelt thanks for your gracious offer to open your house to me, but please forgive me, won't you, if I don't accept this time. I can hardly abandon my friend Henri Amic, who is travelling with me. We shall both stay at the Hôtel de l'Europe – I think it's in the Piazza di Spagna . . .
> You will forgive me, won't you, for writing you such a short letter, but someone's waiting for me. I mean that the guides are waiting for me, as I am just about to leave for Etna.[7]

In Rome, the friendship was firmly established. On 5 June, Primoli reported to Popelin: 'Maupassant has left us for Cannes, where he is to stay for a few days; then he will go to Paris, where, he assures us, the first person he visits will be the Princess.'[8]

*　*　*

It was a year for composers as well as novelists. Primoli entertained the ageing Liszt and the young Debussy. As the winner of the Prix de Rome, Debussy had just come to spend three years at the Villa Médicis. Primoli met him, took a liking to him, and invited him to stay that summer at his seaside villa at Fiumicino. Debussy was grateful to escape the Roman heat and to work in a luxurious setting, far from 'the abominable villa'.[9]

On his return to Rome he was beset, once again, by melancholy and by his desperate longing for France. In 1886, wrote Tienot in his *Debussy*,

> Count Primoli must have witnessed a scene arranged with an imagination worthy in every point of that of the fantastic Berlioz in a similar situation . . . The fiery composer of the *Symphonie fantastique* recalled in his *Memoirs* that he had simulated suicide to rouse the pity of the director, Horace Vernet, so that he forgave him for having impulsively escaped from the Villa Médicis. If we are to believe Count Primoli, Debussy threw himself at Hébert's

128

feet and threatened to take his own life if Hébert prevented him from leaving.[10]

This was perhaps another occasion when Primoli indulged in invention. There is no confirmation of his story. But Debussy returned to Paris before his three years in Rome were completed.

* * *

In the summer of 1886, Primoli himself spent a few days with the Duc de Bassano in the Isle of Wight. He had also been invited, with Maupassant and Henry James, to visit Baron Ferdinand de Rothschild at Waddesdon: the palatial mansion which had recently been built for him near Aylesbury. In the first days of August, from the Baron's London house, Maupassant wrote to Primoli:

> My dear friend,
>   When I received your letter, which crossed mine, I wrote to you at the Isle of Wight.
>   As I thought that you couldn't come on Saturday, I asked you, on behalf of the Baron, to come and visit him on Monday or Tuesday. I don't know if your plans can be altered, but personally I should prefer to see you come on Monday. And this is why.
>   On Saturday the house is absolutely full, and they won't be able to let you stay overnight. So you will be obliged to go back during the evening. Besides, it will be a grand official reception, since the Prince of Wales's son will be there; and this kind of festivity is not always entertaining. On Monday we shall have some agreeable women, so it seems, plus Henry James; and you would give the greatest pleasure to Baron de Rothschild, who is an absolutely charming man, if you spent a day or two with him. He has asked me to tell you so, most warmly . . .[11]

Primoli's plans were duly changed. On 4 August, this time from Waddesdon, Maupassant wrote to him again:

> What a pleasure, my dear friend, to see you in London! I shall be there on Tuesday the 10th to meet you. I hope that you will stay there the following day, the 11th. I should like to introduce you, that evening, at the house of a delightful woman where you will find Breet Hart [sic], the American novelist, and also, I think, Henry James.

129

I am here in an English mansion, surrounded by Englishmen – the Archbishop of Canterbury, the Prime Minister, etc., etc., plus the German Ambassador with whom I have talked a lot because he doesn't know any more English than I do (at least that's what he says). Not many women here – a young girl, Lady X (I can't possibly remember her name), and the Archbishop's wife, who doesn't give me any desire to make the eminent churchman a cuckold. My host, M. Ferdinand de Rothschild, is a charming man. I greatly prefer him to all his guests.

How I should like to have you here!! Oh, what chats we'd have! Write to me at F. de Rothschild's, 143, Piccadilly, and tell me if we'll be able to see one another on Tuesday.[12]

A few days later, from the Hotel Continental, in London, Maupassant scribbled to Primoli: 'Meet me at the Café Royal, Regent Street. I am lunching there .. Come as soon as possible.'[13]

It was a social visit to London. Bourget had given Maupassant an introduction to Henry James, and James invited him to dine at The Prospect of Whitby at Greenwich. Twenty-eight years later, James enquired of Edmund Gosse: 'Have you any recollection of going down the river with me to Greenwich, ... in company with Maupassant, Du Maurier and one or two others?'[14] One of those others was Primoli, on whom Gosse made an ineffaceable impression. In 1914 he wrote to James to ask Gosse's address – he had remembered him all those years.[15] Gosse was, it seems, more interested in James and Maupassant; he had not yet acquired his taste for the aristocracy.

Others had a taste for it. In Rome, in December 1886, the singer Emma Calvé recorded: 'A big dinner yesterday at the Villa Médicis, my neighbour at table was Count Joseph Primoli, a witty man, great-nephew of Napoleon I [sic]. A great friend of Eleonora Duse. I told him how I admired the great tragic actress, and how I had followed her on her first tour. He promised to bring her to hear me at the Opera, as soon as she came back.'[16] He was to keep his promise; in the meanwhile, she noted: 'I often go to [hear] the choirs in the Sistine Chapel. Count Primoli has given me an introduction to Mustapha Pasha, "the last of the Castrati", who sings with an extraordinary voice.'[17] Soon afterwards, Primoli welcomed Maurice Barrès to Rome.[18] His social circles were all-embracing.

They included Flaubert's niece, Caroline Commanville, now Mme Franklin Grout. Jacques-Émile Blanche recorded that

> when our great shipping companies arranged cruises with lectures by scholars, archaeologists and men of letters, the Grouts were among the first passengers . . .
>
> On their return from these cruises, Caroline and Franklin stopped in Rome, at Gégé Primoli's. The Count welcomed the friends of his aunt, Princess Mathilde. What a harvest of flattering acquaintances![19]

> Here is an anecdote which Joseph Primoli told Diego Angeli, and Angeli has kindly repeated to me [wrote Lumbroso, in his *Souvenirs sur Maupassant*] . . .
>
> Guy de Maupassant and Paul Bourget were passing through Rome at the same time. This was, of course, before M Bourget married. Joseph Primoli piloted them more or less everywhere in *Cosmopolis*. One evening, these three gentlemen decided to visit the pot-houses and the brothels of the Eternal City. Primoli conducted his friends to a . . . how can I put it? . . . a *Maison Tellier* of the lowest order: a soldiers' brothel, very near the palazzo Primoli, via Tor di Nona, opposite the Ponte Sant' Angelo.
>
> The ladies made efforts to please, and tried to charm their guests. Maupassant was attracted by the abundant charms of one of the prostitutes, and left the salon with her. A few minutes later, he came back, and found Paul Bourget sitting in a corner, all abashed: in the same corner and the same position in which Maupassant had recently left him.
>
> And then the Norman writer cried out gaily: 'Now, my dear fellow, I understand your psychology!'[20]

Maupassant seemed unshakably vigorous and audacious. On 8 July 1887, he sailed in a balloon over Saint-Gratien, so low that he and his fellow-passengers heard the Princess and her guests in conversation on the verandah.[21] He paid a visit to North Africa, saw Tunis and the ruins of Carthage. Primoli could hardly have guessed the fate so soon to overtake him when he sailed with him on his new yacht, *Bel-Ami II*, along the Côte d'Azur.

Maupassant had syphilis, and by 1890 it was clear that his reason was failing. In 1892 Dr Blanche took him into his asylum; he died there in 1893, hopelessly insane. Primoli made a pilgrimage to Antibes to see the *Bel Ami* abandoned in this melancholy little port where it waited for its master, and will no doubt find a buyer. I was told [he wrote] that when they came to fetch Maupassant to take him away to Dr Blanche's, the poor man, who was all strapped down, with tears in his eyes, begged his minders to carry him to the seashore to take a last look at 'the boat so dear to his heart'. Don't you think that these touching farewells to the confidant of his dreams recall those which Lohengrin addressed to his swan when he was about to quit the land of the ideal to grapple with the rock of reality? Alas, I sometimes wonder, as I look sadly round me, if those who have whole hours of oblivion do not suffer less than the rest of us, who are constantly aware of our miseries.[22]

4

Princess Mathilde had her anxieties. On 11 July 1888, the faithful Grandjean wrote to Primoli:

We went to St Gratien on Sunday . . .

The poor Princess is rather worried about Popelin's state of health, and so is everyone there. The doctors don't seem to have recognized the real trouble at once. It was the little doctor at Enghien who put his finger on it. Popelin's general condition was poor, he had disturbing symptoms and a touch of pleurisy as well. They hadn't noticed the pleurisy, and, when they detected it, it was very late. This seemed to be the reason for the last crisis.

Today, things are getting on quite well. He will recover, but they think it will take a long time. I thought he looked quite well, tired but not despondent.[1]

The Princess herself was despondent: more anxious than Grandjean understood. On 15 July, Primoli noted: 'I have had such unhappy letters from my dear Aunt Mathilde that I am going to visit her at Saint-Gratien. She is always saying that I have the gift of raising her morale and amusing her.'[2]

* * *

Before he left for France, another family drama claimed his attention. This was the controversial marriage of Princess Marie-Laetitia, daughter of Prince Napoleon and Princess Clotilde, to her uncle the Duke of Aosta.

Turin, 17 July

King Umberto . . . has left a few rooms on the ground floor of the

133

royal palace in Turin at the disposal of Princess Clotilde, so that she can rest when she arrives from Moncalieri.

That is where she asked me to meet her at two o'clock.

These rooms are miserably furnished with what could have been luxurious sixty years ago. Armchairs, upholstered in red and blue silk – faded and discoloured, torn and ill-matched – dirty blue curtains, and bad pictures on the walls. The décor of a royal palace, certainly, but a palace on the stage of a fifth-class theatre.

I am always surprised to find that the descendants of the oldest royal dynasties have less need of luxury and comfort than the bankers' sons of today. I myself, who can be content with so little, and have a horror of display, could not see myself among all these things which clash with one another and have nothing in common but bad taste. My eyes feel what my ears would feel at some horrible cacophony.

The décor is forgotten as soon as the characters come on stage. The door opens. The maid of honour, all in black in imitation of her mistress, with a curtsey to you, a double curtsey in the direction of the princesses, leads you in, in utter silence, and presents you.

Princess Clotilde is standing there, erect in her more than monastic black woollen costume, with her silver hair drawn back on her forehead, her thick neck, her sensual lips contrasting with her angelic smile. She half extends her ungloved right hand, like someone who is hardly used to extending it except to have it kissed or to give alms . . .

Near this shadow half effaced from the world, a smiling contrast, as in Holbein's series [of pictures], life is shining in all its brilliance: her daughter Laetitia, tall, dazzling, happy, all in pink with enormous emeralds at her ears, round her neck, on her arms, on her corsage, at her waist – like radiant beetles settled on a rose. It is an Italian Marguerite decked in the jewels given to her by her fiancé. These garish colours, this display of jewels in broad daylight, may not be a sign of irreproachable taste, but not only does one not dream of reproaching her for either, one is even grateful for such innocent sincerity, for this complete harmony between the dress and the soul: it is the childlike happiness of the girl who is leaving her monastic existence, her nun-like apparel, her sombre, tranquil past for a future which seems to her as rosy as her dress, as dazzling as her jewels.

The transformation has already taken place. She says 'Amédée', when she speaks of her uncle who is about to become her husband. She is already her mother's sister-in-law; she seems to take her under her protection. She must consider her as beyond the things of this earth, beyond the world – and she feels that she must support her so that she does not fall as she walks and gazes at heaven.

This marriage is the topic of the day in Italy. For the past month it has been the subject of every commentary. People want to see it as a marriage of convenience, but it is a marriage of love! While her Father tried to marry her to a rich private citizen in Rome, while her Mother took her to Vienna in search of some Archduke, while the Empress looked around her in England, the Queen of Italy leafed through the [Almanach de] Gotha again and again – and while they ran into problems of money, situation, age and religion – Laetitia found, all by herself, just beside her, in her own family, the husband she wanted. In this solemn Italian Court, Laetitia was the ray of sunshine, the welcome burst of laughter. At first it was pity that she inspired, little by little pity became sympathy and, when she was eighteen, sympathy became admiration. As a child, despite her delicate features, she was frankly ugly. The head might be a pretty shape, but it was so sunk down between her shoulders that people simply felt sorry for her. Ill-made corsets and excessively tight corsages confirmed the unfortunate impression. One fine day the bosom was set free, the pretty head emerged from the shoulders, and . . . she shone in all her brilliance . . .

As soon as she appeared at Monza, everyone was happy and laughing with her: the King took her on his lap, the Duke of Aosta pinched her, the Queen dressed her and did her hair, and she herself was teased by her cousins, and defended herself. Her holidays were very short, and then she went back to her sombre tower at Moncalieri, where no Prince Charming came to rescue her. One day a regiment was sent to garrison the castle. Moncalieri came to life with the clatter of weapons, and the happy young girl followed the various manoeuvres from one window to another, and knew all the brilliant officers by sight. One of them, it is said, more innocent or more astute than the rest, even tried to pass a note to her. The unfortunate Mother, followed by her maid of honour, did not know which way to turn, and spent her day in pursuit of her daughter, who could not stay still. At last, in a hassle, Princess Clotilde wrote to the King and asked him to have the officers moved, and, though nobody ever knew why, the regiment was despatched to the depths of Calabria.

After these fireworks, the sombre castle became more melancholy than ever, and the young Princess felt her isolation even more. As Célimène said, isolation frightens a woman of twenty.

And then, so they say, her cousin, the only man admitted to Moncalieri, the eldest son of the Duke of Aosta, went in search of his father and said to him: 'Poor Laetitia is so unhappy that we must do something about her. She will find it hard to find a husband, because the Queen won't have a private citizen, Prince Napoleon won't have a German or a Bourbon, Princess Clotilde won't have a Protestant. So I have made a big decision, which is to marry her myself – and I've come to ask for your consent.' 'This good feeling does you honour,' answered his Father, 'but you're too young, you are a year younger than she is, you still have to work. But I promise you that I will do something about your Cousin.' And he asked her in marriage himself.

When he returned to the Palazzo de la Cisterna, Prince Amedeo solemnly assembled his three children and his military household. When he came to his eldest son, he stopped and said to him: 'I announce the betrothal of Amedeo of Savoy to Her Imperial Highness Princess Laetitia Napoleon. What have you to say?' 'Cosa ne dite.' The young Prince, pale as Don Carlos, bowed low to his father, and murmured submissively: 'Contento lei contenti tutti.'

The various permissions were not hard to obtain. The young Princess's difficult situation made people pass over any incestuous element in this alliance.[3]

* * *

19 July

. . . At last, at 5.05, at the Gare Saint-Lazare, I caught the train for Sannois, where I found the little omnibus which took me to the Château de Saint-Gratien . . . There she was, my beloved aunt, she came to meet me, and held me to her heart . . . And yet my delight was clouded: I found her changed, disturbed, and anxious. Her friend Poliphile [Claudius Popelin] has been ill for six months, and they cannot exactly diagnose his illness. There had been a faint suggestion of angina . . . The fact is that, despite the overwhelming attentions he is given, he is not getting better. He is so weak that he cannot eat at table and, as soon as he moves, he has fits of giddiness . . . The other day he nearly fell into the poor Princess's arms. There is talk of sending him to the South of France. Her own life consists entirely of habit and domesticity, and it is completely upset – and she finds it hard to hold back the tears which rise to her eyes. The Princess was Life and Health when I left her, two years ago; now she is the embodiment of Anguish and Despair. I know what I'm talking of, alas! Yesterday she was forty-five – today she is over sixty! . . .

I did well to come, but I shall only be able to give her moments of forgetfulness. I shan't be able to raise her morale, it is too deeply affected. A cure of two months is not enough.[4]

* * *

The Princess's entourage is not made to cheer her. She is so fundamentally good that she tries to surround herself with people she can help rather than people who can be agreeable to her . . .

Her maid of honour, a very good and respectable person, has neither physical charms nor intellectual accomplishments. She has little in common with the Princess, who puts up with her unpunctuality, her prudery, stupidity and ignorance, out of regard for her absolute respectability . . . Paul Bourget christened her Dame Pluche . . . For all her sixty years, she has kept the naïveté of first youth, and at the same time she wants to know everything and to seem ignorant of nothing . . .

[Count Vincent Benedetti, the former French Ambassador to Berlin], is about sixty-eight. He is small, bald, slight, spry, dapper, even elegant. The cut of his suits is irreproachable.

* * *

The invalid is Claudius Popelin. Despite the falsity of the assertion, and the denials which appeared in the papers, posterity will recall that one year, in 187–, the *Almanach de Gotha* married Princess Mathilde to Claudius Popelin. The 'marriage' took place at Mons, in Belgium, during the War. This supposition, however false it may be, gives a fair idea of P's position in the Princess's household. He is a morganatic husband, loved and esteemed by everyone. His personal talents as an artist and as a poet, his situation as a man of letters and his artistic nature, his virtues as a gentleman and a philosopher, his breadth of mind and kindness of heart and, above all, his patriarchal serenity and his considerable fortune set him above malevolent commentaries.

Towards the end of the Empire, the poor Princess, still dazzling but already nearing her fifties, saw herself monstrously betrayed and abandoned by the man to whom she had sacrificed her life – and this at the very moment when she believed that the death of her infamous husband would allow her to legitimize a liaison of twenty years. In order to destroy her illusions, he himself was obliged to tell her – because she had never been able to believe other people – that he had promised marriage to a young girl! 'A fine young lover for her in her youth!' she murmured, as she described the scene to me. He had even said to Giraud: 'I don't understand why the Princess doesn't want my *tendresse transfor-*

137

mée'! 'What use would she have for your transformed tenderness?' Giraud enquired. [Nieuwerkerke] found his behaviour quite natural. The Princess was the mistress whom he had once loved, and what he needed, this aged and exhausted [philanderer], was a young girl whom he respected. – And he dared to let her understand this . . .

As soon as she understood, she dismissed him from her house immediately, and threatened to make a scene if he did not leave at once – and I recall how she told me about it, in a whisper, while he was a few feet away – and added this feminine touch: 'And he had to go on foot across the fields, because I didn't order a carriage for him.'

This was, alas, her one revenge! 'From morn till night, in the park at Saint-Gratien, undulating as far as the eye could see, along the hills of the Loire, there was the wild rush of a hunted, wounded animal, an animal which paused for a moment, dazed with exhaustion, and then set off again, with a stab of pain . . .'[5]

Gradually, as she released it, her anger subsided, . . . and, when her confidant came back, he found her in floods of tears. 'I've seen Nieuwerkerke,' he said to her. 'Well?' 'He is very downcast.' 'Ah!' she said, with a gleam of hope. 'Yes, he said to me: "Now that the Princess has ceased to protect me, she will have me stripped of all the places she obtained for me. I have a great many enemies, and as soon as they know that I am not protected any more, they will come down on the fallen man . . ."' . . .

It was in fact She who had disguised the nullity of her lover by making him Surintendant des Beaux-Arts, Sénateur, and Membre de l'Institut, rigged him out in all three cloaks of the official carnival . . . In the presence of such weakness she felt her hatred die like her love, and leave in its wake just a vast compassionate contempt.

'That's right,' she murmured, 'he mustn't lose all his official functions and sinecures because he's stopped loving me . . . Let him dine here on Thursdays and Sundays, I agree to that because I have company those evenings; but if he ever once dares to address a word to me in private, I shall expose him and give him his public dismissal. That's settled.' And he accepted!

He humbled himself to come and dine with her on Thursdays and Sundays during the winter and the summer of 1870 up to the War. He returned as a stranger to the salons where he had been the master, in order to mislead the Court, which was not to notice anything. All etiquette and conversation, a perfect gentleman on the surface, he schooled himself not to let anything become apparent. She was a passionate, open, loving soul, unable to hide her impressions and feelings; she had constantly to control herself so as not to burst out and spit out her contempt in the face of this contemptible creature who sat facing her at table, flirting with his neighbour, . . . this immensely handsome coward whom she had loved so much, this coward who should be dead for her since she was dead for him . . .

What feelings had she obeyed when she agreed to suffer this torture? Was it pure compassion, or did she want to hide Nieuwerkerke's desertion from the world? Was it that she wanted to see him again or that she wanted to cure herself of love by making him seem more contemptible in her eyes? Did she cherish some vague hope of his return, or some vague plan of having her revenge? . . .

* * *

However, at the end of the table there was an artist with azure eyes and a sharply pointed fair beard, a real prince of the Florentine renaissance . . . His bright and gentle eyes never left the Princess's eyes . . . He had adored her for twelve years . . . He felt like an earthworm enamoured of a star . . .

Every new work he published was to him a pretext for laying his devotion at the Princess's feet. He had his book superbly bound, set an exquisite enamel in the binding, and, on the first page, he wrote a sonnet in the depths of which he buried his timid homage, which the great lady, accustomed to tributes, confused with the rest. Lost in her love, which she believed as eternal as eternity, she saw no man except the man she loved.

And so he contented himself with following her from afar, . . . and the day when she found herself deceived, betrayed and abandoned, he emerged from his obscurity and held out his hand.

'Surprised, she looked at him.

'It was one morning when she began her solitary walk with her dogs across the park . . . Suddenly, at the corner of a path, he appeared. "Let's walk together," she said, gaily, cracking the long whip, with the short handle tipped with silver, which she used to rally her pack. From the first moment he spoke of love, of the sadness she would feel if she lived alone, and finally, quite simply, he offered himself . . . The Princess raised her head with a quick movement of pride . . . But the outrage to her dignity was a tribute to her fading beauty, and the sudden blush on her cheeks showed as much pleasure as indignation . . .

'There was such respectful piety, such deep adoration in his face that she was soon persuaded to take his arm . . . From that moment she felt appeasement, a sweet new lease of life which changed her walk and voice, and she became a different woman.'[6]

She made a marriage of reason which made her forget her marriage of love.

The War broke out – then came the fall of the Empire . . . P considered their respective situations. He was still young, a widower, rich and good-looking, while the poor woman would be old in a few years' time . . . He understood, he confessed to me, . . . that, left to herself – she was so demented at seeing her family exiled, her house ransacked [sic], her friends all scattered – she would be capable of anything. She was alone, and there must be a man to control her. He resolved to be this man, the man who must devote himself to her, body and soul, and never leave her. He did not hesitate. He sacrificed his life, his independence, his museum [sic], his country and his son to her – and he left with Her. She did not want it. 'Everyone,' he told me, 'understood the decision which I had imposed on myself, and everyone was grateful to me.'

The Princess, accompanied by her maid of honour, by Popelin and Giraud, therefore made her way towards Dieppe. At Rouen, Gustave Flaubert and Alexandre Dumas *fils* came to meet her to urge her to turn back; her arrival had been signalled at Dieppe, and they intended to give her a rough reception. She was accused of taking away the treasures of the Louvre. The Princess! It was then that Dumas wrote those two noble letters which were so courageous and eloquent . . .

After various vicissitudes, the fugitives arrived in Belgium, at Mons – where, it is said, the marriage took place at Claudius's wish. He gave up his freedom, and he would have liked to bind his mistress for ever. Personally, I repeat, I do not believe that this ceremony took place, because I think that my aunt, honest and sincere as she was, would certainly have proclaimed aloud her marriage to the man of her choice . . .

At last, in the spring [of 1871], they returned to France . . . Each of them went home: Popelin to his *hôtel* in the rue de Téhéran, and the Princess to the rue de Berry, first to no. 18, and then to the little *hôtel*, no. 20, which she bought . . .

Whether or not it is legalized by marriage, this liaison has lasted, now, for eighteen years, and it is sanctified by the couple's honesty. They have managed to make the world accept something more difficult to take than a liaison – a *second* liaison. It is true that there is no more peaceful, more domestic life. Every morning, at 11 o'clock, Popelin leaves his little *hôtel* and goes to *déjeuner* with the Princess. At 1 o'clock he goes home again. And twice a week she devotes herself to her painting lessons, once to her music, twice a week she deals with her affairs, and on Sundays she receives those [friends] who cannot come in the evening. At half-past six Popelin returns by cab, he talks with her for half an hour in her little room on the first floor. On the stroke of seven, the Princess goes to her bedroom to dress for dinner. They dine, the Princess works [at her embroidery] on her little sofa . . . At 11 o'clock she rises, everybody leaves, and Popelin walks back to the rue de Téhéran . . .

Nothing troubles this model ménage except a dark cloud which looms larger every day on the horizon, and threatens to burst in a real storm. When the child is not the connecting link, it is the apple of discord. Popelin has a son by the wife who died twenty-five years ago. This son, unsocial and distrustful, cannot hide his aversion for the Princess, although she has always been motherly to him . . . Does he reproach her for taking his father away? For preventing him from having a home since he always takes his meals with her? Has someone maliciously repeated some idle talk to him? . . . Is there some woman who would like to take revenge on the Princess? Whatever it is, Popelin spends his time protecting these two people whom he loves from one another, and putting ointment on their respective wounds. They constantly drive him into a corner, and burst into reproaches about each other, these two people who share his heart . . .

The other dark cloud is Marie Ab[batucci]. Marie Abbatucci is a nice girl of about forty [sic]. Her father, Charles Abbatucci, the Deputy for Corsica, had been such a fanatical Bonapartist that he had ruined his family in the cause . . . He had been entirely absorbed in his idea, and he had seen nothing outside politics. Her mother, on the other hand, was slightly unbalanced; she had never left the house, and she had never seen beyond her casserole. The lugubrious household had not been enlivened by the presence of an idiot daughter [Marie's sister]. Marie herself, very brave and very Corsican, had not even had a bed; she had slept on top of a pile of books, in an alcove. Sometimes she went out with her father, and her greatest pleasure was to visit us [the Primolis] in the rue de Varenne. One evening Mother took her to my aunt's. The Princess saw her again in Brussels, where she reminded her of France.

The Princess was tender-hearted, and sensitive to hidden misfortunes. She took an interest in the girl. She took her under her protection, drew her into her household, and kept her there, and gradually Marie seemed to fulfil the functions of a lady-in-waiting. What also helped to interest the Princess in Marie, was that she knew that a handsome young man, who had seemed a good young man, had asked Marie in marriage. On the eve of their wedding, he had left her to marry the well-endowed daughter of Mme Alexandre Dumas.

In return Marie attached herself to the Princess and the excellent Popelin. He had known the poor girl's sad situation. She had been left alone in the world on the death of her father and mother – and he tried to brighten her life with a mass of little kindnesses . . . She repaid him with grateful attentions and filial devotion. The Princess had been made mistrustful by a first betrayal; she did not mean to be a victim a second time. It would have been ridiculous, had it not been profoundly touching, to see the poor Princess leaning out of her window at the seaside, watching anxiously, as Marie and Popelin bathed together. Perhaps then, for the first time, she was cruelly aware of her age.

Popelin fell ill. Marie attached herself to his bedside and refused to leave it. Once again, the Princess repressed the anger which was always ready to burst. She did all she could to vie with her in attentiveness, she would have gone down on her knees to put on his slippers, she would have watched at his bedside all night. But she was too nervous, too preoccupied, she could not give that continued care, that security indispensable in a nurse, and she had to yield her place to the impassible Marie.

There is nothing as touching as this alternate mistrust and abandon. Sometimes she looks at her askance, lets out two-edged words . . . Sometimes she bursts into insults – sometimes she bursts into tears and falls, in despair, into Marie's arms. 'I entrust him to you, I only have confidence in you, promise me never to leave him, what would become of me if you left him, we think of you as our child . . .'

And, resigned and triumphant, Marie resumes her task and her place beside the invalid – whom these two women have sworn to snatch from death.[7]

* * *

Saint-Gratien, 20 July

I found Popelin better than I had hoped. Very pale and very weak, he came down to the salon. The good Princess gave him her arm and they went for a walk in the sun in the kitchen-garden where I took some photographs . . . The portrait which I like the best, the one which gives the best impression of reality, is the group where the invalid is leaning on the Princess, and they are followed by a dog. One sees the couple from behind, but one would know them anywhere, and, as they pass, our hearts are moved, we feel the emotion we should feel at the sight of Philemon and Baucis.[8]

The Princess's anti-clericalism and her free speech may make her pass, perhaps, for a free-thinker; but she has kept intact, in the depths of her heart, the principles of her Italian religion. And so she eats meat on Fridays, but . . . there is always a fish dinner at her table for scrupulous people . . .

On Sundays, in Paris, she goes to Mass at 11 o'clock at Saint-Philippe-du-Roule, and at Saint-Gratien she goes to High Mass at 10 o'clock. Her prayer-stool in petit-point is embroidered with violets and bees.[9]

27 July

To Paris, after *déjeuner*, in a carriage with the Princess. She has to go to Worth's to order her Court mantle for her niece's wedding, which she cannot refuse to attend. In the evening we discussed the length of the train, and the ladies tried to make curtseys, which ended with tripping up and bursts of laughter . . . The Princess called these curtseys *chinoiseries*. Then she murmured, with her eyes on the past: 'The only pleasure in official ceremonies is the glance you exchange at solemn moments with someone dear to you.'[10]

1 August

Alphonse Daudet uses and abuses *romans à clef*. Until now I defended him, because he only attacked people who didn't matter to me. Today [in *L'Immortel*] he is involving people very dear to me, I am obliged to discard him (and to agree that his books are neither those of a *gentilhomme* nor a *gentleman*). He does not even know how to give an accurate portrayal. He takes the salient and superficial features of some famous personality: the eye-glass, the cut of the coat or hair (if it is a man), the dress or the carriage if it is a woman, and he endows them with the most vile or the most grotesque features, and he wilfully distorts their lives . . .

And so all Paris has recognized my poor Princess under the lovely shoulders of the Duchesse Padovani. I have been disturbed and revolted, not knowing whom to blame. The other evening I spoke frankly to Edmond de Goncourt, the great friend of Daudet, and the only one who could have revealed certain details to him. He swore, by all the gods, that he had not seen a likeness. When I quoted the rupture with the Prince d'Athis and the second liaison, he retorted cynically: 'Oh, it's always the same story with every woman who has had two lovers.' However, he had to agree that

Daudet had been wrong to talk about the Duchess walking in her park with her little dogs, and that he had been wrong to make her Corsican. In any case, I told him, thank God, the poor Princess does not suspect anything, I found the novel on her table, the [bookmark] was still in the first pages, because the book bored her. So I picked it up and hid it in the library. And she will be spared this new grief.

The insensitivity of these literary pontiffs is to me beyond all belief. Goncourt said to me: 'Daudet sent his book to the Princess, and the Princess answered with a note that was only just polite.' It was on this remark that I left.

I must confess that my aunt, who loves her peace, her tranquillity, her independence more than anything, has been cruelly hauled over the coals for some time. First the filthy memoirs of Viel-Castel, and then the Goncourt journals have handed over her name, her sayings and her gestures to the Press. She expresses herself quite honestly, and, carried away by her conversation, she often says more than she intends. She has found herself condemned to have spies around her, noting her sayings and doings, interpreting her smiles and her yawns. Even the two [Goncourt] brothers, who imagined that they were vindicating the Princess, make her say things about this person or that which put her in a delicate situation as regards these people. This evening, as if to excuse Edmond de Goncourt, I told the Princess that he had gone as far as to undress his dying brother and show him to the public. 'But,' she said, comically, 'I am not his sister!'[11]

28 August

Paris with the Princess. Had *déjeuner* with the excellent Poliphile [Claudius Popelin]. His sweet serenity, his long silky beard which smells of violets, his blue eyes which reflect the skies of Greece and Italy: all give me the most perfect idea of the philosopher of classical times. He is still suffering from a sort of malady, an inexplicable lassitude which disturbs all those who love him.[12]

29 August

Edmond de Goncourt to dinner. He comes here when he likes, without announcing himself . . . She is not so fond of him since his memoirs were published . . . Some people are even surprised that she still receives him.[13]

On 11 September the Princess's niece, Marie-Laetitia, the

daughter of Prince Napoleon, was to marry the Duke of Aosta in Turin.

5 September

The princess is vexed at the idea of going to Turin, and irritated by the account of the festivities and the etiquette to which she must conform: *chinoiseries*, she says, in her no-nonsense way.[14]

Next day Edmond de Goncourt went to dine at Saint-Gratien. He found the Princess

half lying in an armchair, in one of those desperate attitudes she has when it's a question of leaving Saint-Gratien on some little journey . . .
  Her nephew Primoli and Benedetti arrive from Paris, bringing the newspaper *La France*. It announces a few cases of cholera in Paris. They tell her, jokingly, that perhaps this will mean a quarantine between Italy and France. She listens to them, gravely, in silence, lost in thought; and then, in all good faith, in the wild hope that this may prevent her journey, she asks: 'Do you think that the declaration of quarantine could appear in the papers tomorrow?'[15]

On 7 September, Primoli returned to his diary.

The poor Princess greatly moved me this evening . . . The doctors have decided that Poliphile should go to Arcachon. In her wonderful unconscious devotion, for She is so attached to those She loves by all the fibres of her heart that in the end She is part of them – the Princess has no doubt that she must go with him . . . And so she expected that Poliphile would wait for her to come back from Turin before he left Paris . . . He has just let her understand that he would leave without her, that his son would go with him and She could come and join them . . .
  Driven into a corner, he finally confessed that his son detested her, and was jealous of her. He had told him that he wouldn't even come and see him if he found him living with her again . . . The poor woman was stupefied . . . And she told me all she'd borne for the past year. 'Every morning this winter, at 7 o'clock, whatever the weather, at the age of sixty-eight, . . . I went to ask Gustave for news . . . He never seemed to show any gratitude for the care I took of his father . . . And he didn't bother with the poor man! . . .

Sometimes it was snowing, it was raining in torrents, it was cold, and he didn't ask me once to stay for *déjeuner*, though he always asked Marie in front of me . . . It was he, in his hatred, who thought of putting Marie between us . . . And she used to stay while I came home alone . . .'[16]

8 September

The Princess is better this morning. She came into my room while I was still in bed to tell me that Poliphile had promised to wait for her at home in Paris. Poor woman! This concession gives her back her serenity – but it makes me terrified for her peace of mind. It shows me the influence of Marie. Yesterday evening I told the poor girl – I am sorry, too, for her false position – If you want some friendly advice, persuade Poliphile to wait for the Princess, and don't appear to hasten his departure. And the Princess said to me: 'Marie behaved very well, I must admit.'[17]

Saturday, 8 September [*sic*]

This evening we leave for Turin: the Princess, the Baronne de Galbois, the Vicomtesse Benedetti, her father-in-law and myself. Before we leave, dinner with Poliphile who is back in Paris. I was convinced that the Princess had not read *L'Immortel*, or, at least, that she had not recognized herself in it. Suddenly, at table, I was painfully struck by the sadness in her voice. She said, without anger, but with deep grief and what seemed to be a gentle reproach for ingratitude: 'She hadn't done anything to him, that Corsican woman . . .'[18]

On her return to France, she and Popelin and Marie Abbatucci left for Arcachon. On 6 October she told Primoli:

I have been here for a fortnight . . . We are in a perpetual squall of rain, wind and hail – one can only just take a step or two outside between the downpours. You can imagine how I feel.
People say that the country here is wonderful – it's terrible . . . I think that in another three weeks my miseries will be over, and I'll bring my dear invalid back in good form.[19]

Charles Grandjean saw Popelin the day after his return.

He seems to me transfigured [he told Primoli]. He looks like he

146

used to do, his voice is firm, and he really seems to be strong. He still complains of minor troubles: fits of giddiness, for example. But let me say that Potin, the great heart specialist, burst out laughing when he was told of Dieulafoy's diagnosis. In his opinion, Popelin had pleurisy after his rheumatism, and, if the pleurisy had been attended to in time, there would probably have been no complication.[20]

It was, it seems, in January 1885 that Grandjean wrote again to Primoli:

Must I tell you of a rumour which is going round Paris? There is no indiscretion in revealing it, for the least informed people know about it, the people who are least familiar with the Princess. They say . . . that she has half broken with Popelin becuse of Mlle A. This is definitely said. I know absolutely nothing. But, even if one eliminates all the hearsay, one is tempted to believe there's some truth in it.[21]

5

That summer, Primoli found himself once again in Paris. The city was *en fête* for the International Exhibition. He settled in the rue de Berry in order to be near Princess Mathilde.

1 June

In the evening I allowed myself to be taken back to the Exhibition, with our charming and excellent friends M. and Mme Hébert, by my poor dear Aunt Mathilde. This year she is only seeking an excuse to go out, in order to get out of herself.[1]

I go up to have *déjeuner* with her. She is finishing her toilette, and she has me shown into her room. I find her cruelly changed. She has been wounded to the heart, and no winter has ever been more cruel than the last. 'You very nearly didn't find me here any more,' she said to me, as she embraced me with a wan smile. And then . . . she added, in a tone of melancholy triumph: 'If you'd come five minutes earlier, you'd have found Popelin here. He's just gone.' I understood from her manner what She must have suffered to have him back again. And she let herself go. She opened her heart to me and, walking up and down the long gallery, she told me, simply and honestly, what certain letters and indiscretions had already half suggested to me . . .

For twenty years the Princess had given herself body and soul to Claudius Popelin, and their liaison had been accepted as a marriage. Some feelings are more sacred than sacraments, and, seeing the independent situation of this adorable woman, and the perfect respectability of the artist, even her family had gradually grown accustomed to consider Claudius as one of themselves: Princess Clotilde, like Cardinal Bonaparte [brother of Charlotte Primoli], had received him with esteem, and the Empress had sent

148

to ask for news when he was ill. Through her affection, the Princess had had him accepted by everyone. She had given him social standing, while before he knew her he had only had a comfortable fortune and a pretty talent. And so his vanity was satisfied.

Ten years ago, said the Princess, in 1879, their physical relationship had suddenly been 'cut, *cut*, as if by a knife'. Naturally, although she still felt a woman, although she was still loving and tender, she said nothing. Her dignity prevented her from complaining, or from running after him. He said that he was ill, absorbed by his literary work. So, during these last ten years, love was nothing more than friendship on his side. Then, last year, he was struck by a mysterious illness which made him constantly collapse. The Princess, in alarm, had installed herself at his bedside like a sister of charity, and, throughout the winter, whatever the weather, she was at his apartment at seven o'clock – and she usually found Mademoiselle A[bbatucci] was already there. And then, when the Princess tore herself from the sickroom to go home, with death in her soul, Mademoiselle was triumphantly kept there for *déjeuner*; while not once did they do her the civility of asking her, and they often let her go in the midst of the rain and snow.

And for eighteen years Mlle A had had *déjeuner* and dined every day throughout the winter at the rue de Berry, and had spent six months in the summer with the Princess, who had shown her every kindness and had even given her an allowance as well as dresses and presents.

At Saint-Gratien, Popelin continued to be ill, and Mlle continued to lavish her attentions on him, although she was perfectly aware of the umbrage which her attentions caused the Princess. She installed herself at the invalid's bedside at every hour of the day and night, performing the most intimate tasks, which she might have left to a servant . . . As soon as dinner was over, she disappeared from the salon to go and sit by his bedside all the evening, and the poor Princess, kept among her guests by her duties as mistress of the house, had found it hard to be patient. Sometimes, unable to bear the strain, she had followed her upstairs, and then there had been scenes, explanations half suppressed because of the invalid's condition. The unfortunate woman was preyed upon by cruel anxieties about her friend's health, and about the treachery which she suspected.

Dr Potin, called in for consultation, and seeing Popelin affected by this inexplicable weakness, asked him if he had made some exertion. P must indeed have been weakened by illness, because he proclaimed what the most insensitive man never admits. He told the doctor: 'I haven't had any relations at all with the Princess for ten years [sic]!!!'

Well, the poor Princess is so frank and honest about her weaknesses that she did not so much mind that P had admitted their liaison to the doctor as that he had announced to him that it was completely over. In the meantime, the Princess had to go to Turin to attend her niece's wedding, and, during these festivities and ceremonies, she had only one thought in mind: to go home, and to go back to him. When she reached Paris, she did not even go to the rue de Berry, she had herself driven directly to the rue de Téhéran, where she found Mademoiselle installed. Going round the *hôtel*, she discovered her rival's dressing-gown and slippers. Her indignation knew no bounds, she burst out, but it was a short-lived blaze of anger which the invalid and his nurse soon extinguished, and they left, all three of them, for Arcachon, which had been prescribed by the doctors. It was a lugubrious visit, and an observer might have heard the dull rumbling of the storm in the *hôtel* as he heard the roaring of the sea outside.

In Paris, the storm burst. There were now simply two women who looked at one another with hatred. The young lady twice gave in her resignation. These were sham exits: she arrived in the evening, P made her go back in the morning. At last, for the third time, she wrote to the Princess. It was the eve of Popelin's departure for the South of France. This time she did not return.

The Princess wanted to go to Cannes. P sent her a telegram to say that, if she arrived, he would leave the same day. He also wrote that he would not return to the Princess unless she received the young lady. For some months he did not appear in the rue de Berry, and the young lady went to see him every day.

And then there was a terrible change in the Princess. Her splendid health was affected, her habits altered, her nature was no longer the same. She was both hurt in her self-respect and wounded in her love. She could no longer sleep, and her faithful Julie told me that when she went in to her at 7 o'clock in the morning, she found her already up, she had been up since 4 or 5 o'clock, the first light of dawn had made her rise from her bed of grief, she would settle down at her little desk and then immediately get up and walk all round the *hôtel*, cursing and weeping. She even turned detective . . . She did not only have Marie watched, she used to watch herself. 'It's quite simple,' she said to me, in the broken-hearted tone of a woman who has drunk the dregs of humiliation, 'I took a cab, and stopped it at the corner of the rue de Téhéran and the boulevard Haussmann, and, through the little window in the back, I could see the entrance to his house and the people who went in and came out. And I saw her go in every day, but I didn't always see her leave . . . Once I saw her arrive in a carriage which was full of flowers – can you understand that, what a hussy! –the concierge and his wife came out to take the vases that she brought, she paid the driver, and she went in, radiant, with bunches of roses in her hands . . . Then I stopped the cab, the driver told me that he had picked this lady up at the marché de la Madeleine, and I took the number, to have a palpable proof of this effrontery and of my misfortune . . .'

And yet she wanted to continue to put on a brave face, to show that she was not defeated by age. She dressed herself up, put on her jewels, and received her guests as if nothing had happened. The news had become known, and it roused a shudder of indignation, a surge of pity. People came to visit her, and said nothing, but their eager presence was a sign of their respectful compassion. She told me that she had seen people who had for years forgotten the way to her *hôtel*. In the meanwhile P, who had sworn that he would not return there without the young lady, made his appearance once again. Perhaps he understood that opinion was against him, perhaps he hoped to deceive people by his presence. He came back for *déjeuner* and dinner once a week, Monday and Wednesday, and in the morning he deigned to pay a visit of a few minutes – a doctor's visit to a poor invalid. He maintained that he had neglected his son too much for the past nineteen years, and that he could not desert his hearth and home – and beside his hearth the young lady warmed her feet and waited for him. From time to time the Princess rebelled in fury at the thought of sharing him; she wanted to give him her ultimatum: 'Choose between Her and me' – but she was too afraid that he would say 'Her'. . . . And she was silent . . . She contented herself with a gleam of hope: that, without promising anything, in the distant future he would tell [the young lady] that he would not see her again . . . 'I am ashamed of my cowardice, my lack of dignity,' she cried, with tears in her voice and in her eyes, 'and other people can certainly reproach me for my weakness since I accuse myself!'[2]

4 June

Meissonier came to announce his marriage to Mlle Robinson, with whom he has been living for thirty years. He is over seventy and she is over fifty. What divides them most is their stature: she is built like a big Englishwoman in a vaudeville, and he is as small as one of his pictures, with a long flowing beard . . .

We talked about the eternal question of the love of Musset and Mme Sand. Alexandre Dumas owns the correspondence. We were discussing which of the two was the more in the wrong.

'Take a plough,' said Dumas, when he was asked, 'harness a cow and a goat to it. The cow will pull conscientiously. The goat will gambol about unbearably in every direction, until the cow grows impatient and disturbed in its own work, kicks it away, and continues its work alone or with another companion. That's how it was with Mme Sand and Alfred de Musset.'

Mme Sand spent her life seeking the sensations of love, and was never able to feel them.[3]

Wednesday evening 2 o'clock in the morning [*sic*]
12 June

The poor Princess was wonderfully eloquent and extremely touching this evening. When her guests had gone and only the dear Héberts, Louis Ganderax and myself were left in the salon, she, who had controlled herself all the evening, and tried to please the guests who did not matter, let herself go. She began to pace up and down the lighted empty salon, superb in her ample grey silk dress, with her wonderful pearls round her neck, and a ruby drop falling on her breast like a little drop of blood . . . And she grew animated, she talked, fire and tears lit up her eyes, her voice was trembling with grief and indignation, her heart overflowed in words . . . 'I'm ashamed of my cowardice,' she said, 'my lack of dignity . . . One night he came in to me, ten years ago, he made me make my will, he asked me to leave a sum to Marie, and I left her 100,000 francs; it's infamous!

'And at Arcachon, under the table, they were pressing one another's feet, and looking at me, and saying: "You're not eating anything, Princess, you're not well, what's the matter?" The wretches! . . .

'And now, when he comes, when he looks at me, I feel he's looking avidly to see if I have another wrinkle, another white hair. And he reproaches me for not knowing how to grow old . . . My misfortune is to have kept too young a heart . . . And I'm not saying all this as recrimination, because I'm ready to forgive and forget . . . But let him stop seeing her, or at least let him give me some vague hope that one day he will stop seeing my most mortal enemy . . .'[4]

[June]

She touches me profoundly by her sincerity, her frankness and her fidelity. What she regrets most bitterly, it seems to me, are the ten lost years, . . . during which he had given her to understand that he had to work: [the ten lost years] that he was spending, she says, under her roof . . . 'It's infamous! Cut, *cut* as if by a knife!' she repeats, with a heartbroken smile, a smile which makes one weep.[5]

[June]

Henri Meilhac gave us a big *déjeuner* in the Javanese village [at the International Exhibition] . . .[6]

16 June

To the races in the Bois de Boulogne, Grand Prix de Paris with my Feltre cousin [the Duchesse de la Feltre] and her husband.

Photographed the President of the Republic, Carnot, in his stand, Mlle Pierson, Mme Benardacki, the stand of the ladies of the Jockey Club, with Mme de Metternich and Mme de Pourtalès standing out among them.[7]

153

6

The old order and the new converged in the Bois de Boulogne. The Republic was now solidly established. It did not only tolerate the presence of a Bonaparte Princess, it accepted an Orleans Prince in France. By a decree of 9 March 1889, the Duc d'Aumale, the fourth son of Louis-Philippe, had been permitted to return from exile. As Primoli recorded:

The Duke had paid dearly for his return ticket to France; he had agreed to bequeath his château [at Chantilly] to the Institut on condition that he was allowed to live there until his death. His brother Joinville sometimes teased him about his generosity, and usually referred to him as 'the Benefactor' . . .

*   *   *

One day the Duc d'Aumale was sitting to [Léon] Bonnat. Someone had brought in a portrait of the First Consul. 'What a fine classical head!' cried the Duke, in delight. '. . . Princess Mathilde also had some features of the imperial face. When I saw her at the Tuileries, in my young days, I was very taken with her!'

After the sitting, Bonnat was walking down the avenue des Champs-Élysées, smoking his cigar. At the rond-point he met Princess Mathilde, who was walking her little dog. She stopped him and held out her hand, and, with her kindly smile, she asked him to continue his walk with her.

'What are you doing at the moment?'

'A portrait of the Duc d'Aumale.'

'Oh!' she said, with a sigh. 'He was very handsome!'

'Indeed. He was telling me a moment ago that he had been very smitten with you.'

'Well, I've always adored him.'

'He'd be delighted to see you again.'

'Can I go and meet him in your studio?'

'Whenever you like. He sits to me every afternoon.'

'I'll come next week, but . . . if he sees me as I am, he would be too disappointed. I'll wear a veil.'

The artist reported the conversation to his sitter, who replied with enthusiasm:

'I shall be delighted to show my collections to Princess Mathilde, if she would care to honour Chantilly with her visit. I shall go myself to learn her wishes.'

The Princess agreed to go and have *déjeuner* at the château, and the host sent her a list of mutual friends: Bonnat, Augier, Gérôme, Dumas, [Auguste] Laugel, etc.

The great day arrived. The Princess, who was always most elegant, took particular trouble with her dress . . .

Bonnat described to me, not without a touch of emotion, the coquetry displayed by both these veterans, each of whom claimed that they only wanted not to horrify the other, but both of whom really hoped to please the other still.

The Duc d'Aumale had kept nothing of the handsome, manly face of his youth except the blue of his bright eyes. To the authority of a retired general, he added the slightly melancholy grand manner of a dethroned prince; his figure would still have been young had it not been for the gout which bent him painfully and obliged him to lean on a stick.

'You should have seen him on the steps of the château,' Bonnat said to me, 'dressed with the rather excessive, rather awkward elegance of a soldier disguised as a civilian. He was wearing a buttoned-up frock-coat, grey trousers, and white spats. He waited with feverish impatience for the Emperor's niece . . .

'There was the carriage. At the window, framed by a little black velvet bonnet with white feathers, was the kind, smiling face of the Princess . . . The Duke took off his hat, which he balanced on his stick, and offered his right hand to his illustrious visitor: a hand whose fingers, deformed by gout, attempted to conceal themselves in large pearl-grey gloves.

'In order not to hurt his pride, the Princess pretended not to see his embarrassment. She did not lean on the trembling hand which the poor gouty man held out to her, she scarcely brushed against it, and she stepped out of the carriage unaided.

'With the frankness of a woman who has nothing to hide, she boldly picked up her violet poult-de-soie skirt and revealed, in a billow of Valenciennes lace, a small foot shod in a bronze half-boot, and a still slim leg whose curves were emphasized by a pink cashmere stocking. Never could she bring herself to accept black stockings, she thought that everything which touched the skin should be white. Nor could she admit tailored costumes: she didn't, she said, like women disguised as men. She kept to silk and lace.

'The Duke complimented her on her taste, which had not allowed itself to be corrupted, he offered her his arm, and the royal couple passed into the dining-room, followed by the two retinues which merged into a variegated procession. One had the vision of some golden wedding in a fairy-tale: these were really a Prince and Princess of olden times.

'After the meal, the Prince, as the proprietor, took the Princess on a tour, beginning with a long pause in front of Gérard's Napoleon, which, she told him, was her favourite of all the portraits of her uncle. He also showed her several mementoes of the Duc de Reichstadt which came to him from his wife – the Princesse de Salerno, a cousin and friend of the unfortunate Aiglon.

'He repeated how pleased he was to do her the honours of his domain.

' "And I, Monseigneur," replied the Princess, "am doubly delighted with my visit, when I think that, thanks to your generosity, these marvels will not be dispersed, and that they will always belong to France."

' "If I hadn't taken these precautions, who knows if the works of art which I have so lovingly collected would not have been scattered to the four corners of Europe and America, and if these buildings would not have become an annexe to the race-course?" '

* * *

Every spring, after this visit, the Princess went to *déjeuner* at Chantilly, and every winter the Duke came to dinner at the rue de Berry.[1]

* * *

Meanwhile, in the summer of 1889, Primoli continued his diary.

Paris, June

[Jules] Lemaître [the critic] is flattered because Mme Straus tells him that he has become Right Bank, and he felt himself terribly Left Bank. Not even provincial, he said. In fact he has kept college attitudes, and perhaps he affects them. When he talks about the races, he asks: 'Who won the first prize?', and not 'the cup'.[2]

156

To Triel with Meilhac, the Strauses and the Lippmanns to visit Guy de Maupassant, who has rented a châlet on the Seine to write his novel *L'Âme étrangère*.

Heard Maupassant talk literature for the first time. He told us that he had never found a book so hard to write as *Fort comme la mort*. He had certainly worked very hard, he must have lived in constant mental tension, because this work is not in his nature. 'I wanted,' he said, 'to write the history of a feeling at a certain period in life. The characters are almost entirely symbols, that is why they are vague and remain in the background . . .'

I believe that the acquaintance and friendship of Mme K[ann] have a great influence on Maupassant's talent: she gives a soul to his books. I believe that she can be as salutary to the author of *La Maison Tellier* as [she was] fatal to the novelist of *Un Crime d'Amour*. She has too many affinities with Bourget, their union makes me think of a marriage between first cousins which could only produce imperfect offspring.

Maupassant told us that Bourget had accused Mme K of having given him the subject of *Fort comme la mort* which the author of *Mensonges* was in process of treating himself in *Cosmopolis*. He abandoned it on the appearance of Maupassant's book. Here and there it really is a question of a rivalry between mother and daughter, but this point of departure doesn't belong to either of them. And then they have two such different styles that it would have been particularly interesting to see them treat the same subject. Maupassant shows us mother and daughter at the same time, while in Bourget's novel the mother is dead and the hero falls in love with the daughter because of her resemblance to the mother whom he had loved . . . Maupassant and Bourget are certainly the leaders of the new school. Maupassant has more relief, Bourget has more depth; both of them have a very great and quite unquestionable talent.

Three comments on Paul Bourget. The first comes from a witty woman, who has dearly loved him: 'Paul Bourget's heart is a stone,' she says, 'but if you strike it very hard, you sometimes strike sparks from it.' The second comes from Barbey d'Aurevilly: 'Paul Bourget is charming, but he is often . . . ailing.' The third comes from Alexandre Dumas: 'He looks so hard at the movement of a watch,' so he maintains, 'that he forgets to notice the time . . .'

. . .

To Alexandre Dumas' at Marly with the Comtesse de Mailly-Nesle *née* de Goulaine, Widor and Paul Bourget, for whom I feel a real attraction. Dumas warmly and sincerely congratulated him on

Le Disciple, though he criticized the ending – the conversion of the old scholar; he found it in contradiction with the portrait which he drew of him at the beginning. For all his hostility, how concerned Alexandre Dumas always is with religious questions! I remember what Monseigneur Mermillod said to me about that noble soul: 'He isn't an enemy of the faith, he is only exiled from it.'[3]

1 July

I have come to instal myself at Saint-Gratien with my dear Aunt. After some negotiations, P has come here to occupy his usual room, but he looks like a man condemned to death. He doesn't speak to the Princess's maid of honour [Mme de Galbois], whom he accuses of having informed against him. And it would be amusing, were it not so painful, this situation in which two people live side by side and don't speak to each other. Each of them addresses themselves to a third party. If one maintains a theory, the other denies it to somebody off stage; the first one takes it up again, and so on. There are scorn and hatred in the looks they give one another. The poor Princess came into my room, as a mother would, while I was still in bed. She sat down on my bed and lamented: 'He has just left for Paris, and he was all scented! But he wasn't scented yesterday . . . Can you understand it? He's writing verse, and I can't write a line!'[4]

[Late July]

I left Saint-Gratien to visit the Empress at Farnborough . . . The Empress took me to see the chapel which She has built on a hill in the park in memory of the Emperor and the Prince Imperial. It consists of two churches, one above the other. The crypt is silent and imposing in its simplicity, it has three places and contains the two identical tombs of Father and Son. It has its private door through which the Empress enters, and it has no open communication with the Church above, which has its worshippers. I photographed the poor Mother going to pray at her son's tomb.[5]

Paris, 25 July 89

Returned to Paris [from Farnborough] for the tragedy and comedy competition at the Conservatoire, which amuses me as much as ever. *Déjeuner*, as last year, with Mlles Réjane and Pierson, Jules Lemaître, Jacques Normand, Le Corbelier, du Tillet, the painter Degas, and Hugues de Roux, who was the secretary of Alph. Daudet.[6]

Princess Mathilde is furious about the Memoirs of Viel-Castel, and she is more than justified in her disgust.

'I shall write my Memoirs, too,' she cried, 'and they will see!'

'You won't write them,' Lavoix told her, bravely.

'And why not?'

'Because one always sees servants who speak ill of their masters, but one never sees masters speaking ill of their servants.'[7]

[August]

To the Eiffel Tower with Edison, whom I photographed on the fifth platform. *Le Figaro* and the correspondents of the American papers asked me for my little snapshots . . .[8]

That summer, the summer of the International Exhibition, the Shah of Persia visited Paris. Primoli continued:

Thursday 8 August

The Shah is a man of medium height, between 50 and 60 years old, he looks hard and dirty, he has a badly dyed brown moustache, he is dressed in black with a clerical frock-coat, grey silk gloves, a big diamond, cut in the shape of a heart, with a gold chain through it, spectacles, and a lion in diamonds on his astrakhan cap . . . Some years ago, the Shah found himself at Enghien, where he had the colic. This is an inconvenience to which his diet must quite often expose him: he eats throughout the day, apparently the dishes are set out on sideboards, and he eats standing, picks up the meats and delicacies with his fingers, eating and spitting everywhere. Someone therefore pointed out that Princess Mathilde's château stood on the other side of the lake, and that His Majesty might fittingly seek hospitality there. Apart from the fact that the Shah was very curious to see the niece of the great Napoleon, Persian etiquette demanded that he should relieve himself in a princely house. Since the Princess was in Paris, the butler did the honours in Her Highness's absence, and led the Shah where the King goes alone but the Shah sits in company. The Court protested, His Majesty was not accustomed to use any throne except his own. The high dignitaries of the Crown seized a splendid Sèvres vase from the mantelpiece and set it in the middle of the salon; it was there that the Shah relieved himself to the great scandal of the butler. This time the servants, well aware of His Majesty's habits, brought some more ordinary vases down to the library, where he retired

159

quite shamelessly with his entire Court ... The Shah, once relieved, came back to the verandah where he ate cakes and toyed with ices, drank champagne and tea, and talked to the ladies for a little while. Then we all went with him to Enghien, where he rejoined the carriage procession with the escort of cuirassiers.[9]

[8 August?]

The poor Princess is still in misery. P is taking the waters at Uriage with his son. She shows me the letters that he writes her. They are very correct, and dry, and he addresses her as *tu*. This cold-blooded intimacy disturbs and revolts me. You address a woman as *tu* to tell her that you love her, not to tell her about your colds and cascara. She told me that he had never called her *tu* in his letters, even at the time when he loved her most. I think I understand that he used this form to stop her from showing his letters, but she doesn't care a rap for these conventions. What has been has been, and it is not her fault if it has ended. She is wonderful in her sincerity. She answers with letters which are touching and passionate in their grievous regrets, and worthy of Mlle de Lespinasse. There are observations like this: 'You reproach me for not growing old. Well, you needn't worry, I'm growing old if growing old means detaching oneself from everything.' And again: 'You regret that you can't find any more subjects for verse, I envy you for regretting only that.' And again: 'There is someone who interests me more than all the world, and that is myself; there is someone whom I loved more than all the world, and that is you.'

Nothing shows more clearly than this correspondence the chasm which separates these two human beings. They speak different languages. One writes grand sentences, the other struggles to find some feeling behind these fine, empty phrases, and answers with a cry from the heart.

Just now we went to the haberdasher's at Enghien where P and M used to go every morning, and I am still petrified by this snatch of conversation between the haberdasher and the Princess. 'Ah, Princess, you're back again?' 'Yes, I've been back a month.' 'How is Mr Popelin?' 'Very well.' 'And Mlle Abbatucci?' Mathilde, very coldly: 'She's dead.' 'Dead! She can't be!' 'Why not? Why can't she die like anyone else?' 'What a dreadful thing! Do you hear that, *mesdemoiselles*? You remember Mlle Abbatucci? She used to come in every morning with Mr Popelin? She's dead ... And where did she die, Princess?' 'I don't know, in Spain or Italy ... Show me some veils.'[10]

160

7

On 19 August, Primoli left Saint-Gratien on his way to Italy.

[Venice,] 23 August

At Florian's I found the joyful [Jean-Louis] Forain, [the artist and engraver], all in white flannel. He introduced me to his pretty companion, with whom, so he says, he is having a honeymoon before marriage. It is She who refuses to marry him, and hesitates to tie herself for ever. She remains his pupil and his mistress. She is the daughter of an austere schoolmaster, and at 14 she carried off the novels which her father confiscated from the boarders, and read them in the attic: that was how she had her education. She is barely twenty, she is so adorably pretty that we watch the triumph of her beauty: people follow it, dazzled, from the bridges and piazzas. The men contemplate it in silence and the women list her graces in their sweet Venetian tongue . . . Spent three days in a gondola, taking photographs . . .

My fleeting visit to Venice has left me with the impression of a fantastic fairy-tale, with Forain for an agreeable friend and the pretty Jeanne Bosc for my good angel. Her coquettish metamorphoses reminded me of Josepha's comment to Baronne Hulot: 'We can be *all* women in one.' She was, alternately, Muse and hoyden, artist and girl, coquette and art student, Parisian and Venetian, an Englishwoman from a keepsake and from Baedeker [*sic*] – but she was always graceful. The pretty pictures frame her charming silhouette in the window of a gondola, in a flurry of pigeons, on the Rialto bridge, on the Giants' Staircase, on the edge of the well at the ducal palace, on the steps of the *loggietta*, her arms curved round her head in harmony with the curve of a bridge . . .

[And] those changes of view perceived from the depths of the gondola: those boats full of vegetables and fruit, a Venetian woman crossing a bridge, draped in her shawl, . . . some gondoliers asleep under a pergola, the movements of the rowers, the bases of the marble palaces, young girls working, framed in an ogee doorway . . .[1]

The photography continued. On 8 January 1890, Romain Rolland, staying in Rome, reported to his mother that he had just met 'Prince Primoli' at a *soirée*.

He is a curious character, this prince. He is agreeable, a good sort, and quite distinguished. But he has a passion for photography. He photographed the Pope in his garden, frail, and leaning on his stick; he photographed Madame Carnot, getting out of a carriage, seen from behind; only yesterday, at the Capitol, he photographed the Empress of Germany. Loulou [his brother] is even madder about it; in company in a salon, you suddenly hear: 'Clic! Clac!'; and there it is, you're photographed. They carry microscopic cameras in their hats, in the buttonholes of their coats [*sic*]. There's nothing you can do about it; everyone's snapped in turn.[2]

The clic-clac seemed to be endless. On 1 March, Primoli recorded:

Sunday. Snow and sunshine! I leap out of bed, order the carriage, and, armed with my two cameras, I go in search of a corner of Rome – a snow scene! I look over the Tiber, I go through the ghetto, the piazza de la Bocca de la Verità, and in the shelter of the temple of Vesta I come across an encampment of *ciociari*; then I go to the Palatine. Never shall I forget that luminous vision of the spring. Those Farnese gardens in which the ruins mingle with the verdure, stones and foliage merge in harmony under a veil of snow which is sparkling in the sun. Wonderful view over Rome, the country and the distant sea . . . And those thousands of invisible birds singing like classical choruses in the pure white almond trees, the pure pink peach trees . . .[3]

On 16 June, at dinner, Romain Rolland met him again: 'Prince Primoli, with the bored expression, a few carnations in his buttonhole [*sic*], and a few bundles of snapshots in his pockets . . .'[4] On 30 June, Rolland was exasperated:

I had received an invitation from Cardinal Mermillod to his taking possession this morning . . . After the ceremony, a buffet: ices, little cakes, and marsala . . . Primoli impertinently placed himself facing the cardinal, barring his way to the sacristy, with his

162

ridiculous camera. And at the buffet, two or three times, he photographed the little cakes, and the guzzling guests . . . This mania is irritating, and even insolent.[5]

For some it had a certain charm. On 9 August, at Saint-Gratien, Edmond de Goncourt recorded: 'After dinner, Primoli gave us a magic-lantern show of his snapshots, in which I saw myself on the threshold of my house at Auteuil, life-size.'[6]

* * *

Primoli was occupied; but his social life, his travelling, his mania for photography, all disguised his inner emptiness. In the autumn of 1890 he learned, from the papers, of the marriage of Jeannine, the daughter of Dumas *fils*.

There seems little doubt that, had he wished, he could have married her. Four years earlier, Grandjean had told him that his interest in her was widely known. 'The young girl loves you, and she has said so to the Princess.'[7] Jeannine was clearly hoping that Princess Mathilde would use her influence on a reluctant suitor; and the Princess had tried in vain to arrange a marriage for him. She understood his reluctance all too well. 'He isn't unhappy,' she explained to Grandjean. 'There isn't any [unrequited] love that has to be uprooted from his heart. That's all just words, it's only literature. He's obstinate, and if he loved he would get married. He is held back by countless little things which I thought he could overcome . . .; and then he is consoled by his laziness!'[8] Primoli had chosen not to marry Jeannine; and now she was someone else's wife. He tried to rationalize his decision. On 12 October, from Ariccia, he sent Dumas his congratulations, in a letter which seemed a premature farewell to youth and hope.

Mon cher Maître,
    The papers tell me that Jeannine has just got married. I have sent my good wishes directly to your dear child, but I must send you my congratulations. Should I confess to you that this marriage extinguishes the last ray of light which still illuminated my future? . . .
    I had either to sacrifice my mother to my wife, or to sacrifice a young girl by transforming her into a sister of charity. It was therefore myself that I sacrificed. It was the only loyal solution . . .
    While Jeannine was free, I should never have married another young girl; now she is married, shall I ever marry? I am

163

thirty-nine, I am ugly and bald . . . I am the man you still marry, but no longer the man whom you love.[9]

Dumas' answer showed his understanding of the least marriageable Bonaparte.

My dear young man,

I think your imagination is greater than you realize yourself, and that it makes you see things in the wrong light. You and I are on the terms of a virtual son and an adopted father. If you had had as deep and enduring a feeling for Jeannine as you believe, you would have opened your heart about it, and this confession would not have committed you to anything. I should have told you, better than anyone else, about the pros and cons of such a marriage, and we should have looked together to see if happiness for both of you might lie there. Your mother was a secondary reason.

If you had married Jeannine, your mother would not have lost a son, she would have gained a daughter. Jeannine was not a society woman, and there would have been no sacrifice or effort on her side to love the people whom you loved. You kept up a long correspondence with her; the Princess urged you to marry her; if you didn't, it was because you didn't want to do so. It wasn't for me to be the first to mention it to you. What a situation I'd have put you in, and what a position I should have given myself with you and your family! I should have looked as if I'd sought a princely alliance . . .

Can you see this cardinal's nephew thinking of marriage to the daughter of a heretic like me, a woman who was not baptized, the sister of a woman [Colette Dumas, Mme Lippmann] who had only had a civil wedding with a Jew? They would have laughed till Kingdom come in the Eternal City, unless they had blushed for all time. You recoiled from all this fuss, in spite of all the Princess's exhortations – and she'd got this marriage into her head. She never talked to me about it; but she discussed it with Colette, and, when Colette came to tell me, I said: 'If it were serious, Primoli would talk to me about it.' You didn't talk to me about it. And therefore it wasn't serious. The truth is that Jeannine, as I know her, would have been an intelligent friend for you, a companion of the opposite sex with whom one could make the journey of life. I could have given her to you, but I really couldn't have offered her to you. I had too much to gain or lose by it.

And then, who knows if St Paul isn't right? You are still my son, and it costs you nothing, and I love you dearly for yourself and yourself alone. Perhaps it is better that way . . .[10]

Four

1

Melancholy reflexions [noted Primoli, later that month]. My life has been a failure, and I regret that I haven't married, because I was born to be a husband and father and I shall die an old bachelor. Now it is too late. I blame my brother a little, because, as far as marriage is concerned, he has been selfish, and he has only thought of his own interests . . . All my friends would be in favour of my getting married, but I am going to be forty![1]

His age would hardly have been a barrier to matrimony. One doubts if he had ever seriously thought of married life. As he wrote himself, he had inherited his grandparents' uncertainty of soul; and that was why he had 'hesitated to bind himself by a lasting liaison or a fragile marriage.'[2] He had a feminine sensibility, he delighted in talk and gossip, he had enjoyed warm relationships with older men; yet it would be surprising to learn that he was homosexual. It would also be surprising to find that he had ever had a significant liaison with a woman. The idealism which he had confided to his diary in his boyhood, and to Dumas *fils* in middle age, concealed, perhaps, a lack of libido, a distaste for sex. 'I have vowed to myself to remain a virgin until I am in love, really in love, with a woman.'[3] So he had written when he was seventeen. Probably he never made a serious physical commitment. The deepest relationship of his life was, without much doubt, his relationship with his mother; the only one to approach it was his relationship with his great-aunt, Princess Mathilde. 'Really, if she were younger, and I were older, I should think myself in love with her.'[4] So he had written, again at seventeen. Now that his mother was deranged and virtually lost to him, he turned increasingly to the Princess.

167

She herself turned to him gladly. She was still tormented by Popelin's liaison with Marie Abbatucci.

I think of nothing except my present situation [she had confessed to Primoli in January]. I want to get out of it at any price – even by death. That is what they really want, and what he desires. They would be free – and I have had my day! Oh, they're infamous! *She* and the son are villainous . . . And he's so weak! . . . He writes poems and he's consoled – he has no preoccupations. He says he doesn't think or feel any more, he says he's fond of me! That's ludicrous, and doesn't deceive a soul![5]

She continued to love him and to condone his duplicity, and she continued to share him.

If the poor man wasn't bullied and harassed by *her* and Gustave, it would all have been forgotten long ago [this to Primoli on 20 September] . . . I am thinking of my return to Paris – and I am more disturbed by this change than usual. Alas, I must admit that I am no longer the valiant person that I used to be. I have been wounded and I shall never be cured. I shall vegetate, live on with a broken heart. I was young and brave so long. I've become a tearful woman, and nothing can get me out of the sadness which envelops me. I dread waking up in the morning.[6]

I am more miserable than ever [this on 1 October] – my feelings are sad and gloomy.
    I have no reason at all for that, no news. For some time *he* has been coming back more often, and relations are even better. It will pass. I hope so, because I feel I'm not being reasonable.[7]

Primoli was sympathetic; he was also conscious that this passionate Bonaparte should be recorded. He asked her, now, if he might write her life.

I am quite willing to let you do so [she answered]. But what a sad subject! Had it not been for my good health and courage I should have died – and under the appearance of a brilliant and enviable life there are only disappointments, false positions and ingratitude. In 1836 I was betrothed to the Emp[eror] for four months, he dropped me for the Strasbourg affair. In 1840 I was married to Mr D[emidoff] – I suffered all his ill-treatment for the six years I remained with him, and it's lucky that my health wasn't ruined.
    From 1846 to 1869 God knows that I was deceived, and finally I

was abandoned. From 1870 to 1890 I no longer need to tell you what happened. I was sustained by an affection which I thought would last, and I did not foresee having to share it . . . I was sure of my own personal devotion, for the past two years I have not lived . . .

This nothingness is breaking me.

My family have only served to oppress and harm me. I have given them a great deal, and I have been disowned in return . . .

I will tell you all you want to know – explain it all to you . . .[8]

Early in November she told him: 'I shall fight to the end – but without illusions . . . It is my fault, my fault, my very great fault! I only blame myself!'[9]

Soon afterwards, he returned to France; he found her still obsessed by Popelin.

The situation [he observed] is fundamentally unchanged, but the acute condition has become a chronic illness. The Princess, who doesn't admit half-measures, . . . wants Popelin, to whom she has given herself for life. Popelin wants the young lady, who finds herself compromised because of him by the Princess's outbursts. He divides his life in two. He comes to the Princess's in the country from Saturday evening to Monday morning – from Wednesday evening to Friday morning. The rest of the time he stays in Paris to receive Marie. This sharing exasperates the Princess, but she must certainly resign herself to it if she wants him. From time to time she rebels, bursts out, and sends him a very dignified letter of dismissal. But the next morning . . . he appears at the usual time . . . And, as usual, he goes into the Princess's room an hour before dinner, lies on the green chaise-longue, says he isn't well, and asks her to stroke his head with her little gloved hand . . . And – to flatter her – he tells her she does him good . . . And She's happy![10]

She was not only betrayed by Claudius Popelin; she was also betrayed, again, by Alphonse Daudet. In his novel, *L'Immortel*, he had described the Princess's break with Nieuwerkerke; now, in his play *La Lutte pour la vie*, he presented Paris with an account of the Popelin affair. On 11 December, Primoli recorded:

I have just been to a performance of *La Lutte pour la vie* by Alphonse Daudet. I was oppressed all the time, I felt a weight on my stomach . . . It was all the more poignant for me as I was seeing my poor Duchess Padovani in flesh and blood. Paul Astier is P[opelin], more than blackened; it isn't the weak and honest man I know, but the Duchess is undoubtedly Her. Since Daudet has known her, he has drawn her noble figure in two novels, in *Les rois en exil* and, more especially, in *L'Immortel*. The novelist is always something of a seer, and he describes the scenes that are to come. Having tried to get under the Princess's skin, he thought: 'What would she do if she thought, or knew, that her lover had deceived her with a young girl who owed her everything?' – and he guessed right.

And I have heard the deeply wounded woman express her anguish in the very tones of grief and anger that Daudet has given her. As I have used certain pages from *L'Immortel* to describe the Princess's break with Nieuwerkerke, I could use actual phrases from *La Lutte pour la vie* to describe the second betrayal.[11]

* * *

It was a time for seeking comfort and family affection; and the Princess had always had a very strong sense of family.[12] On 15 December, writing from Rome, Prince Napoleon assured her: 'As soon as I see Primoli, I will give him your commission for my photograph – though my aged face is hardly attractive to reproduce.'[13] On 3 January 1891, he continued: 'Joseph Primoli, whom *at last* I sometimes see, hasn't mentioned taking my photograph any more, when he asks me I will sit for him.'[14]

Soon afterwards Gégé Primoli took the imperial likeness of the man whom the Goncourts had called *un César déclassé*.

2

Prince Napoleon died two months later: on 17 March 1891. He was sixty-eight.

> The Prince's death won't bring any sort of political change here [so Grandjean reported from Paris on 26 March]. It is more likely to lessen the power of the Bonapartists. Some elements of the party will go over to the Republic and others to Orleanism. France will not change its government at any price. It has had a surfeit of politics. It wants to be undisturbed.[1]

For Princess Mathilde, her brother's death was a sharp reminder of mortality. 'Since he died,' she wrote to Primoli on 4 September, 'I have been haunted night and day by the thought of Death. What can I do? Live and suffer and gradually fade away, and complain as little as possible.'[2]

She did not cease to complain to him. Her unremitting misery continued. '*She* and *Gustave* are as one – the poor Father isn't happy,' she explained on 3 December. 'He doesn't hesitate to say so, but he can't change anything. My mind is cracked and gone, I don't know what to think! Pity me, think of me, write to me, love me, these are consolations I deserve . . .'[3]

In the new year, 1892, the situation was grievously settled. On 17 May, Camille Doucet sent a telegram to Gégé: 'Princess entrusts me sad task of informing you sudden death of Monsieur Popelin.'[4]

* * *

Primoli went to see her, and to take the burden of her grief and her regrets.

171

For the past four years, she told me, there has not been a day when she has not wept. She suffers both from the loss of her friend and from his betrayal, as if he were still alive. She rediscovers around her a thousand traces of this liaison which seem to her to be tangible proofs . . . Here is an enamel which he had done of the other woman, there is a photograph in which the two accomplices are looking at each other . . . And then, at dusk, when she finds herself alone again, on the little sofa near the big armchair which he used to sit in, and when she tells herself that he won't come, . . . she bursts into tears! . . .

Her life had been turned upside-down by this *mariage de raison*, she had had to modify her tastes, age herself by twenty years to be in keeping with the poor invalid who was weakened, she [now] believes, by his betrayal . . .

The liaison with Nieuwerkerke began in Paris in 1845 . . . The break occurred in 1869 . . .

The Princess shows me [the draft of] a fine letter which she sent to the Emperor at the time of the formation of the Ollivier Government. They tell me, she wrote to him, that because of the constitution of the new Cabinet, M de N[ieuwerkerke] would be dismissed. Do not increase my unhappiness, Sire, by making me the cause of an unhappy man . . .

Then Popelin. She did not want to. He insisted, followed her to Brussels. *Mariage de raison* . . . She gave herself entirely. On their return she refurnished his *hôtel* in the rue de Téhéran, which had been ransacked by the Commune . . .

Yesterday [at Saint-Gratien], when her mind was wandering, she said to her lady's maid: 'Where is he? What's become of him? I can't live like this!' And she burst into tears. Today she told me: 'I'll blow my brains out in the end.' And she meant it when she said it, but she won't do it, and she will suffer for years from the love that was stolen from her and from the strong right arm that she has lost.[5]

* * *

Primoli left France, but she continued to send him letter after letter. 'My poor dear Aunt [he told her on 25 June], I can't help thinking that our friend Grandjean is not entirely wrong in prescribing a little of the diversion you need so as not to be fixed on one idea . . .'[6] Grandjean and his wife went to stay with the Princess at Saint-Gratien. On 7 July, from Ariccia, Primoli wrote to her again:

As usual, our thoughts crossed one another. I can quite understand that your grand dinner on Sunday did you more harm than good. It is harder to mend a heart than to wound it . . .

I am delighted that our Friend Grandjean has arrived, for no one has more good sense than he has, . . . and he appreciates you as you deserve. And so you can confide in him *blindly* . . .[7]

She confided in him, and he, in turn, confided in Gégé.

You mustn't judge her condition by what she writes to you [he explained to him in mid July]. She is sad, but she isn't incurably wounded, as we might have feared. She is gradually getting better. She even seems to me better than she was last winter or the winter before. At the moment, there's only one thing which really torments her, and that is Gustave's stubborn refusal to return the letters. It isn't that he's positively refused to return them. But his attitude is worse than a refusal.[8]

Gégé sent her wise advice, but she could not take it.

Everything you say is right, but I can't apply it [she answered on 20 July]. I'm deeply wounded – everything reminds me of him, and the wound bleeds as soon as it's touched by memory . . . I miss him at every moment – I looked after him like a child, he was my concern, my only concern – everything was concentrated in him. My poor dear Gégé, pity me. I have wonderful friends and I try not to bore them by my sadness. I live as I always do, busy myself, but without any zest – with death in my soul and tears in my eyes. What a sad old age I have! Pity me.

No news yet [from Gustave] about returning my letters, and nothing about the legacy which was left to my incurables. He doesn't reply to *anything* or to anyone. I will keep you informed. You're a great consolation to me – and I count on you to console me.[9]

On 1 August, once again, she lamented to him:

My life is finished, it has been poisoned . . . You're right, returning the letters wouldn't have mattered to me if Gustave had been nice to me – it would have been a consolation . . . I know that everything is finished for me . . . Alas, I'm mad – and there's no cure for me.

I was content with so little.[10]

173

On 7 August she continued: 'For the past few years [since my return from Turin, the visit to Arcachon], I haven't lived. I am so sick at heart. I had and I still have a fixed idea of him – Him, always him – or rather the ideal that I had created.'[11] On 15 August:

> For four years I have suffered – but with hope. Today there is nothing any more!
>
> I have some moments which I greatly cherish. I do not lack friends. But he alone was necessary to me – he had absorbed my life!
>
> Dear Grandjean comforts me as much as he can. He gives me plans to occupy myself: to continue my memoirs . . .[12]

On 19 August she wrote, yet again, about the man 'I mourn so much, the man who was all my life . . . My dear Gégé, how hard life is! I regret my bad years! They were still very happy because he was there . . .'[13] On 22 August, once more, she confided to him:

> According to all I see and hear the general conviction is *that he deceived me* for the sake of his self-esteem –that I was his dupe and am now his victim! No one dares to tell me so – everybody thinks so! Do you think so, too? In that case why shouldn't I try to forget him and fortify my heart and mind? Could I do it? Should I be better for doing it? Or is it wiser to drown in the tide of griefs and regrets? Gégé, you must tell me the truth. I ask you to. I must get out of my rut.
>
> Dumas is going to see Gustave and talk to him loud and clear.[14]

'You drive me to despair,' confessed Gégé, from Ariccia, on 7 October. 'If I come to see you I don't know what I can try to say to you to cheer you up a little! You are brooding too much on your grief and brooding too much on your suspicions, you must stop it, or you won't get better!'[15]

On 4 December he arrived, once again, in Paris.

> At the Gare de l'Est I find my dear Aunt's brougham and the kindly faces of Joseph the valet and Léon the coachman, who seem pleased to see me again. At the *hôtel* in the rue de Berry, I find the Princess with open arms, her eyes full of tears, warm kisses on her lips . . . She takes me to my rooms, which are nice and warm and brightly lit, all ready to receive me. It is comfort trying to give me

the illusion of happiness . . . Alas! It is only the effect of a mirage . . . I feel a certain reluctance to let myself be pleased by it, as if my dear departed Mother would be jealous![16]

His mother had not died: she still lingered on in Rome; but, as a human being, she had left him. His relationship to Princess Mathilde was perhaps the nearest he had, now, to that between a mother and a son. It was also the relationship between a passionate woman and a confidant; and the Princess needed more than ever to unburden herself. Gégé listened to her, and consoled her.

She was remarkably faithful, even to those whom she had good cause to mistrust. She had chosen to overlook Daudet's betrayal in *L'Immortel* and, again, in *La Lutte pour la vie*. More than once she and Gégé called on him in the rue de Bellechasse. In February 1893, Mme Daudet recorded:

Saw Princess Mathilde again . . .
I looked at her this week in Alphonse's study. She was accompanied by her nephew, Count Primoli, and dressed in the Second Empire style, not dated because she slightly adapts it to the modern fashion . . . And I was moved to hear her describe the personal drama in her life, the one that people are talking of at the moment, the betrayal in her household by a hand which was destined to close her eyes.[17]

175

3

Soon afterwards, Gégé returned to Rome; but the thought of her did not leave him. 'I come to you when my heart is overflowing with grief,' she confessed on 12 February. 'I couldn't tell you why – but I'm in such a bitter mood that I'd like to hide from everyone and simply weep. Which I don't refrain from doing . . .'[1]

She was lost in grief, and Primoli must sometimes have felt that she was indulging in her misery. Her love of life, her sense of purpose, seemed to have gone. He was soon confronted by an all-confident, exuberant contrast. Before Princess Mathilde's despairing letter reached him from Paris, he found himself absorbed by Sarah Bernhardt. She was spending a week in Rome on her European tour.

13 February

At last she's gone! Who's gone? Sarah the Great, Sarah Bernhardt herself. It is true to say that all roads lead to Rome. She stayed for a week, gave eight performances. After living her social life for 48 hours, I am played out: she must be made of steel . . . I had her to *déjeuner* with the Princesse de Venosa, and I had her to supper one night after the theatre. This little festivity really rather worried me, because I wasn't sure how it would go, but everything went off better than I could have hoped. To begin with, she had written to say that she would not come, she was so tired, and I had to insist, and tell her that she was expected . . . She arrived at about 2 o'clock in the morning [*sic*], wearing a pretty peach-coloured dress, wrapped up against the chill in a blue fox boa . . . I gave her my arm and led her into the red salon, which was nice and warm and brightly lit, and filled with the prettiest women, to whom I

176

introduced her. On the way I presented Princess Brancaccio, the Marquise Theodoli, Lady L, Princess Odescalchi, etc., to her, as if she were a queen. We finally reached her little table, where I installed her between the Héberts and Princess Doria. Then came Comtesse Pasolini, Mme Le Ghait, Princess Pallavicini . . . I gave her her menu with her portrait which I had taken the day before. I had hung a gold coin with [the head of] Justinian on it, in memory of Theodora.[2]

Sarah returned to Paris to buy the Théâtre de la Renaissance and to prepare for a tour of South America. On 14 February Primoli, who was more than six years younger, lamented: 'I am writing nothing, nothing. I am leading a puppet's life: dances every evening!'[3]

Rome, 9 March

A very busy day, if not a full one. Went out in the pony-cart at ten o'clock. Bought the *Débats* at the kiosk in the Piazza di Spagna. It contains articles by Voguë and Deschamps on Taine, who died the other day. I read these interesting pages as I went along, whipped by the wind, borne away by the gallop of my little mare. As we passed through the Porta Salara I thought of the chapter in *Voyage en Italie* on the typical Roman campagna, which must have had a very special interest for the author of the theory of environments. And I remembered the only time, I think, that I saw him. It was in 1866, I was spending my holidays at Saint-Gratien, Taine came to dinner one Wednesday evening with Sainte-Beuve, Saint-Victor, Théophile Gautier and the Goncourts. My Aunt showed him some verses which I had just written without great prosody but with a certain sense of harmony. He asked me to recite 'Lucie' [by Musset]. You can imagine how nervous I was, and my voice was trembling; he was none the less delighted and touched, because we were fifteen years old, the poet and I, and he murmured: 'He feels it and says it as it was written.'

And I remember that, twenty years later, on that same verandah, on a starry night, the great artist Baudry told me an anecdote about Taine which he had had from Edmond About. It was at the École Normale in about 1849. About and Sarcey were discussing love; Taine had looked up from his Spinoza, and said: 'I think that love . . .' 'Oh, you,' retorted About, 'you don't have a say in the matter: you don't know what a woman is. Go on with your book.' Slightly impatient at this reproach, Taine picked up his hat and left. 'Is he really angry?' they wondered. Twenty minutes later, Taine came back, somewhat flushed and breathless from his escapade. He found his friends still in the heat of discussion. He sat down, crossed his legs, stared at them through his spectacles, and flung at them with a certain disgust: 'Now I *know* what a woman is, and I am entitled to tell you that love . . .' That is Taine in a nutshell, judging a feeling by one sensation, womankind by one impression.

Taine was one of Princess Mathilde's habitués. He broke with her over his articles on the Emperor. His conversation about it with Renan is already history. 'I am most embarrassed, my dear Renan. If I publish my work on Bonaparte, I break with a great lady who has never shown me anything but kindness; if I modify it, I compromise with my conscience. What do you advise me to do?' 'My dear Taine, when I published my life of Jesus, as I perceived it, I knew that I should break for ever with a much greater lady who had brought me up: the Church . . . And I did not hesitate.' The Princess made no useless recriminations; she left her card on him, marked P.P.C. [Pour Prendre Congé]. In December, when I knew how ill he was, I tried to bring my Aunt round to kinder feelings, I should have liked her to send for news of him. 'Never!' she cried, angrily. 'A swine who said that my grandmother was *dirty*! And that the Emperor slept with his sisters!' She had tears of anger in her voice, and I dared not insist. For me the thought of the happy hours which Taine has given me effaces phrases in his work which could have ruffled me.[4]

* * *

In that summer of 1893, Primoli was back in Paris. He spent some time with the Empress Eugénie, on one of her discreet visits to the Hôtel Continental. 'We are crossing the Tuileries gardens,' he noted. 'The Empress points out the flower-bed which has replaced the Salle des Maréchaux, and she says to me, sadly: "There I am – I feel that I am one of those rose-trees covered with thorns which have grown up where I used to live."'[5]

However, Primoli had come, above all, to cheer Princess Mathilde. 'What a change in my Aunt,' he had written to her, 'who was the perfect incarnation of *mente sana nel corpo sano*! How badly the spring inside you is working today! It needs some oil, I mean some affection, you must let yourself be loved, . . . and you will still enjoy what is sweet in your memories and forget what is bitter about them . . . I have high hopes of the sun – one cannot stop that great accomplice from coming in through the window and entering the gloomiest of hearts.'[6] Now he resumed his familiar occupation as her escort.

Took my Aunt Mathilde to see Alphonse Daudet in the rue [de] Bellechasse. He was alone in his study, and unable to move. He still has his handsome head: the head of Christ rising from the tomb and bearing the traces of the Passion. He talks about Zola without bitterness. The author of *L'Immortel* says that the Académie cannot elect him because it would appear to accept his works, and that a mother who saw 'de l'Académie-Française' on Zola's books would have the right to buy *Nana*, *La Terre* or *Pot-Bouille* for her daughter, and trust to the Académie's recommendation. 'Zola is mad to stand for election,' he said. 'He has children by his wife's maid. His wife knows, and she suffers anguish over it. There have been terrible domestic scenes. She now holds back her tears, and takes out the children of the husband whom she adores – the children whom she used to see in secret.'[7]

Paris, 21 June

The great success of the moment is the *Walkyrie* at the Opéra. The Gluckists and Piccinists are once again enraged. People are discussing [it all] in the cafés and salons with enthusiasm and animosity. I determined to take my Aunt Mathilde to the Opéra. Nurtured on Italian music, she is completely antagonistic to Wagner, she can find no harmony in him. She was quite frankly indignant throughout the performance, and her honest indignation pleased me more than conventional admiration . . .

Gounod told me he doesn't believe that this enthusiasm will last in France. It's a passing whirlwind, he said. He certainly doesn't despise Wagner, and he finds him 'very decorative'. He also said 'it's a musical fresco' – but he prefers *Don Juan*.[8]

Saint-Gratien, 22 June

Gounod came to spend the day at Saint-Gratien with his old consort. He had come back to her one day, after all his escapades in England with Mrs Weldon. He had thrown himself at her feet, asked her to forgive him, and said: 'Madame, I bring you THE BUST of Gounod' [*sic*].

I put Gounod among the four greatest charmers in Paris. They are for me (since Théo's death) Alexandre Dumas *fils*, Sardou, Alph. Daudet and Gounod. Dumas has the most wit and depth,

Sardou most erudition and vitality, Daudet has the most verve and poetry, Gounod has most eloquence and youth . . . The composer of *Mireille* is astonishingly young and eloquent. With his blue eyes and his white beard he looks like Faust in person: [you feel] his false beard is about to fall off and he's going to be twenty. He would be a prophet if he were not Anacreon, and the wreath of roses would suit him as well as the tongues of fire. He says things which seem to be engraved on some oriental talisman, and they fall, perfectly chiselled, from his lips. You have only to pick them up. 'One is attached to people,' he said, 'according to what one gives them. Debtors are often ungrateful, but benefactors can never be . . .' 'My ultimate dream,' said Gounod, 'what I should have liked as a swan-song, would have been to set the story of the Passion to music with only an organ accompaniment. In order to inspire myself I should have needed to meditate in a Gothic church when a thousand human voices echoed from the roof. In fact I always try out my religious music in the vastness of a cathedral, and I wait for the echoes to answer, in order to judge the effect . . .' . . .

Gounod and Princess Mathilde felt their memories awaken at the magic name of the divine Malibran. Gounod recalled how, when he was at college, he had been allowed to attend the St Charlemagne banquet, and his mother had rewarded him by sending him to the [Théâtre des] Italiens where they were performing *Otello* with Malibran, Rubini and Lablache. It was perhaps that wonderful ensemble which revealed his vocation to him. 'One evening,' he told me, 'when Garcia was playing the part of Otello, La Malibran saw him change daggers, and fainted in terror. She thought that he would carry out his threat, and really kill her.' Princess Mathilde said that she was twelve when La Malibran arrived, bringing letters of introduction to King Jerome. 'My father asked her to dinner, she accepted, and asked permission to come in her costume as Amina in *La Sonnambula*. She was pretty, agreeable and delightful. Afterwards we went to applaud her at the theatre, she had to repeat the finale of *La Sonnambula* seventeen times, and she did not sing it the same way twice running.' Chateaubriand says in his *Mémoires* that, when La Malibran wanted to identify a bird whose name she had forgotten, she imitated its song.[9]

22 June [*sic*]

Princess Mathilde lets herself go this evening and tell us with a melancholy verve, a sad half-smile, about the agonies of her childhood. They have produced a wonderful result, but they have made her unable to see her mother except as a torturer who was jealous of her ... The poor Princess has never forgiven that virtuous and sensual German for calling her in, without modesty, after she had been shut up with her husband, to help her to sew the button back on her pantaloons. It was offences like these, so acutely felt by a young and delicate soul, which in a certain sense denatured the Princess's natural feelings, and made her set Love far below maternal Love, and gave her the prejudice of virtuous women. To listen to her, you would think her childhood was a time of virtual tortures. There was a box in which they made her stand, to oblige her to curtsey correctly ... And those poor little feet, which they hooped up in iron [*sic*], and those little hands which they set on a piano and shut down under a bar, and the stiff, high corsets in which they imprisoned her! One day she puffed herself out as far as she could so as not to get them on, and her mother thrashed her.

Then there was this procession of tutors which continued throughout her childhood and her youth ... And the governesses who slept with her father ... Her brother detested veal, and she had a horror of pigeon. They had been forced for months to eat veal and pigeon at a little table set in a draught. They had begun by throwing the execrated food under the table, and then they had changed plates with one another, and finally they had come to like what they were given. But why torture children – could it be the jealousy of the old?[10]

Sunday, 25 June

Woken at Saint-Gratien by a ray of sunlight and the birds singing ... Went to see the Princess in her delightful room with its four windows, all sunlit and fragrant ... Waited there while her hair was done, read the newspapers ... She talked to me unreservedly about her grievous regrets, which can all be summed up in a name – Popelin – and about her plans, which all tend to have me beside Her.

Took the 9.30 train to Paris.[11]

[June or July]

Went to Jacques Blanche's pretty studio – he's the son of the excellent doctor – in the rue des Fontes at Auteuil. Took some photographs of the strange daughters of José-Maria de Heredia. One of them writes charming poems. When someone asked her to publish them: 'Oh no, Monsieur,' she answered, with the adorable affright of seventeen, 'oh no, I want to be posthumous!'[12]

4

In the early 1890s, Primoli fulfilled the ambition of Abel Hermant, and presented him to Princess Mathilde.

Nearly everyone I knew belonged to her inner circle [so the novelist was to remember in *Souvenirs de la vie mondaine*], Goncourt used to go there on Wednesdays and Sundays. And, finally, in the Grenier, and almost everywhere else I went, I used to see [her nephew], Comte Joseph Primoli, whom, like all the world, I called Gégé. Yet although I called him Gégé, it had never occurred to him to present me to the Princess, and I admit I was a little piqued.

But that was because he liked surprises. When he came to Paris, he used to stay in the *hôtel* in the rue de Berry where he had a small apartment, a sort of bachelor pad, independent of the main building. I went to call on him there one day, at his express invitation; he wanted to show me his famous stamp collection, which became more famous still when the rumour spread that it had brought him, if I remember rightly, nearly a million.

This collection did not interest me in the least, because I was then unaware of its market value, which would have impressed and also scandalized me. Out of politeness, I pretended to admire the stamps, but despite myself I often turned my head towards the courtyard, hoping at least to catch a glimpse of Napoleon's niece. Strange to say, I had never seen her in the flesh, though nearly everyone I knew displayed a signed photograph of her on the mantelpiece in their salon. Then we went out together, Primoli and I.

As we were crossing the courtyard, he suddenly remembered that he had to fetch something from the hall of the *hôtel*. I followed him, without ulterior motive, and we found ourselves face to face with the Princess, who was about to get into her carriage. He presented me, she held out her hand, hardly gave me time to kiss it properly, and told me that she was at home every Wednesday and Sunday.

She said so in such an imperative manner that I took it for granted, and had no doubt that, as from the following week, I should go to the rue de Berry every Wednesday and Sunday. I have never been presented to someone of that rank with so little etiquette. Gégé, who had disappeared as soon as he introduced me, seemed to be very much amused. He liked jokes and mystifications.[1]

Even Ethel Smyth, that daunting amazon, who was a composer of operas, and the daughter of an English general, was not safe from Gégé's practical jokes. In the early 1890s, 'as a sort of honorary *Demoiselle d'Honneur*',[2] Dame Ethel (as she was to be) accompanied the Empress Eugénie on a two-month cruise in the Adriatic. The yachting party, she recalled,

consisted of three persons only, HM's gentleman in attendance being Count Joseph Primoli . . .

On one occasion a supremely ridiculous incident happened, and to give point to it I must explain that she had a physical horror of relics which no sense of their sanctity had power to counteract. One can imagine her consternation, therefore, when we were informed, on landing at Trau, that a ceremony had been arranged at the Cathedral in her honour, in which the shin-bone of the founder was to play a part. There was no escape, the church was filled to bursting, and, as she knelt at the altar-rails, the organist meanwhile playing a thunderous valse-tune, the relic was not only produced, but as an unheard-of favour presented to her to kiss. I watched the whole scene from the background where I had modestly placed myself, fearing, as a heretic, to desecrate the bone; but the priest, informed by the mischief-loving Count Primoli, that I also was of the Imperial party, made a kindly yet authoritative signal. And no sooner had I pressed my lips to the relic, than a bell was rung and the valse broke off abruptly in the middle of a bar – which is an exceedingly difficult feat to accomplish . . .

I have many vignette-memories of that entrancing voyage: the journey from Trieste to join the yacht at Corfu in a huge liner, empty but for a crowd of Mussulmans on their way to Mecca, who walked about with large, long loaves of bread under their arms in the daytime, and used them as pillows at night; I see Primoli, who was mad on photography, snapshotting the pilgrims, and the Empress's terror lest they should murder us all in consequence.[3]

* * *

183

September 1893 found the inveterate traveller in Italy.

It was [he wrote] in the Bay of Naples at the end of the festivities which had been held in celebration of the [King and Queen's] silver wedding. The Italian Royal Family, with the Emperor and Empress of Germany, other princely guests, ministers and high dignitaries of state, found themselvs on board the *Lepanto*. At the request of the Queen – who knew that punctuality is the politeness of princes – they hastened their return to port. There was a very full programme that evening; it was nearly half-past seven, and they still had to disembark, get dressed, dine at 7.45 and then go to the San Carlo, where all the aristocracy of Naples had been summoned for the gala performance at nine o'clock. And so there was no time to lose, and the ladies were wondering how they would manage to be ready. The young Emperor was listening with interest to the Minister for the Navy, who was telling him that one of his officers had discovered the secret of petrol-fired torpedoes. 'That's very clever,' said William, excited by every new idea, 'could you let me see a demonstration?' 'Whenever Your Majesty wishes.' 'At once.' 'Very well.' Orders were given to launch a long-boat. There was great commotion among the masters of ceremonies: this manoeuvre had not been listed in the programme. They wondered, in terror, who would stay with the Royal Family, who would go down with the Emperor, where they would land, which carriage would wait at the port, etc. During these *sotto voce* discussions, William II leapt into the long-boat with the Minister for the Navy . . . The Queen – of whom he had not even taken leave – stood on the bridge, and watched him go off without a word . . . No doubt she was thinking of these delays, these excitements and festivities – which were derisory for her, since they were supposed to celebrate twenty-five years of unclouded happiness, and had she actually had five years of marriage? Perhaps she was also thinking of that young madman into whose arms Italy had so casually thrown herself, and for whom it was in process of being ruined; with her positive good sense, she must have told herself that he could one day drag it as easily into a disastrous war as into a pleasure outing . . . With an indefinable gaze, she followed him, as he was tossed about by the waves, entirely absorbed by his latest craze; and, at last, unable to contain herself any longer, although her hard profession had taught her everything about the painful art of never complaining, she half turned towards the dignitaries standing beside her, and simply murmured: 'Gentil sangue latino, questo e ancora un barbaro.'

They sat down at table after 9 o'clock instead of 7.45. During dinner, the Queen did not address a single word to her imperial neighbour, who was no doubt aware of the royal *broncio*. She seemed absorbed in a conversation about art and literature with the guest who was sitting opposite. It was the minister Martini, one of the most cultivated men in Italy, and certainly the most French conversationalist in the Peninsula. These two lofty minds expressed themselves in the purest Italian, but they seemed to talk a language foreign to their surroundings, it was so incomprehensible to the two Sovereigns, it was so far above militarism and sport – those two unique battle-horses of modern princes. The Emperor gave up the attempt to attract the Queen's attention, and tossed off comments to some third person with an attempt at flippancy. At one moment, over the Queen's head, he threw the Prince of Naples an apparently insignificant invitation, which might appear a mere polite formula: 'I definitely expect you at the autumn manoeuvres in Germany.' The heir to the throne gave a suspicion of a smile, but before he answered he looked straight at his father, who looked at the minister Brin out of the corner of his eye. The minister made a gesture like Pontius Pilate, it was polite rather than political. The King translated it by an approving grunt in his thick moustache, and the Prince of Naples accepted . . . The trick had been played, and Bismarck's pupil stroked the pummel of his sword and decided that he would lodge his guest at Metz, and celebrate with him the anniversary of Sedan. Under the eyes of France, which had been wounded to the heart, the grandson of Il Re Galantuomo and the grandson of the Emperor William would celebrate the fall of the victor of Magenta and Solferino. 'Gentil sangue latino, quello e ancora un barbaro!'[4]

* * *

The Kaiser returned to Germany; and, once again, Primoli decided to go to France.

> Don't think I'm coming to Paris to entertain you, my dear Aunt [this on 12 October]. *You're* going to entertain *me*! *You'll take me* to see Sardou's play about the Empire, [and] Sarah Bernhardt, . . . one wet day *you'll take me* to the museum at Versailles, another to the Louvre (the museum) and another to the Louvre (the shop). In fact, I intend *to tire you out*, so that when I go you'll say: 'Thank God, now I can have a rest!' . . .

> GG[5]

Nothing, in her later years, restored Princess Mathilde's morale like Gégé's bracing and devoted love. More than once she told Grandjean how happy she would be if Gégé were to settle in Paris. On 13 October, Grandjean told him:

You have given the Princess great pleasure by promising to come this autumn . . .

I am saying this to you now, and I'm speaking very seriously. Never has your presence been more necessary: no, not even after the tragedy last year . . .

I know I tend to take a pessimistic view of things. But things have reached such a point, physically and emotionally, that from now on we need to be doctors rather than friends. Until this summer the Princess held out, badly no doubt, but she held out. Today the collapse has begun. One can still check it, but in three months it will be too late. She will be finished.[6]

Another blow was about to fall. On 18 October Gounod died, and she was in despair. Gégé announced that he would come at once. It is not clear from the correspondence whether he paid a visit in October, or whether he was kept in Rome, by illness, until mid November; but, on 19 October, Grandjean wrote:

My dear friend, believe me when I assure you that, if you hadn't come, it would have been a disaster . . . [My wife] found the Princess even more out of countenance than we expected, even after the worry about your illness and the terrible blow of Gounod's death. For nowadays the death of a contemporary is a stunning blow for her, and how many of them have died in the past year, from Lavoix to Blanche and Gounod! It has reached the point where I tax my ingenuity to find old men of eighty who are well so that I can 'casually' mention them to her.

I cannot see her depressed like this, because I feel that, with her robust health, she has several good years to live. It's only her morale which is affected, and it isn't incurable . . .

And, believe me, it isn't grief that's killing her. Her grief is immense, but it's the kind of grief she can live with. What's killing her is that she is destroying herself by her irritation with everything around her. She is still immensely energetic, and she's only using her energy to fret herself, to create herself subjects for exasperation. So she must be distracted, prevented from having time to get worked up about everything. It's difficult, but not impossible.[7]

* * *

Rome, 25 October 1893

Dined at Hébert's with Émile Ollivier and Lefebvre de Béhaine, the French Ambassador to the Holy See. The amiable diplomat is the brother-in-law of Frédéric Masson and the cousin of Edmond de Goncourt, who constantly mentions him in his *Journal*.

People have been quoting stories of the courage and ingenuousness of Marshal MacMahon, who has just died. His sayings have remained proverbial. People have accorded him some which he probably never uttered, but they only attribute gross stupidities to the poor in wit – who are often rich in feeling; that is why the Kingdom of Heaven belongs to them, and sometimes the presidency of the republic on earth. One recalls the flood of eloquence inspired in [MacMahon], when he was in power, by the sight of some region under water. 'All that water! All that water!' were the only words he found to hearten the terrified inhabitants. Nor has one forgotten the encouragement he gave to a negro soldier who was presented to him: 'You're a negro, carry on!' I don't know if these sayings are authentic, but I myself have seen the letter of condolence which he sent the Empress on the death of the Prince Imperial. The heartbroken mother, closeted in her room, sent this curious missive to me in my study; she had fiercely crossed it out with a slash of red pencil, which looked to me like a line of blood: 'I am,' he said, 'happy to have this occasion offered me, Madame, to remember myself to you . . .'

One might quote some snatches of dialogue which are already classic between the Marshal and his faithful d'Harcourt, who was the President's factotum and adviser . . . Someone said that there were two ambassadors in Rome. 'Impossible!' cried the Marshal. 'I promise you.' 'But . . . let's ask d'Harcourt.' D'Harcourt was summoned, and explained. The Marshal – with stupefaction, at first, then with admiration: 'How does he manage to know it all, that devil of a d'Harcourt?' Besides the grotesque sayings there are the sublime ones said as spontaneously as the silly ones. 'You are off to victory, Marshal.' 'I am off to war.' 'Here I am, and here I stay' was said quite simply, without the Don Quixote panache or the hand on the swordhilt with which they have tried to embellish it. It was the saying of a resolute and determined soldier, they have wanted to make it into a rhodomontade. In spite of this absence of . . . literature, he wrote his memoirs, from which Émile Ollivier, who had actually seen them, picked out this sentence: 'I have regretted all the governments I've served, except my own.' Most of these fake witticisms were concocted by M Thiers. He could not forgive the Marshal for having had the wit to be his successor, and he had christened him MacBette. The truth lies in Thiers' saying, and he said of his successor: 'Not as stupid as they say, or as honest as they believe.'[8]

187

Émile Ollivier talks to me about Prince Napoleon. He knew him very well, and he was alternately his friend and adversary. He considers him the evil genius of the Empire, counterbalancing the Emperor's sane ideas by his fatal influence, annulling them, and producing those contradictions which prevented Napoleon III from gaining the friendship of one side or the other, while contriving to displease them both. One might add that the Emperor hardly had illusions about his terrible cousin. When Émile Ollivier came to power, Napoleon III said to him one day: 'There are two friends of yours whom I want you never to mention to me: one, because he lacks commonsense, that's Napoleon-Jerome; the other, because he's dishonest, and that's Émile de Girardin.' Despite this mistrust, the Emperor always allowed himself to be taken up again by Prince Napoleon. The Prince had kept the right of the small child who had tyrannized over him from his infancy, he had continued by stealing Rachel from him, and he had finally been jealous of his Empire, constantly putting spokes in the wheels of the chariot of State. Prince Napoleon could never resign himself to being second, and wanted to be first. Hence his systematic opposition to his cousin's government and his treachery towards the Prince Imperial. 'How often I told him,' added Ollivier, 'that under the Empire it was a crime to make oneself the centre of an opposition, when all relations and friends should close ranks and let the adversaries break themselves.' When the Empress was about to be delivered, Prince Napoleon was waiting in the next room, with the great dignitaries of the Crown; when they came to announce that a Prince was born, his features grew contorted. He was so overcome that, when the Emperor came in, radiant with joy, he had a certain pity for his cousin, and gently laid his hand on his shoulder. 'Calm yourself, Napoleon, calm yourself . . .' It was three hours before he could bring himself to sign the birth certificate of the person who was taking his place as heir presumptive. On the Emperor's death, there were terrible scenes between him and the Empress; one day, in a burst of fury, he even threw an inkwell at the head of the widow of Napoleon III. When he left the [Bonapartist] party, he tried to justify his conduct by saying: 'I do not seek the Prince Imperial's place; we are not aiming at the same goal, he wants to be Emperor, I hope to be the President of the Republic.' Ollivier answered him: 'As long as the Prince Imperial is there, if there is a Bonaparte at the head of any government, it must be him; you have only to follow him. Your behaviour towards that young man is criminal.'

What he lacked was the sense of duty; he knew his rights, but he did not know what he owed to other people. When he had said: 'That annoys me,' he had said everything, and that was that. He did not understand that in certain positions one has to show a certain consideration. That is what always surprised him in his sister-in-law, the very correct Queen Margherita. She fulfilled her duties as a Sovereign so punctiliously that she seemed to find pleasure in it. 'She enjoys boring things,' he used to say, 'she is never so radiant as when she is presiding over some official ceremony.' These two aristocrats could not get on with one another . . . The Queen used to say, not without a certain regret: 'Everyone extols my dear brother-in-law's intelligence, wit and learning. I only know them from hearsay, because with me he never deigns to open his mouth. I touch on every subject in vain, he always lets the conversation drop.' And yet, with the learned Queen Margherita, he did not have to fear the literary innocence of the young Duchess of Genoa. One evening, this pale, diaphanous, almost bloodless blonde princess, who only wanted to be agreeable and to be amused, found herself at table next to Prince Napoleon. She rummaged in her little head to see what she could find to interest the solemn personage with the scowling face, and she said to him eagerly: 'I adore French literature!' Renan's friend looked her up and down, his eyeglass to his eye. 'Yes,' she continued, happily, 'Gyp, for example! Do you know a writer in any language superior to Gyp? . . .' Here one understands that the Prince was disarmed; he could only smile, and he could not enter into a . . . literary discussion; but, as regards the Queen, his silence meant timidity rather than disdain. He did not want to ruffle, or to lie, and he abstained. He couldn't say anything, if he was unable to say it all . . . Besides, . . . he hardly knew how to talk to women. Yes, this lover of the fair sex did not know the art of talking to these exquisite, delicate creatures. Gallantry and flirtation were not his strong point. He tamed them rather than seduced them. They were charmed rather as the wren is charmed by the serpent which fascinates it and devours it.[9]

Primoli, too, was fascinated by Prince Napoleon's conquests. He left a long manuscript study, *Prince Napoléon et les femmes*, which, alas, he thought unpublishable.

Rome, 11 November 1893

Émile Ollivier says that Prince Napoleon's scholarship is suspect . . . On the other hand he has the gift of assimilation to the highest

189

degree. This does not prove very personal ideas, but it gives an illusion to the public and charms the adversaries whom one wants to conquer.[10]

5

Dinner at Princess Mathilde's [wrote Goncourt on 15 November] . . .

There are Dumas, his daughter Colette, Primoli, who is in Paris for the moment, Pichot, and Ganderax, who came during the day to ask me for my collaboration in a review which is being founded, a sort of second *Revue des Deux Mondes*, of which he is editor.[1]

La Revue de Paris was to be published from the beginning of 1894; Gégé would one day contribute to it. Meanwhile, in his diary, he continued to make notes on the Princess's conversation, her character and state of mind.

[Paris, November 1893]

She was a good German Princess, made to live by her fireside with an adored husband and a dozen children. After the difficulties of her childhood, I must try to set down the turpitude of Mr D[emidoff], to show that it was impossible for the poor young woman to live with this Cossack who was rotten to the marrow. Her very contact with him risked infecting her, and his brutalities hurt her pride . . .

Then Nieuwerkerke had made his entrance into her life.

She was to love him with all her might and with all her soul – despite his infidelities, despite her own exalted station – for 25 years, for all her life, until the day when she was finally freed by her husband's death, and he was on the eve of gaining his own freedom. Then she offered to marry him. He then confessed to her that he had promised marriage to someone else, . . . to a pure and innocent young girl, a girl for whom he felt esteem! . . . This dagger

191

thrust aimed at her very heart killed the love which had, until then, survived everything.

Henceforth she felt a deep disgust for humanity, she who was such an optimist, and God knows what would have happened to her if, as she stood on the threshold of old age, there had not been an artist, poet and philosopher, who was loving and compassionate and held out his hand to her. She took it. As he was a few years younger than herself, she thought that she could expect him to close her eyes, and she began to live again . . .

She had been so shamefully deceived the first time that she had lost the confidence which she had had when she was twenty, the illusion of her first love; she became suspicious, mistrustful of everything and of everyone. As her splendid constitution had remained young beyond the usual limits, she could not admit that it was different with the ageing and rheumatic poet. As he neglected her, she watched him; she thought she perceived that he was deceiving her with one of her intimates, and she discovered that this girl had supplanted her in the invalid's heart. There followed anguish, torture, jealousy, unheard-of scenes, the expulsion of the young lady, quarrels and patched-up reconciliations, a life destroyed for ever . . .

Death intervened too late to settle anything. It bore the poor man away from life more easily than it could tear the love away from the Princess's heart: her regret is complicated by a remorse which she does not admit. She reviles him through her tears. She finds again, in mourning him, the childlike innocence of the first hours of love.

She writes impassioned letters to the dead man and goes and pushes them through the grille of his vault – to which she has been forbidden access. And every morning, at about 8 o'clock, I hear a knock at my bedroom door: it is Her, she sits at the foot of my bed – and begins to cry . . . One must try to heal a deep wound; it is beginning to go septic with continual rubbing . . .

To the Vaudeville with the Princess to see Sardou's new play, *Madame Sans-Gêne*. The prologue entertained us with its very skilful reconstruction of Paris under the Directoire. In the first act, the pretty scenery and the splendid costumes had completely captivated us, when the Maréchale Lefebvre cast an inopportune tirade in the face of the Emperor's sisters, and even listed the names of their lovers. This revolutionized the poor Princess. She felt terribly put out at seeing her aunts insulted on stage, and especially at feeling that every eye in the audience was upon her . . . I had some difficulty in making her stay. However, at the end of the act, as I was afraid of the Emperor's appearance, and a particular scene in Corsican dialect which had been mentioned to us, I took her out by the stage door . . .

The poor Princess was all flustered and upset, and, in the heat of the moment, she vowed she would tell Sardou what she thought of him, and I was afraid that she would finally break with him as she had broken with Taine. I did however obtain that she would not write to him . . . Alas, I only delayed the outburst, for, after my departure from Paris, letters were exchanged . . .

The dear Princess is very personal . . . And so she has a horror of the theatre – perhaps to her the theatre represents an evening away from her round table or, again, the absence of friends who might be with her. For her, the show is a rival to her own dear salon . . .

Sauzay, a professor from the Conservatoire, comes to *déjeuner*. Every Wednesday, from time immemorial, in order to give him pleasure and to have the pretext for giving him a fee of 50 francs, the Princess grows bored for an hour playing the piano, while he accompanies her on the violin. He has the physique of a musician out of Hoffmann: he is over eighty, small, spare, alert, he seems to come out of his violin-case, with piercing eyes behind his gold-rimmed spectacles, a knowing smile, a sharp voice, in tune with his violin, and his memory full of anecdotes.[2]

Sauzay was too promising a character to waste; twenty-four years later, when he thought of writing a book on the Princess and her friends, Primoli returned to his notes, and published an article on 'La Princesse Mathilde et le maestro Sauzay'.

Like most of the Bonapartes, Princess Mathilde had very little feeling for music. She only enjoyed military fanfares, which stirred her patriotic heart, and the Italian airs of Bellini, which recalled her radiant youth in Florence, since they had accompanied the declarations of love that were murmured to her when she was eighteen . . .

The Parisian public must naturally have thought that the Princess was drawn to music as she was to the other arts. Indeed, every Sunday evening, in her conservatory, Beethoven quartets were played with expertise under the baton of maestro Sauzay, and, every Wednesday morning, for an hour or two, she played classical pieces on the piano, while her old professor emphasized their rhythm on his violin.

If one looked carefully for the reason for all the Princess's actions, one would always end by finding affection behind them. With other people one would trace the actions to duty, calculation, taste or whim . . . With her, the heart alone was the secret power which set everything in motion. She loved to love, and she knew how to love. She did not only scatter her graces on poor mortals with her rosy fingers; she knew how to give herself, too, at the risk of drawing troubles on herself. But the little trouble which she caused herself was compensated by the great pleasure which she assured her fellow-creatures.

* * *

One of these private heroic deeds to which, moreover, the Princess was accustomed, was inspired by her affection for her music master, Sauzay. She had little taste for music; but, until her eightieth year, and until the bow fell from the hands of her accompanist, she consented to take her piano lesson like a schoolgirl. It was an ingenious and touching excuse for making the old professor accept the fee, and above all for giving an hour's pleasure to her faithful old friend, who adored her.

He was a ghost from the eighteenth century who seemed to have escaped the scaffold at the Revolution. He reminded one of Consuelo's Porpora or a fantastic character from Hoffman. When he appeared to me for the first time, he was already very old, but still very vigorous, slight, almost diaphanous, a cricket's skeleton dried up by the sun, a pale, bloodless face, a kindly smile under a faded moustache, a sharp and mischievous glance behind his gold-rimmed spectacles. His arms were still supple thanks to the exercise of the bow, and his legs, as thin as spindle-shanks, in his loose trousers, kept the agility of a dancer's; he also had the gestures of a conductor and the movements of a tame monkey. It was, apparently, for him that someone had written the line:

Glissez, mortels, n'appuyez pas . . .

He came to *déjeuner*, every Wednesday, at half-past eleven. Before the war he came to 24, rue de Courcelles; after the 'dreadful year' he came to 20, rue de Berry, and every summer he came to Saint-Gratien. You should have seen him arrive with his violin-case under his arm, his long black frock-coat, his pale waistcoat, his grey trousers, his patent pumps. With what ardent and tender respect he bent over the fine hand, gloved in suede, which was affectionately extended to him! They went in to *déjeuner* and ate with a good appetite, and, when she came back to the salon, the Princess herself overcame the scruples of her guests, and lit her master's cigar, while she grumbled about the smell of the tobacco . . .

As the last cloud of smoke evaporated through the garden door, the guests were dismissed, while the professor tuned his little yellow violin ... Then he came and bowed respectfully to his pupil, who, for a moment, seemed to hesitate between revolt and resignation.

'What a nuisance you are!' she said to him, with a smile which contradicted her exclamation. 'It is too good of me to be bored like this just to give you pleasure . . .' She rose to her feet, he kissed her hand and ceremoniously led her to the piano. The student sat down at the Erard with a sigh and conscientiously deciphered her imposition, then another, and then yet another, and so on for an hour and a half, until they announced that the carriage was waiting.[3]

*　*　*

30 November, 1893

This evening, a private dinner with the Princess. I recited the verses which I had written to her at the Collège [Rollin]; and, poor as they were, they moved her to tears as they brought before her eyes a past which has vanished for ever. With her, the human chord is touched much more easily than the literary chord; she remains insensible to the finest lines in Leconte de Lisle, which she does not understand, but she will be moved by a *cri de cœur*. The heart scarcely beats except to the breath of the breeze which stirred it when it was twenty, it only understands the language with which it loved – and was loved.[4]

Paris, November

I talk to Porto-Riche about our poor friend [Maupassant, who had recently died]; he touches me by saying that Maupassant mentioned me to him several times, with affection. He interests me by showing me that, from certain letters which went astray, it was known that he slept, once, with the delicate heroine of *Notre Cœur*. She was no doubt disgusted by his brutality, and never wanted to submit to a second experience; and so, having left him famished, after she had roused his appetite, she may have hastened the fatal catastrophe. As for this madness, of which they now find traces in his works, Porto-Riche tells me that he himself had given [Maupassant] the subject for some of the novellas which seem the most conclusive. To this one might reply that if Maupassant had not felt ineluctably drawn to this fatal path, he would not have been struck by these disturbing stories, and he would not have told them in his turn.

Poor Guy had literary sense, but he lacked taste, and he who was

195

so simple and seemed so solid, was snobbish about grandeur. His apartment was dressed up, so to speak, in its Sunday best, and furnished with a garish luxury which seemed to have been inspired by some demoiselle Tellier whose ideal he had realized. A certain literary sense survived in him after he had lost his sanity. When Ganderax talked to him about *Musotte*, he said: 'I don't like that.' Of *La Paix du Ménage*: 'It isn't good.' And when they told him that he had been awarded the prize of 10,000 francs: 'They have been using my name again,' he added, bitterly.[5]

December

P[——] to dinner . . . He tries to play Wagner to the Princess, but her Italian heart had woken to the airs of Bellini, her youth was cradled by Malibran, and she shuts her ears to *the music of the future*.[6]

16 December

At the revival of *La Dame [aux camélias]*, in Alexandre Dumas' box. He tells us that Sarah begged him to attend a rehearsal. The day before yesterday he decided to do so, and – as soon as the curtain rose – he saw characters appearing which were unknown to him! During her world tours, Sarah had found that the supper party was too small, and she had added some guests *crescit eundo*! She had thought of giving Saint-Gaudens a natural son who goes on the spree with his father – and so on. In the third act, she added the torn-up letters which are not indicated in the original. She herself is the Original. She got into Marguerite's skin, and lived the story as if it were her own. And so, when we go to her dressing-room, and find the master, Porto-Riche, Ganderax and Montesquiou, and she throws herself into the author's arms, and murmurs in her golden voice: 'Maître, are you pleased?' 'It's very good,' he answers, 'very good, but it's something different,' he adds, in a whisper.

Some green-room tales from Porto-Riche. Sarah was playing *La Dame* very fast. She was in a hurry to be free that evening, she was jabbering. They begged her to speak more slowly. 'If you don't shut up,' she cried, 'I'll kick the bucket at once.'

'God, I'm bored!' she said, one evening, yawning in the foyer of the Théâtre-Français. 'Remember, Mademoiselle,' came the sharp retort from Mlle Favart, 'that you are no longer at the Odéon.' Sarah crossed the salon and, with a deep curtsey, she murmured in her golden voice: 'At the Odéon I should have said b——.'[7]

On 18 December, Goncourt recorded dining with Princess Mathilde and Primoli at Daudet's. 'Little [Reynaldo] Hahn sat down at the piano and played some music which he had composed for three or four poems by Verlaine, real poetic jewels.'[8] Verlaine remained in Primoli's mind. On 20 December, he continued:

Last day in Paris. The final experience is the most delectable of my visit. A rehearsal of *Bérénice* by the divine Bartet: a Racinian symphony which I have wanted to hear for years – and my expectation was not disappointed. During the five acts of the royal elegy, she always wears the same costume: dull gold and pale lilac – love hidden under melancholy tenderness. All that changes is the style of her hair. In the first act, she appears still radiant from the feast with an aureole *à la* Gustave Moreau. In the second, she adorns her brow with a royal diadem which she will reject in the third, as soon as she begins to lose hope of the crown, to appear with the silky hair of Bérénice. At the end, she puts on a veil under which she modestly hides her grief, and she covers her eternal widowhood as with a shroud.

> Her fine head on her small hand lies at rest;
> She listens to the song of far cascades,
> And, in the fountains' drowsy serenades,
> She hears the name of Titus, echo blessed.
>
> She's closed her heavenly eyes of clematis
> To picture, in the heart of the great fight,
> Her gentle hero, captain of delight,
> And, Jewess, in the power of Venus is.
>
> Then she is frightened to be amorous,
> For Roman law, dreadful and barbarous,
> Bans foreign women from the imperial throne.
>
> And, as her soul sobs in black misery,
> Into the arms of her dear minion
> The queen tenderly falters and faints away.

How can I resist slipping between my pages this pure engraved amethyst which sums up my exquisite moonlit vision? *Bérénice* is indeed the plaintive song of departure, the elegy of separation, the heartrending music which cradles the farewells: it should be played on a violin . . . I too am departing, bearing in my ears this harmony which seems to me to accompany the tears falling drop

197

by drop from the eyes of my poor dear Aunt. She is so sad to see me go, and she is afraid of finding herself alone again without the warmth of my affection. And for me, too, as for Bérénice, it is Rome, on the horizon, which is the reason for my departure.[9]

Five

1

Rome, January 1894

In parallel with this notebook, I am once again beginning a diary in which I note my insignificant sayings and doings – so many landmarks placed on the highway, so that I can find my way in the evening when I want to return towards the Past without knocking against the stones in my path. There my steps are counted, here I have marked the stages and the sensations suggested by the hazards of the journey. These are still impressions caught in a photographer's dark-room in quick snapshots . . . This journal of my inner existence might be called 'Around my life – Echoes and reflections'. At long intervals, I shall directly set down the small detail noted in my diary, or the person met at a turn in the road, which has no horizon. Alas! The only moments of enlightenment which they may receive, my soul which is imprisoned by reality, and my life, which is broken against the bars of our *carcere duro*, are real days of suffering which make me see clearly in my grievous and unchangeable situation: they show me the grey in the present, the black in the future, and, no doubt, the rose-colour in the distant past – but what was luminously rose in the dawn takes on a sinister tinge of blood in the twilight, which makes one almost long for utter darkness . . . so as not to see any more. . .

Does the art of knowing how to live consist in replacing intimacy by society, affection by indifference, happiness by pleasure, grief by forgetfulness, the family by acquaintances? One must learn to enjoy life with what one hasn't got, content oneself with substitutes and with understudies. And so I went to hear midnight strike on the clock of S. Marcello and of S. Maria in Via Lata – where my grandmother is buried – at the Princess of Venosa's. She herself is a friend of twenty-five years' standing, but a worldly friend from whom I am separated by a mass of social conventions. We have neither an affection nor an interest in

201

common, and we hardly share the same ideas. But, apart from that, our relationship is as intimate as it can be between two sophisticated people of different sexes, who have not been lovers. What unites us, is that Formosa – as I call her – is perhaps the woman with whom I am nearest to being in love. And she knows that, for me, she has been the most exquisite woman that I've met and she has always remained in my eyes just as she appeared to me one fine morning in the summer of 1871 at the summit of Monte Cavo. Her ideal charm comes from the harmony between her soul and body: 'mente malata in corpo delicato' – an afflicted soul in a frail body – as opposed to the 'mente sana in corpo sano'. The Christian purity of expression merges with the Greek purity of line, and the chaste expression veils the pagan serenity with a cloud of melancholy, [she has] the bearing of a goddess and the head of a virgin. . . Her beauty is the beauty of a good era: it is pure *quattrocentista*; and it is in contemplating the gracious Florentine that I have learned to appreciate the divine Renaissance which she seems to embody in this *fin de siècle*. . .

At midnight, we drank the traditional glass of champagne with the beloved sister of the mistress of the house and donna Lavinia, her sister-in-law, who has been under her spell since her childhood. . . Then, at one o'clock in the morning, to the Palazzo Orsini, had supper with the Princess de Solofra, who had assembled some of her women friends. . . Although everyone was quite willing to be cheerful, this nocturnal feast was as usual rather lugubrious. To be honest, suppers are failed dinners where the guests are drowsy rather than hungry. In order to succeed, a supper must be the end of something or the beginning of something else.

Rose late. Piazza di Spagna. To Axel Munthe's and to Félix Bouchard's. Signed the book at the Quirinal. Went to Aunt Julie's. Mass at noon at S. Antonio dei Portoghesi. Walked with Bouchard, whom I took to see my adorable Pinturicchio de S. Cosimato. Then to the villa Pamphilj and to the Comtesse de La Tour's, whose windows look over the Tiber. These are the only river banks to remain intact, and poetic as they used to be.[1]

Rome, 1894

A moment of rebellion against Axel: violator of conscience, destroyer of the *vortex* of illusions which surrounds me, the man who forces his entry into the depths of my heart to study its beating, who goes to seek in the depths of our brainbox the tiny hope which remains huddled there, hidden, forgotten, . . . the

hope whose caressing breath is enough to sweeten us, restore us to
life. . . He breaks its action, bruises it and wounds it, and with an
ironic smile he makes it come unsoldered, evaporate – and he puts
nothing in its place. He takes me by the hand and obliges me to
contemplate reality in its most brutal form; and who can assure me
that it is the Truth? Everything is an illusion, I recognize that; but
life is a dream, man is a shadow, and Truth is Faith. I do not say
that Faith is Truth. Since you can put nothing in its place, do not
snatch it from me.[2]

15–29 May, 1894

Arrived in Naples Tuesday 15th at 6.30 p.m. . . .
By train from Naples to Rome. I read *Le Trionfo della morte* by
d'Annunzio. Brunetière claims that the second part is the author's
masterpiece. He seems to err a little by the display of knowledge
which he does not possess: resounding names, arrayed as they are
in Hugo's poetry, behind which one feels the absence of learning,
and the desire to create an illusion for the innocent reader who is
more ignorant than himself.[3]

* * *

While Primoli was criticizing Gabriele d'Annunzio, Eleonora
Duse, his most famous interpreter, was earning royal and
imperial acclaim. On 18 May, at Windsor Castle, Queen
Victoria noted in her journal: 'At a quarter to ten we all went to
the White drawing-room, where a little stage had been put up,
and the Italian actress, Signora Duse, acted in a piece called *La
Locandiera*. She is nice-looking, with a most attractive voice
and way of speaking, and her acting is admirable. She was
presented to me afterwards.'[4] Three years later, in 1897,
possibly with help from La Duse, certainly with a little
invention, Primoli gave his account of the event.

Four or five years ago [*sic*], when La Duse was passing through
London, Queen Victoria sent to ask her to come and act at
Windsor.
What could she perform for Her Gracious Majesty without
shocking British *cant* [*sic*]? Princess Louise suggested the fifth act
of *La Dame aux camélias*. When they made objections to her:
'It's very simple,' she answered, mischievously. 'We will tell my
mother that it's about a pure young girl called Daisy. Her fiancé,
Armand, is in India; he comes back too late to marry her, and she
dies in his arms.'

203

The ingenious plot might have succeeded, in spite of Marguerite's hesitation, when the Queen solved the problem by letting it
be known that she wanted to see *quelque chose de gai*, something
cheerful.

In this case the last act of *La Dame*, even arranged *ad usum
Reginæ*, no longer fulfilled the required conditions, and La Duse
went to Windsor to act in *La Locandiera*.

The performance was not given in the theatre [*sic*], but in the
White Drawing-room which, it seems, is a privilege reserved for a
few celebrities. . .

When it was over, Her Gracious Majesty asked for the delightful
actress to be presented to her.

It was like an apotheosis in a play. A semi-circle of princesses
and ladies in full evening-dress surrounded the old Queen who,
like a good fairy, leaning on her magic wand, talked to the pretty
Locandiera. . .

In order to put her at her ease, and show her that she was among
friends, the Queen began by saying:

'My daughter, Victoria, has often talked about you. . .'

And La Duse, who had not shed the mischievous and innocent
soul of Mirandolina, any more than she had shed her costume,
murmured to herself:' Well, well, little Duse, I hope you can boast
of your fine friends! . . . Here is an Empress of India who deigns to
speak to you and remind you that you know her daughter –
another Empress!'

And then they told her that the Empress Frederick had talked a
great deal about her and that the Emperor William was very eager
to see her. He had come to Windsor the previous week, and they
told her the bit of gossip which had delighted the Court ever since
the visit. There had been a great family dinner; on such solemn
occasions as this, the Queen arranged the seating according to
closeness of kinship. . . The Emperor of Germany, treated as a
grandson, was relegated to the end of the table. . . At dessert, when
one of the guests proposed a toast to the Queen of England,
another to the Empress of India, and a third to some of the other
grand titles of the mighty Sovereign, – the Emperor raised his
glass, like a child sent to stand in the corner, and just said, with a
mischievous smile:

'To Grandmama!'

It was the grandson's answer to Granny.[5]

It was an engaging story, but there is no record in Queen
Victoria's journal that the Emperor had then been at Windsor.

2

Late that autumn Primoli was once again in Paris. On 8 November he called at the Daudets', where he found Edmond de Goncourt at dinner.[1] Three days later he appeared at Goncourt's Grenier at Auteuil.

> Primoli arrives [wrote Goncourt], and takes a photograph of [Jean] Lorrain and me.
>
> Then he talks about La Duse, with whom he has just spent a week in Venice, La Duse, the Italian actress who has been mentioned to me for playing *La Faustin* in London or in Germany. He says that she lacks many things as an actress, but, in spite of that, she is a very great artist. He paints her as an actress of great theatrical independence, only applying herself in the acts which appeal to her talent. In the others, which don't please her, she either eats grapes or indulges in some other diversion.[2]

* * *

While Primoli was in Paris, Émile Zola was in Rome, to document himself for the second novel in his series 'Les Trois Villes'. The first of his cities had been Lourdes, the last would be Paris; now he was preparing to write a novel on the Eternal City. On 14 November, Goncourt continued: 'Primoli read me a letter from an Italian whom he had put in touch with Zola, an ironic letter in which he writes that Zola questioned him about the *donna romana* and told him that he would devote the last three days of his stay in Rome to the study of the Roman woman.'[3] A fortnight later, Goncourt added: 'Primoli confides in me that Zola is now at his palace in Rome. He is looking at projected photographs, with which he will be condemned to describe in his book all that he has been forbidden to see.'[4]

On 5 December, according to Paul Arrighi, Zola was received by the King of Italy, and then by Queen Margherita. The Queen also granted an audience that day to the critic Ferdinand Brunetière. These two conversations, explained Arrighi, were 'described for us in some unpublished notes written by Comte Joseph-Napoleon Primoli, who has kindly let us consult them.'[5]

Zola was presented first [before Brunetière], and, thinking that he would conceal his inexperience of Courts, he adopted an unconstrained, almost familiar attitude, and, after a perfunctory bow, he sat down on a low chair, at the feet of the fair-haired Sovereign, and put his hat down on the floor beside him. . . And, in answer to a question from the Queen, the writer described his triumphal journey: 'They are very interesting, Your Majesty, all the cities of your beautiful kingdom,' so he began, mopping his brow as if he had travelled through them on foot, 'but the most civilized is certainly Milan; and of course this superiority is natural, since it is the one nearest to Paris!' The Queen, we are told, greeted this blunder with a smile which the writer took for approval, and, since she was unable to talk to him about his earlier works, which she had not read, she questioned him about *Rome*, which he was writing. The author replied that he had already seen everything, and that it only remained for him to study Roman woman, which would be the affair of a few hours. . . Margherita of Savoy did not take up this second observation, but, taking advantage of a moment when the conversation lagged, she told Zola that she was sorry to have to let him go, but she had to receive one of his compatriots who was waiting for his turn.

In the ante-room, the satisfied pince-nez of Zola crossed the sly pince-nez of Brunetière. The director of the *Revue* [*des Deux Mondes*], on the threshold of the room, made the low bow which was demanded by ceremonial, and, casting a glance towards the door through which Zola had just vanished, he excused himself as follows: 'What a lot of Frenchmen in one day for Your Majesty!' Then, encouraged by the Queen's attitude of consent, 'he made [we are told] a brilliant autodafé of his colleague, while appearing hardly to brush against him with the tip of his academic tongs.' And, while Zola repeated that he was 'enchanted with his visit,' Queen Margherita must have been more convinced of the bankruptcy of Naturalism which had been proclaimed seven years earlier.[6]

Primoli himself had not lost his taste for practical jokes, and he had gaily played one on Arrighi. This account, wrote René Ternois, in *Zola et son temps*, was 'pure imagination'.[7] 'People have gone so far as to take certain sketches by Comte Giuseppe Primoli quite seriously. He was a genial practical joker,' wrote P.–P. Trompeo. 'He enjoyed mixing real events with imaginary ones in his journal.'[8] As for Primoli, continued Ternois,

Zola probably saw him in Paris. The Count paid a call on him to thank him for a novel he had sent (probably *Rome*), and, having found he was not at home, had left his card: 'I very much hoped to meet you in Paris since I had had the misfortune to miss you in Rome, and I hope I shall have another occasion to shake you by the hand.' And a few years later he sent his good wishes on a card on which he had pasted an amateur photograph (a very pretty one, incidentally) of some lazzaroni sunning themselves at the foot of a wall, with a few words distributed in the four corners: 'Best wishes – 1899 – Rome – Joseph Primoli'. They were always anxious to be original in that family.[9]

* * *

Meanwhile, on 2 December 1894, Goncourt recorded: 'Primoli came today to photograph the regular visitors to the Grenier. There were about twenty of them, and there were poses in the Grenier and on the steps. Charpentier [the publisher] arrived too late to be photographed, and made the comical lament: "Oh, I don't belong to any group, myself!"'[10] Three days later, Goncourt noted:

Primoli went to see Réjane in her dressing-room today, and brought back this amusing story. Some years ago, when she went out with her daughter, she used to be followed by a man who gazed affectionately at the child. At last, one day, he approached Réjane and said to her that he would like to leave the little girl 80,000 francs in his will. He wanted to leave a legacy of this value to the child of an actress – and of an actress who was not married. Réjane did not refuse the gift, and she felt a certain curiosity to know the man's name – but that was impossible! One day, she received a box of chocolates for her daughter, from the stranger; she went to the shop and asked for his name, but they did not know it. At that time, the rumour of her marriage with Porel was going around Paris, and she thought she saw that the man was avoiding her. Then, finally, when the marriage was settled, the man completely disappeared. She never saw him again.[11]

* * *

Primoli, who had a taste for gossip and ephemera, was also conscious of history, and aware of those who helped make it. First among them, in his affections, remained Princess Mathilde.

> The Princess [he noted] has the rare and precious gift of being an anti-snob about things and of having the courage to proclaim her taste. . .
> The Princess's friends were the charm of her life, and they will be its glory. . . And certainly she did not choose the part of the good fairy with the ulterior motive of earning admiration from posterity; she chose the part instinctively. . . She told herself that Fortune had smiled upon her, and that all that was most distinguished in France must share the favour which her cousin lavished upon her. . . And so when I asked her what she regretted most about the Empire, she answered honestly: 'The good that I could do' – the good that she continues to do today.[12]

Primoli loved her and he admired her; and she, in turn, loved him and depended on him. On 22 December she wrote in despair: 'My dear Gégé has gone. I am all disorientated. . .'[13]

3

I aspire after Ariccia rather than Paris [wrote Primoli in April 1895]. Paris is oblivion in the midst of the noise and bustle – but Ariccia is serenity in touch with nature – meditation in isolation. I should like to write a book there with the noble title which Huysmans wanted to give his *En route* – *Là-haut*. It is in fact up there that I hover over the abyss of verdure with the shining sea on the horizon, all golden during the day beneath the eyes of the sun – and silvered at night by a moonbeam.[1]

On 20 May, none the less, he arrived in Paris; two days later, Goncourt met him dining with the Princess.[2]

* * *

Gégé is in Paris [Henri de Régnier was to write]. These words, exchanged here and there, signified that Comte Joseph Primoli had left Rome and his palace in the Via Torre di Nona to come to Paris for one of his annual visits. In Paris, as in Rome, he had numerous friends in every world and every milieu, and the diminutive *Gége*, by which people readily referred to him, showed that he lent himself with a good grace to the most diverse familiarities. In fact, this Napoleonide, the son of a Roman patrician and a Bonaparte princess, was devoid of all arrogance and free of many prejudices, but his smiling condescension and gracious affability were none the less evident to anyone who failed to take account of the imperceptible distance that he expected people to keep from him; and he knew quite well, with a very Italian delicacy and a very French politeness, how to emphasize, when need be, the dignity of his birth and the illustriousness of his relations. Gégé once again became Count Primoli, just for the moment that it took to put people and things back in perspective.

His imperial kinship made him, in Paris, the guest of his aunt

209

Princess Mathilde. As long as she lived, he would stay with her, and his presence in the rue de Berry was welcome to the Princess, who was very fond of this nephew, and treated him rather like a spoilt child. He took advantage of this treatment to indulge a certain taste he had for jokes and mystifications. He took a malicious pleasure in embarrassing people by indiscreet questions or disconcerting remarks, and nothing amused him more than bringing people together who would have preferred not to meet. These pastimes gave him infinite amusement. There was, in fact, something childish about this big, pleasantly corpulent man, with the rather slack Napoleonic face, and the fine fair beard. From childhood he had kept his pretty tricks and his insatiable curiosity.

This curiosity led him into every world and every milieu, the most exclusive and the most accessible. He knew as many nonentities as he did crowned heads, but, however cosmopolitan he was, he still remained, as he liked to say, 'the most Parisian of Romans and the most Roman of Parisians'. Indeed, he was rather European. He had frequented every celebrity in every country, and he had, in fact, photographed most of them, because he rarely travelled without his camera, which had provided him with countless snapshots. . . One of them, which he was proud of, showed Pope Leo XIII walking in the gardens of the Vatican; but the pictures were not enough for him, and he completed them by numerous notes taken from life. These notes would have been material for most interesting memoirs, if he had not been too lazy to make use of them.[3]

* * *

He continued, none the less, to write them.

Paris, Sunday, 10 November 1895

Auteuil, Goncourt Grenier. Toudouze, Charpentier, Raffaelli, Descaves. Poor Alphonse Daudet arrives, leaning on Léon Hennique in the absence of his own Léon, who is travelling round Spain with Georges Hugo. It is characteristic, this persistent friendship of the two ex-brothers-in-law: it has survived the divorce which should have separated them. Gossip says that the young husband thrashed the young wife, and that the young wife took revenge by beating the mother-in-law: 'Se non e vero e ben trovato' – by a Labiche.

Daudet still has the handsome head of his youth; under his curly hair and his curled beard, growing silver now like an April stream, one can easily rediscover the poet of the Amoreuses, but, alas! the

210

Mother and child. Rome, *c.* 1890.

The unknown woman. This brilliant, imaginative photograph was taken in Rome at the end of the nineteenth century.

Un César déclassé. Primoli's imperial portrait of Prince Napoleon was taken early in 1891, just before the Prince's death.

Princess Mathilde in later life. She is wearing the pearls which Napoleon had given to her mother.

Princess Mathilde in her studio at Saint-Gratien, *c.* 1895.

'Sarah the Great, Sarah Bernhardt herself.' A photograph taken in Rome in February 1893.

King Umberto I and Queen Margherita enter the Quirinale gardens for a reception on the occasion of their silver wedding, 26 April 1893.

The Duke of York, later
George V, in Rome for
the silver wedding
celebrations. He is seen
leaving the Quirinale on
24 April.

Princess Mathilde and
Charles Gounod
photographed at Saint-
Gratien, probably on
22 June 1893.

Auteuil, June or July 1893. Jacques-Émile Blanche paints the portrait of one of Heredia's daughters.

Edmond de Goncourt with the regular visitors to his *Grenier*. A photograph taken at Auteuil on 2 December 1894.

Saint-Gratien,
c. 1894. Princess
Mathilde with
Alexandre Dumas
fils and other
friends.

Princess Mathilde
with a gardener at
Saint-Gratien. This
enchanting
photograph
suggests a post-
Impressionist
painting.

Amoreuses have indeed ravaged their too loving poet. He falls, bewildered, breathless, on to the red divan, and, before he even recovers his breath, under his vast cloak, groping like a blind man, he seeks, he seeks and finds the relieving and deadly morphine needle. Then, his ulster thrown back, like a Prince Charming in disguise, he emerges from his scarves, and appears in his silky velvet jacket; and he begins to speak: he is the only one. They all listen, the rest of them, hanging on his lips, which bestow upon the enchanted audience the honey of the heavenly Plato. His winged, poetic, vibrant, impassioned talk rouses new ideas with certain turns of phrase. He has the *rare* epithet which, says Goncourt, makes the great writer. It is not a spectator who has seen, it is a man who has lived what he describes, and all the feelings he has known come alive again at the evocation of memory. Continual pain has refined his sensibility, and resignation has brought him to an indulgent philosophy. If much understanding brings much tolerance, much suffering makes one very compassionate, and, besides, as a final touch, he has kept a little of the malice of le Petit Chose which gives the poet's bouquet a scent of its own.

We discussed the duel of the moment. 'When someone,' said Daudet, 'comes to ask you if he should fight, it means that he doesn't really want to and of course you have to answer "No".' Last winter, T came to consult him in a case of this kind. 'Cher maître, you've read the article about me... It wasn't pleasant, but is it unpleasant enough for... I mean, what do you advise?' Daudet, questioned like this, answered feebly that there was nothing in the article (which, incidentally, is atrocious) which seemed to him to merit a duel...' It doesn't, does it?' cried T in triumph, rising to his feet. 'Well, just think that when my wife read that incriminating paragraph, she was quite frightened, and said to me: "Go..." "Go and fight?" "No, go to Daudet and do what he advises." So I'll do what you say, but ... could you – for her, just for her, you know what women are ... could you give me a little signed note to say that, in your opinion, there is no cause for a duel in my case – and that you advise me not to fight?'[4]

It was next day, 11 November, that Dumas *fils* arrived from Marly with his young wife, to have *déjeuner* at the rue de Berry.

I went down to meet him in the courtyard [Primoli recorded], I fell into his open arms, and he gave me two kisses, two big smacking kisses which were so resounding that I don't remember having any like them and the courtyard reverberated with them. He was

211

as good and affectionate as ever, but he seemed to be pensive. . .

Edmond de Goncourt came to dinner, as he has done every week for thirty years. He is the sole survivor of those Wednesdays with the Princess. That evening she used to gather a whole battalion of writers round her table, under the presidency of Sainte-Beuve: there were Taine, Renan, Saint-Victor, Théophile Gautier, Giraud of the Institut, Lavoix, etc. All of them gone!

Goncourt tells us about his interview yesterday, which is reported in this morning's papers . . . A reporter found his way in and violated his thoughts, to wrest from him his feelings about Berthelot, the new Ministre des Affaires Étrangères. His friend Renan had written his epitaph: 'One might write on his tomb,' he is supposed to have said, '*Here lies Berthelot, in the only place which he never solicited.*' Goncourt had resisted, at first; then, under the gimlet of this skilful . . . burglar, he had gradually opened, and revealed the depths of his thoughts, and he had gone even further. They had also made him gossip about Renan, while, as he said himself, the most ardent polemics should die out after death, and he had decided not to mention the author of *La Vie de Jésus* again. By treacherously half-quoting him, the reporter distorted the mystic free-thinker's profession of faith.'It doesn't really matter to me,' Renan was reported as saying, 'whether Napoleon or William reigns, provided,' so he added, 'that one has the right to think freely.' . . . The journalist simply reported the first half of the sentence. Goncourt is furious, and swears – but it is rather late – that he won't be caught again. Isn't it incredible that he should have reached his age, with his experience of the Press, and not known that one should only tell reporters what can be repeated? . . .

Besides, poor Goncourt's unconscious innocence can only be compared to the opinion which, as he grow older, he has formed of himself and of his mission in the world of letters. His intimates, the friends who will no doubt belong to his Académie, are the first to smile at this *Journal* – which, personally, I find absolutely absorbing – this *Journal* which is really the journal of the illness of a man of letters: hypertrophy of the Self. It is the condition of a Hindu idol which has gazed so long at its navel that it has finally taken it as the centre of the world and sees nothing more around it. Last year, on 25 June 1894, he announced the death of Carnot: 'No luck!' he adds (and he is not talking of the President, or the assassin, or France). 'Really, I have no luck with the publication of my books. *En 18—*, my first volume, appeared on the day of Napoleon III's coup-d'état; the seventh volume of the Goncourt *Journal* . . . has its advertisement and reviews cut short by the assassination of the President of the Republic.' It is the triumph of unawareness, it is the most perfect incarnation of impersonality in literature but of the personality in existence. He reminds me of those difficult horses which wear blinkers so that they don't see to the right or left and concentrate all their attention on the road. . .

What makes me excuse this enormous and unconscious simplicity is his almost touching good faith. So it was that Huysmans said one day to his friends: 'I promise I'll make him put what I want in his *Journal*.' 'Maître,' he confided to him, on his return from some travels in the North, 'they told me that every educated Norwegian has one of your books at his bedside.' 'Indeed! That really is a triumph,' said poor Goncourt, with his kindly, trusting smile. And that evening, conscientiously, he noted in his *Journal*: 'Huysmans assures me that no educated Norwegian goes to sleep before he has read a few pages of mine.' Once the thing was written, it was ineffaceable. He no longer allowed that he might be deceived, or deceive himself, or deceive other people. Ludovic Halévy asked him to cut out some lines which were offensive to the memory of his unfortunate friend Prévost-Paradol. All that Goncourt could do was to keep the passage, print Halévy's letter as a note, and add: 'I do not consider myself entitled to cut what I have written.'[5]

* * *

Dumas had had reason to feel pensive on his visit to the rue de Berry; no doubt he had been aware of the imminence of death. On 20 November, Goncourt recorded: 'The Princess and Primoli have been to Marly today, to see Dumas, who is ill . . . The Princess entered the room after Primoli, who had been struck by the change in him and by his weakness. When she went in, Dumas pulled himself together, and braced himself up, and exclaimed: "Ah! you come of a family which is not afraid to see someone with the plague!" '[6]

On 27 November, at the rue de Berry, as Goncourt and Coppée were demolishing the latest play at the Théâtre-Français, Primoli came to tell them: 'Dumas is dead . . . The Princess has just had a telegram.'[7]

He himself went to the funeral; and his thoughts of Dumas mingled with admiring thoughts of Maupassant, when he recalled the occasion in 'La Route de Marly'.

. . . Bougival awakens in me the joyful and dismal memory of Guy de Maupassant. I used to go and eat *matelote* with him in the little

213

suburban tavern where – perfect oarsman that he was – he felt himself at home. Despite his terrible end, I still see him as if he were alive, and living fully, living well, in Rome and London, Triel and Tivoli, because I always refused to go and visit him in the asylum, in spite of the invitations from the kind Dr Blanche. 'If he doesn't recognize me,' I thought, 'what misery for me! If he does recognize me, what humiliation for him!' However unexpected it seemed, the fate in store for him, you might find the presage of it in some of his books, especially in *Le Horla*, which seems like his diary written in advance. I remember walking him home one evening to the rue Boccador, and, when I left him, he said to me: 'You think I'm going to be alone. . . Well, when I open my study door, I'm going to find my double, sitting writing at my table.' I thought he was joking.

Alexandre Dumas admired talent wherever he found it; he became a fanatic about Maupassant's short stories, and wanted to meet the author of *Boule de suif*. He had been struck, he told me, by the prodigiously simple art with which my friend drew a character in three strokes, three lines of the pencil. He preferred the beginnings of his matchless novels to the endings, which were often commonplace. And so he found no words to express his admiration for the first pages of *Monsieur Parent*, which had just appeared. What a long time ago it was, that *déjeuner* at Durand's which I organized to bring these two honourable, gifted men together! I invited not only Maupassant and Dumas but Paul Bourget and Louis Ganderax. I still remember the conversation, in which my guests vied with one another in wit. Alexandre Dumas, in particular, showed a flattering and irresistible coquetry to people whom he wanted to charm. I have since found traces of that endless rain of fireworks in more than one novella by Maupassant (the idea of which it suggested), in certain pages on love by Paul Bourget, and in an article in *Le Figaro*, called, I think, 'Alexandre Dumas et les femmes', signed by Henri Meilhac, who must have been informed by Ganderax. When Maupassant died, Alexandre Dumas undertook to finish his little play, *La Paix du Ménage*, and he had it performed at the Théâtre-Français. I wrote to Dumas: 'I didn't congratulate you on the success of *Le Père prodigue*, but I cannot refrain from shaking you by the hand after the success of *La Paix du ménage*, which you will appreciate much more. The first is only a satisfaction for your self-love, the second is a joy for your heart. The idea of doing a service to someone you support, and someone who can never know or acknowledge it, bears within itself a delicate and subtle recompense which only a soul like yours can enjoy. Yet I feel that I should thank you, too, because it is I who introduced this poor friend to you. And then your kindness sweetens my regrets. I reproach myself because I introduced him to two pretty women in the formidable category of flirts, who had, perhaps, an inauspicious influence on the second part of his life. Your friendship is so beneficent and so disinterested that it compensates him for these *liaisons dangereuses*, and he would forgive me for them because of this. . .'

Alexandre Dumas answered: '. . . I was very glad to do something for poor Maupassant, whom I dearly loved, no doubt because I had known him through you, but also because I knew that he was full of courage and I felt that he was very unhappy. After *Le Horla* I feared for his reason; after *Fort comme la mort* and *Notre Cœur* I had other anxieties. I saw him seriously involved with trivial women whom he should have used only once. When robust souls like that allow themselves to be manipulated by such spiders, they crumble and fall to pieces in the webs they weave around them.'[8]

Primoli comes early [Goncourt recorded on 1 December], and we have a long talk before everyone arrives. He talks to me about Dumas, about the last night before the funeral, when he watched by the corpse, to give his daughters a rest, about Dumas' vanity about the beauty of his feet, . . . and he tells me that Dumas has left him the manuscript of *L'Affaire Clemenceau*.

Then he talked about his journey to Spain with the Empress, in 1877. At Ronda, the manager of the hotel wanted to keep such wealthy guests as long as possible, and, in those days when there was still no railway, he maintained that, for the moment, there was no means of transport. The Empress sent Primoli to a toreador, who was passing through with his company, to ask for places in his diligence; she assured him that toreadors were the most gallant men in the world. And the toreador immediately put his carriage at the disposal of the Empress, and said that his companions would ride on horseback or on the roof of the carriage. And the Empress and Primoli paid the bill and fled from the hotel, as if they were insolvent, and had themselves met on the main road. And the toreador took them, I think, to Seville, and refused the slightest payment. It was sent to him later from London by the Empress, who sent him diamond shirt-buttons.[9]

As for Primoli, he continued to serve both Empress and Princess. On 4 December, Goncourt recorded him projecting his slides at Princess Mathilde's. He found it curious to see the tiny slides enlarged to give life-size illusions.[10] Primoli not

215

only entertained Princess Mathilde, he still had an unequalled talent for soothing her. 'The poor dear Princess,' he noted, 'says something which touches my heart: "It is only when you are there," she tells me, ". . . when I know you are in the room above mine, that I don't wake up crying at night."'[11]

He had his own profound regrets; and now, an ageing bachelor, he recognized what for years had been his own dearest wish:

> Sainte-Beuve says that if you look in a writer's work for the word he is most inclined to repeat, you find the adjective which describes him best; and so in Edmond de Goncourt's books, on nearly every page, I find the adjective *distinguished*. That is what marks his talent and his character. And, as for me, when I listen to myself, I catch myself usually calling servants, or a friend, *figlio mio*! . . . my child! . . . That is indeed the harrowing regret which comes from my heart.[12]

4

As Primoli recorded, the annual dinner for the Duc d'Aumale had been first postponed, this year, by the mourning for Cardinal Bonaparte, and then by the death of Dumas *fils*, who was to have been one of the guests. Finally, it took place.

There were fifteen of us at table: the Princess, the Duke, the [Auguste] Laugels, the Marquise Flavie de Casa Fuerte, the Comtesse de Clinchamps, Anatole France, Léon Bonnat, Gérôme, Giovanni Borghese, Louis Ganderax, etc. The Princess accorded the Duke every honour: she seated him at the centre of the table, in her own place – a concession she only made to the Empress – and she sat on his right. She, who was always served first, took the trouble to have two services, so that the dish could be presented to Monseigneur at the same time as it was to her.

The Duc d'Aumale is particularly interesting, because he represents a whole epoch which is already distant – beyond the Second Empire. His memory is prodigious – a Prince's memory – and princes have the duty to have one – as well as the memory of a learned man. He recalled piquant anecdotes and characteristic details in the style of Stendhal. He talked a good deal, like someone who had had to live abroad for a long while, and was making up for it. And to this shrewdness of observation he added a vivacity which made one think of another, Southern race.

In fact, he himself unwittingly provided the clue to the enigma – when he mentioned Queen Marie-Amélie. 'My mother,' he said, 'was calm and serenity itself; but, as soon as she began to speak Italian, everything in her began to move: her eyes, her face, her lips, her nostrils, her arms and fingers. She was the living image of her native city, all Naples passed before us!' . . .

Scratch the French officer and you would soon revive the latent flame of that Vesuvius which nothing could completely extinguish.

He softens his military stiffness by Italian courtesy, which delights in being agreeable and in sympathizing with the listener. So it was that he deigned to approve a guest who maintained the truism that most society people – like most of the common herd – knew the history of France through Alexandre Dumas, in spite of his factual inaccuracies. The master storyteller had also reflected local colour and justified his famous observation: 'History is a nail from which I hang my novels.' However, history is not the chief attraction of his work: that is the dramatic element.

The Duke told us that, in his childhood, on 1 January, he regularly used to notice the mulatto giant towering over the group of employees who came to present their new-year wishes at the Palais-Royal. 'Later on,' he told us, 'Alexandre Dumas was to write the history of my elder brother's regiment, and I had him invited to Neuilly with our most distinguished officers, so that he could question them at leisure – and have the necessary information for the work which he was doing. When they rose from table, Alexandre Dumas, back to the fire, talked throughout the evening, without addressing a single question to the guests who had been invited to answer them. . . At about midnight, the Duc d'Orléans said to the inexhaustible – though unwitting – lecturer: 'You entertained them a great deal, but they didn't teach you anything.' Did the volume ever appear?

I had asked the Princess to invite Anatole France to this dinner. He was standing for the Académie, and he wasn't certain to have the vote of the Duc d'Aumale. I had no doubt that, during the evening, the subtle writer of *Le Lys rouge* would know how to plead his cause. . . In fact he gained it, but in a very unexpected way. The Duc d'Aumale found himself in high spirits in this sympathetic atmosphere; he started to talk at the beginning of the meal, and he did not stop until he heard the clock strike, when he rose and said: 'Gentlemen, we have tired Her Imperial Highness enough, we must let her have a rest.' He kissed the hand of the Princess, who accompanied him to the door, he bade an affable farewell to each of the guests, and, as he reached Anatole France – the Princess had whispered something about him – he grasped his hand in a significant way. It was understood that by this handshake he gave him his vote. France had hardly been able to speak, but he had listened to his future colleague. This sympathetic attention had been more eloquent than the finest speech.[1]

On 23 January 1896, Anatole France was elected to the Académie-Française. He duly sent his thanks to Primoli.

It was not the only occasion on which Gégé Primoli found himself involved in Academic politics. In time he advised Cardinal Mathieu, Louis Bertrand, the novelist, Henri Bergson, the philosopher, and Georges de Porto-Riche, the dramatist, one of his closest friends. It would be remarkable today to find such candidates enlisting the help of a socialite in Rome.

5

The socialite was uncommonly kind. Early in 1896, Marcel
Prévost set out for Italy. He took with him a rough sketch for
his new novel, *Le Jardin secret*. During the fortnight he spent in
Rome, Primoli invited him to *déjeuner* at his villa at Ariccia.
'The setting and the house so clearly enchanted me,' recalled
Prévost, 'that my host suggested that I chose a lodging
somewhere in the vast palazzo and that I settled there when I
wanted.'[1]

Years later, Prévost was to draw a portrait of this genial
Maecenas:

Count Joseph Primoli's face, with its fine and noble features, its
pink complexion, its largely bare forehead and its snowy beard, is
[he explained] truly European. There is no capital whose society is
not familiar to him, no capital where he does not enjoy close
friendships. But he is above all Roman and Parisian; and if he
himself really knows which of the two he is more (I think I know,
too), that is scarcely evident to someone who just meets him in a
salon in Rome or Paris. As a Parisian, he was educated at the
Collège Rollin, and he has never broken off his relationships with
everyone who matters in Paris, not only in the world which is his
natural milieu, but also in the arts and in literature. As a Roman,
no one, not even Stendhal, has known Rome better; he belongs to
its present and its past, there is no fragment of its marbles, no strip
of its paintings, that he has not examined, appraised and
catalogued. His curiosity, in the best sense of the word, is
inexhaustible. . .

And yet it would be unjust to him to suppose (as some have
done) that this curiosity is his only motivation in his relationships
with his contemporaries. Besides his curiosity, he also has the

wish to increase the fortune, glory and happiness of his friends. . .

I can't remember how many years I have known Count Joseph Primoli: I really can't remember. I cannot imagine the beginnings of a literary life in Paris without his figure on my horizon. . . As for him, the years have scarcely changed him. They have simply emphasized the delicate, yet majestic character of the face, and changed the golden beard to a silver beard.

As I have said, this kind patrician invited me to live in his *villino*, or palazzo, in Ariccia. . . Are not Italian pomp and Italian simplicity expressed in the fact that the same building is called a palace or a little villa, according to taste? To be honest, if the apartments at the casa Primoli, at Ariccia, have no pretentions to splendour, they have the imposing dimensions of a palace. Standing at the end of the Corso, which is the long street in the village, looking over the Valle Riccia, with nothing between one's eyes and the far-off sea some forty kilometres away, it would certainly house a community in its numerous apartments. . .

I settled there on 24 March [1896], and in the big house, where the coolness was precious to me, I resumed the hardworking, solitary life which I had led in Siena and Perugia, working in the morning, and sometimes spending the afternoon in Rome. . .[2]

He finished his novel in Ariccia. That September it began to appear as a serial in the newly established *Revue de Paris*.

* * *

Primoli himself was in Paris in the spring and summer of 1896, flitting in and out of the Goncourt *Journal*. On 26 April, with Jacques-Émile Blanche and Maurice Barrès, he burst into Goncourt's Grenier 'like a hurricane'.[3] On 27 May, Goncourt recorded:

Dinner at the rue de Berry to celebrate the Princess's birthday. She is seventy-six today.

Before dinner, there is a diplomatic conference between the Princess, Mme de Galbois and Primoli, which rather intrigues me. We were thirteen at dinner, and, as Mme de Galbois refused to dine with her niece, Ganderax kindly left to have dinner with his daughter. . .

The evening ends with a serenade arranged by Primoli in honour of the Princess. Italians, dressed as mummers, play and sing us Neapolitan songs.[4]

She needed the serenade, and, even more, the sympathy. 'Paris has never been so empty,' she had written, once, to Gégé. '. . . No one has asked me to dinner for a fortnight. . . I grieve, and work, and sleep as much as possible. I linger on, and think of you, and want you with all my heart.'[5] On 16 July came the death of Edmond de Goncourt; and 'when all is said [this again to Gége], he was one of my old friends, often unbearable – but he was there, and full of good intentions. It is a new shock and a new grief. What a sad life! Everything is crumbling around us. . . I keep on seeing poor Goncourt's face. And his poor house, what will become of it? How horrible death is! Oh, why must one live since one has to go?'[6]

Increasingly she needed the genial presence of her confidant. It is said that she did not count the money which she lent him, or the arrangements which he chose to cancel.[7] If this is so, it was because she knew his feelings for her were disinterested. She had known, now, for many years, of his devotion to her. She liked to feel that he was in Paris. So Gégé stayed, and gave her entertainment and comfort, and photographed the salon at Saint-Gratien, and, unremittingly, focused his lens on all the celebrities of the age.

That autumn she was suddenly swept out of her unhappy solitude. She was recalled to Paris by the visit of Nicholas II and his wife. Determined to strengthen Franco-Russian understanding, President Faure asked her to receive the Tsar and the Tsarina at the Invalides; and, aware that the interests of France were at stake, the Princess agreed to take part in the ceremonies of the Republic. On 6 October she was present when the imperial couple arrived in Paris; and next day, as Napoleon's niece, she greeted them at the Invalides.

M. Faure introduced me [she told Gégé], and we all shook hands. I thanked the President for giving me a box at the Théâtre-Français, and he answered: 'I hope that this isn't the last time I can do something for you.' We shook hands, and Their Imperial Highnesses [sic] continued their visit. In fact the Tsar stopped at the Emperor's tomb. All the generals and aides-de-camp remained round the crypt. I went home to change and set out again for the déjeuner. I thought it would be only me, but there were forty-eight of us.

The Tsar is simple, he has fine and searching eyes. He is a small man, and he doesn't look like an emperor. She is tall and beautiful:

a nice expression, but her face and neck are brick-red – which doesn't improve her. She was, she said, astonished to find that I was still so young. She had expected to see a very old lady with white hair! . . .

In short I had a good impression. She is simple and agreeable, he is thoughtful and serene. They would certainly have liked to stay another few days. They are leaving happy. They were given a splendid reception. . . Paris went mad for a week, there were such crowds in the streets.[8]

The visit of Nicholas II marked the end of her public life. In the Dreyfus Affair, two years later, she showed the last signs of political activity. From the beginning of the Affair, Primoli supported Dreyfus. She sent him a severe reprimand: 'Your letter makes the scales fall from my eyes. You are with the wicked, with the enemies of our society and our country. . . Why believe in our enemies? Your sad aunt, Mathilde.'[9]

6

In the spring of 1897, after a long interval, Primoli met an old acquaintance: Francesco Paolo Tosti. Born in the Abruzzi fifty-one years earlier, Tosti had written multitudes of graceful drawing-room songs; they had enjoyed great favour, and earned him the post of singing-master to the Queen of Italy. To Primoli the songs recalled his old, unspoken love for the Princesse de Venosa – the love which haunted his imagination. Now, once again inspired by his imagination, as well as Tosti's recollections, he recorded Tosti in England.

Nice, 14 March 1897

After fifteen years, I have met Paolo Tosti again: the delightful musician of my twentieth year, the harmonious accompanist of my youth, the one who lulled my earliest dreams. How many castles in Spain rose up before me as he sang, castles which have since collapsed like the new buildings in Rome! I remember the yellow salon in the palace where I used to go and spend the evening: I used to listen to *him* as I looked at *her*, and I saw the youthful beauty of Formosa bloom, as she enchanted us by the grace of her movements and the purity of her attitudes: it was like a chaste pantomime that we witnessed to the sound of the music which had blossomed under the starry sky, under a moonbeam which came through the half-open window. And then the hand was kissed, the curtain lowered, and, at about one o'clock in the morning, Carlo [Cecconi], Tosti and I walked home, talking about her. . . We all three adored her, and she loved none of us. Thanks to this absence of love, no doubt, we were able to keep our friendship.

The palace has collapsed in ruins, only a gaping hole marks the spot where it once stood; the pretty princess still has her virginal figure, but she is fifteen years older. Poor Carlo, I saw him die of

224

cancer of the stomach, fighting against atrocious pain. And, as for me, how many loved ones have died around me? How many have died within me? And Tosti, the brilliant and sentimental maestro from the Abruzzi – that blessed province which gives Italy its great artists, or its humble stable-lads, Gabriele d'Annunzio, Michetti, Barbella, etc. – Tosti had vanished! . . . It was only yesterday, it seems to me, that the young musician with the golden beard, the blue eyes, the sensual lips, newly arrived from the Abruzzi, made those memorable evenings in the Roman *salons*. He set simple music to a simple poem which had been given to him by the most fashionable poets of the Peninsula, from Ferdinando Martini, the future Minister, to Gabriele d'Annunzio, the future high priest [*sic*]; then he hummed his songs to his own accompaniment. This spontaneous melody, which seemed to sing of its own accord, this melody one remembered without thinking, gave Italian ears a rest from the encroaching music of Wagner. . . With Tosti, you only had to abandon yourself. As Gounod said about Saint-Saëns, it was certainly not *equilateral* music, but it was the accompaniment to dreams. And so people invited him, argued over him, snatched him from one another: 'Figaro su, Figaro giù!' – 'My good friend Tosti!', 'My dear maestro!', 'Ciccillo mio!' . . . They called for him everywhere, and everywhere he would arrive with a smile and a song on his lips: he would sit down at the piano and stay there late into the night. And some people listened to him, and others flirted to the music. . .

It was a delightful life, but, when the cricket had sung for several winters, summer came and it was destitute. Tosti decided that it was time to seek his fortune in the country where music is not an innate need but a luxury [*sic*], not a wild flower which blossoms everywhere, but a hothouse bloom which is purchased at great cost – and, singing as he went, he left for England. . .

Paolo Tosti had been in London for some time, trying to delude himself by sometimes taking the fog on the Thames for the smoke from Vesuvius. He had indeed found some young ladies he knew who recalled a winter spent in Rome, and continued their lessons in London, but he wondered if, after all, the occasional fees were a compensation for the tedium of travel, the sadness of exile, and above all the absence of the sun – which he needed to give life to his music. He was homesick, and no doubt he was about to decide to go back across the Channel and the Alps. One evening, he had dined at a gentlemen's club, and while the English, as they always do after the meal, remained at table to smoke and drink, he went over to the piano and, *sotto voce*, began to murmur some of his most sentimental love songs. . . Gradually the table was deserted

225

for the piano, and they all remained hanging on the *maestrino's* harmonious lips. The enthusiasm reached its peak when Tosti began to sing a Neapolitan song. . . At the end of the evening, a young gentleman came up to him and said to him very formally, but very politely:

'Since you are so obliging, Monsieur, would you come and make a little music for a lady who is very ill and very old, and sang with Lablache?'

'Of course.'

'Tomorrow at 6.30, then.'

'What is the address?'

'St James's Palace.'

'Who is the lady?'

'The Duchess of Cambridge.'

The following evening, at 6.25, Tosti got out of his cab at the palace gates, where a horse-guard was on duty. The butler, who had been informed, came to greet him, and entrusted him to a valet who led him upstairs. On the landing he was handed over to a majordomo who in turn escorted him to a room where he found the young lord who had invited him. The peer shook hands with him, and led him through a series of rooms into a vast dim drawing-room, which he entered on tiptoe, and in silence. Here, with a gesture, he showed him the piano which was concealed in the bow-window, and made him a sign to sit down at it and sing. In the dim light, on a chaise longue, buried under a flood of lace, Tosti glimpsed a very old lady who appeared to give no sign of life: was she paralysed or asleep? She did not seem to notice his arrival. He hesitated to break this silence, but at a sign of encouragement from the young man he sat down at the piano, somewhat nervous, and, with his thin Italian voice, he began by singing, at first *sotto voce* and then, as he grew bolder, with more passion, one of his most poetic Tuscan *stornelli*. . . And, at this harmonious language, this melodic music, the old inert woman who seemed to be nearer to death than to life, looked up as if she were leaving her tomb, and came to life again: her dim eyes half opened and lit up, a vague smile passed across her pallid lips, and her hand, which was resting on the lace, gently beat time. . . Tosti observed this resurrection, and in an almost triumphant tone he began the final refrain: 'Ed io risorgerò. . .' And then one heard a sigh rather than a human voice, and this sigh said: 'Ancora!. . .' And Tosti, more assured, repeated his *stornello*. A passion had survived in the old duchess, it was music. Every evening they brought her some musician to divert her, but, usually, it was some virtuoso who only thought of pushing himself forward, and ended by making the invalid dizzy,

226

instead of lightening her suffering. And so, when, instead of these bravuras and garglings, she heard this frail voice sighing these refreshing melodies, she was deeply moved and charmed. When Tosti had finished, she called him over to her to thank him. She looked into the bright eyes of the man who had done her so much good, and she begged him to come back: it would be a good deed, she told him in Italian, 'un' opera caritatevole'.

He went back the following evening, then he went back every evening. . .

Gradually the old grandmama was charmed by the young artist; she became attached to him, called him 'my sweet nightingale', and conceived a grateful affection for the joyful southerner with eyes which were as blue as his own skies. And then she showed maternal affection for this exile, who must long for his sunshine, she made it a duty to take the place of his absent family (the family which perhaps she prevented him from joining), and she said to him:' It won't be for long, . . . although you prolong my day, and warm the evening of my life with a last ray of sunshine.' On one occasion, it was he who fell gravely ill. She demanded that he was brought to St James's to be looked after by her household; when they opposed the idea, she went into bursts of rage which gravely affected her health, and they had to tell her that he was installed in the Palace, and at every meal she sent him special dishes, jellies, etc., which they pretended to take to him: she was giving food to her nightingale. . .

Every day she gave him a present. She even gave him precious family heirlooms. Tosti had to pretend to accept them so as not to vex her, but he regularly took them to her brother, the Duke of Cambridge [sic]. The situation of the old Duchess's favourite musician naturally excited jealousy and jokes. One day the Prince of Wales, who always entered rooms unannounced, found Tosti at the invalid's bedside. He was leaning over her to hear what she was saying to him in her tremulous voice. 'Aha!' said His Royal Highness, 'David Rizzio!' Tosti made no reply, but he promised himself that if another unpleasant comment was made to him, he would answer. The occasion soon arose. A few days later, the Prince of Wales passed Tosti in a corridor; he gave a low bow, drew aside, and said: 'After you, Uncle!' (Hadn't people spread a rumour that the aged Duchess had offered to marry the young maestro to attach him to her for life?) At this fresh insult from the irreverent nephew, Tosti could no longer contain himself. He went to complain to the Duke of Cambridge. 'Your Royal Highness,' he said to him, 'I am quite willing to visit Her Royal Highness as an employee or as a friend, because I am deeply devoted and grateful

227

to her; but, if I am to be ridiculed, I shall not come again.' His help was too precious to be lost, and henceforward no one laughed at him. During the ten years she lived on, Tosti came back to sing every evening, except on Sundays when he came for dinner but no music. One evening Queen Victoria ventured to ask her aunt to lend her her musician at the time of the usual visit, and – something unheard-of in England – the Queen met with an absolute refusal. . .

The good fairy's illness was chiefly old age, and, at certain moments of crisis, when the doctor was called and was powerless to help her, he used to send for Tosti, and prescribe . . . another song, which revived her. At last, one evening, summoned in all haste, Tosti arrived to find the big room crowded with people. As usual, he went to the piano, counting on his daily miracle. They told him that it was no use: 'Love's labour's lost!'. . . And then he went up to the deathbed, and, slipping amongst the Princes of the Royal Family, he knelt behind the Queen of England and the Princess of Wales. The charming old lady half opened her eyes, and recognized her 'caro mignolo'. She smiled at him, a last grateful smile, drew him to her, and, gently laying her trembling hand on his head as if to bless him, she murmured as she enveloped him with a last tender gaze: 'Ever faithful!'[1]

Augusta of Hesse-Cassel, the widow of Augustus, Duke of Cambridge, represented an era of English history: the daughter-in-law of George III, she was also the grandmother of Princess May of Teck, the future Queen Mary. She died in 1889, at the age of ninety-two.

A few days after the angelic creature had gone to hear the songs of the seraphim, the Princess of Wales [wrote Primoli] sent Tosti a ring. On the bezel she had had engraved her aunt's farewell to the musician: 'Ever faithful'. And she herself, the poor Duchess, showed fidelity from beyond the grave. To reward him for the poetry with which he had filled her final years, she left him a small pension which let him unite his destiny with that of a charming woman who seems to be both his mother and his daughter:

> La compagne parfaite
> qu'il faut au solitaire et qu'il faut au poète.

And now, his golden beard is as silver as an April stream. He is no longer kept in England by his protectress, or by Queen Victoria, who had taken him over from her aunt. Will he take the sunlit road to Italy again, will he come and sing his swan song at the foot of Vesuvius? Or has London really become his second home, and will the joyful Bohemian settle there and become an *old gentleman*?[2]

Tosti was to settle there, and to become singing-master to the Royal Family. He died in 1916, at the age of seventy: Sir Francesco Paolo Tosti, KCVO.

7

As Renée Lelièvre observed, in her book on Italian drama in France, Primoli played the part of a benevolent cultural attaché. He was the natural patron for Italian authors:

> He intervened with translators, publishers and theatre directors. In their letters to [Georges] Hérelle, [the translator], Butti, Ojetti, all the Italian men of letters constantly made use of his name. 'Giuseppe Primoli and I hatched a fearful plot in Rome,' wrote Gabriele d'Annunzio. It was a question of having [La] Città morta performed in Paris. It was in fact the Count who negotiated with Sarah; it was he, again, who, in 1897, wrote a long article and presented La Duse to the [French] public. It was he who introduced the first of d'Annunzio's works to be performed in Paris.[1]

For some years he had eagerly furthered d'Annunzio's career. He had persuaded him to give an interview to Gaston Deschamps, the critic of Le Temps.[2] In the spring of 1897 he encouraged him to write Il Sogno d'un Mattino di Primavera. On about 13 April, d'Annunzio announced to his translator, Hérelle: 'Primoli is extremely interested in these performances, and he has urged me very strongly to write this new play – we have decided that the French text of the Songe should be published in the Revue de Paris on 1 June. The first performance will take place at the Vaudeville on 4 or 5 June.'[3] On 18 April, Primoli duly recorded:

> Visit from G. d'Annunzio, on his way back from Albano where he retreated for a week to devote himself completely to his drama. . . His eloquence gave me the illusion of sincerity, and it conquered

me. He had the exaltation of the man who has lived far away from all human contact, or in the company of dreams and madmen. All these impressions came from him, came from every pore: they showed his awareness of his strength, his genius creating its own future; he was a seer, a prophet, the *vates* in all his wonderful intensity, with his second sight. . . In his eyes I saw them pass, the dreams that he formed, the cycle which was being composed. As the walls of Jericho crumbled at the sound of the trumpets, the walls of his ideal theatre rose up at the sound of his magic words. The wonderful cycle revealed itself to my enchanted eyes, a midsummer night's dream, the fire of an autumnal twilight, the death of a winter evening.[4]

* * *

Rome, 1 May 1897

At the Hôtel Bristol, I ask for Madame Duse. She is about to leave, and she is coming down the stairs. She sees me, and waves a wonderful book-binding: some old embroidered material tied with green silk moiré ribbon.

'I've got it!' she cries, triumphantly.

'What have you got?'

'Gabriele d'Annunzio's manuscript!'

'What is it called?'

'*Le Songe d'une Matinée de Printemps*!'

'It's the right time of year.'

'And I'm going to put it into its setting: I'm off to the country with my company, and we'll rehearse in the fields, and under the trees, among the flowers. . . Ten days – just ten days – of rest, and then Paris!'

'What will you begin with?'

'I can't make up my mind between *Magda, La Femme de Claude, La Dame [aux camélias]*. . .'

'So you're limiting yourself to Sarah's repertoire.'

'Sarah's repertoire?. . . It's universal, it goes from *Phèdre* to *Spiritisme* by way of Victor Hugo's dramas and Alexandre Dumas' comedies! . . . It is the whole of the French theatre, which is really the only living theatre, . . . except for a few dramas or comedies sprung up here and there through the inspiration of genius. . . And, personally, I am going to the Renaissance for the honour of playing a small part in the French theatre. Am I right or wrong? Who knows?'

'Trust in your name.'

'No one knows it in Paris.'

231

'Then trust in your anagram.'
'What do you mean?'
'Hugo would have told you: *Duse – Deus.*'
'Well, I'd never thought of that!'[5]

On 1 June she began a month-long season at the Théâtre de la Renaissance. That day *Le Songe d'une Matinée de Printemps* appeared in the *Revue de Paris*, in the same issue as Primoli's tribute to her.

* * *

1 June

Ten years or so ago, in Rome, at the [Teatro] Valle, among those who followed La Duse's performances most assiduously, I noticed, at the back of a box, a man whose solid build (in spite of his unhealthy face) revealed him to be German, while his vague and searching gaze behind his gold-rimmed spectacles announced that he was an artist. It was, in fact, the celebrated Bavarian artist Franz Lenbach.

He did not take his eyes off the stage, and he followed every movement of the actress as if he had wanted to fix them in his mind and then transfer them to canvas.

At the end of the theatrical season, Lenbach begged Madame Duse to come and spend an afternoon in his studio at the Palazzo Borghese. She went there rather against her will, she has such an aversion to posing. What was her surprise to find the panels of the huge room hung with pastel sketches which showed her in different attitudes! Her likeness was reflected as if by innumerable mirrors.

They were all like her – and they were not like one another. . .

In short, there were thirty sketches, and there was no portrait.

That is rather what I dream of undertaking, to give some idea of this creature of a thousand souls.

I am going to seek out personal notes, a correspondence with Alexandre Dumas, passages from letters written or received, newspaper articles, and produce a series of snapshots from them. . .

* * *

Last year, on a visit to the little town of Chioggia, near Venice, I read an inscription over a portico which made me pause. 'Calle Duse'. Already! The Duse who had given his name to the street was in fact the ancestor, the grandfather of our actress, a performer

232

famous in his day, but since forgotten. . .

In the *calle Duse*, along the canal, [Novelli, the Italian Coquelin, and I] encountered a strange procession. We saw a fat woman who, under her black mantilla and her flashy golden chain, one would have recognized anywhere in the world as a midwife, and a good rustic whose beaming smile revealed the happiness of a brand-new father. Between them a wet-nurse, in all her finery, bore a crystal coffer like the ones which hold wax images of the infant Jesus. This new-born child was not wax, it was undoubtedly flesh and blood, and it would certainly have broken its glass prison if its little feet and arms had not been firmly bound by its swaddling clothes.

And suddenly I remembered the baptism of the little Eleonora Duse, at Vigevano, and I understood the astonishment of the Austrian soldier who, seeing the approach of the mysterious tabernacle, had imagined that it contained some precious relics, and had, respectfully, presented arms.

And so, as soon as the procession had got home again, Signor Duse had gone up to his wife:

'Forgive me, my dear,' he had said, half pitiful and half triumphant. 'Forgive me if, in exchange for the daughter you have given me, I cannot offer you a handsome gift. Instead I have brought you a happy augury. Our child will be celebrated, I promise you: they presented arms to her.'

And, rooted in the hearts of these worthy people, with the power of a conviction, this idea restored their courage in times of hardship, and more than once the mother told her daughter:

'The present doesn't matter, I am sure of your future. When you entered the world, they presented arms to you!'[6]

Her future had indeed been assured.

A real triumph for La Duse [continued Primoli], that is what Verdi said one evening as he was walking on the seashore, in the moonlight, with the confidant of all his thoughts. He was talking about *La Traviata*: 'I could not do it again today,' he said, 'and I shall never do anything better. . .' And he added: 'That little Duse! . . . If I had heard her before I composed my opera, what a wonderful finale I might have planned with that crescendo of "Armandi" which she found, simply by letting her heart overflow!'

*   *   *

There is Verdi's testimony. The personal verdict of Dumas she will not, alas, have known. 'She will die without my seeing her,' he had

233

written. She is still alive, but he has never seen her, at least on stage.

On one occasion, between trains, she ventured to present herself at Marly. She was just recovering from a serious illness, and, during her long convalescence, in which she had been condemned to rest, she had learnt French; and so he was absolutely delighted to observe that she scarcely had a foreign accent. . . Time passed quickly, she had to go, he escorted her to the station. He had wanted to give her all the roses in his garden; while they were tying up the bouquet, the train began to move. With the agility which he was to keep all his life, he ran after the train, and held his roses out to her; she put her arms out of the window, and caught the bouquet in flight. . . That was the first and last time she saw him; and, since then, she has always seen herself borne away by a stream-train, condemned to wander about the world. And he, the great benefactor, appears to her escorting her and offering her the roses from his garden, destined to give fragrance to her journey.[7]

Now he had died, but the journey continued, and it had led to Paris. Primoli had for years urged La Duse to go there; now, in the summer of 1897, with the entire Italian Embassy, the Ambassadors of Austria, Russia and the Netherlands, and the French Minister of Public Instruction, and with Mme Doche, who, forty-five years earlier, had created the part of Marguerite Gautier, he and Princess Mathilde saw La Duse in *La Dame aux camélias*.[8] On 15 June came the first performance, in French, of d'Annunzio's play. *Le Songe d'une Matinée de Printemps* enjoyed a *succès d'estime*, and La Duse created a profound impression. The introduction of the actress and dramatist to Paris was an undoubted triumph for Primoli.

8

1 February, at dawn. I cannot sleep. Yesterday evening Dr Mazzini told me that my poor Uncle [Napoleon, the last Prince of Canino] has only a few days – perhaps a few hours – to live. . . The diabetes has degenerated into tuberculosis [*sic*]; one lung has gone, the other is affected. He doesn't eat and doesn't sleep, he is growing thinner and weaker. . . He is a shadow and a breath: only his voice survives, in loud and sudden bursts, and it produces a singular effect as it comes out of this skeleton. . .

A troubled week, disturbed by the ups and downs of the death–struggle of my poor Uncle Napoleon. . . Only his voice and glance survive, and recall the colossus which he still was some months ago. The other morning he said to me: 'I am beginning to like these feverish nights which pass between waking and sleeping, in which all my past existence reappears to me. . . The present is effaced, and I see the past again with such intensity that shapes rise up before my eyes, precise in every detail. . . I am reliving my campaigns in Africa, Mexico, 1870 . . .' And he let himself go, and opened his overflowing heart to me, told me about his last disappointment. After a hard battle at Metz, in which he had been one bullet away from death, he had seen all his officers die before his eyes, one after the other, he had replaced them at the same post, certain to meet the same fate, and he could not explain how he had been spared by the shells that were raining down around him. . . On the evening of that terrible day which would no doubt be repeated on the morrow, believing that this time he could not survive, he withdrew into his tent, and poured out on paper all that welled up from his heart. His soul rose up towards God, and his thoughts turned towards his country, towards those who were absent, towards his father's house, towards his wife, who bore, in her womb, the child which perhaps he was destined never to

235

see. . . All this overflowing love, this faith, this hope, all the feelings which overcame a soldier who had been under fire and would be so again – he poured out in a letter which he sent to Rome, to the woman who had so nearly been a widow.

The other day, after one of those feverish nights which called up those supreme visions, he recalled this eve of a possible death in the middle of the watch which was, this time, the last, and he wanted to re-read his impressions and asked his wife for the letter. At first she didn't understand what he meant. . .

'The letter I wrote to you from Metz.'

'Oh, yes?'

'Well?'

'I haven't got it any more.'

'What have you done with it?'

'I don't know. . . I must have torn it up. . . . Thrown it away.'

'What?'

'I didn't know that you minded so much, otherwise I'd have kept it.'

And he finally discovered that he had never been understood by the woman whom he had chosen, among all women, just for her dazzling beauty. At the apogee of the Empire, on the morrow of the Italian campaign, when he was not just a match but an alliance, in the face of the whole world he had chosen this young girl who had brought him nothing but her beauty. And she had even refused to give him a son. When she seemed to have recovered [from childbirth], she had taken her two small daughters into her room, on either side of her bed. She had prevented her husband from approaching her and from continuing that branch of the Bonapartes in which the fusion of Joseph and Lucien – the best and most intelligent of the Emperor's brothers – had for a moment made people believe that that was where the race would be perpetuated.

This episode of the letter was the final blow. It touched him to the heart. Since then, he had been unable to hide his dull rancour against this woman. 'Yes, yes, she feels remorse,' he says, 'but now it is too late.' And this soldier who is so good, so upright, loyal and affectionate, looks at her with hatred when she comes into his sick-room to fulfil her wifely formalities, to sit near the door at a certain distance from the bed and ask him how he was the previous night. . .

I watched the invalid being moved from one bed to another with the aid of a sheet: to me it seemed a shroud and a laying in the tomb. The poor body is reduced to the state of a diaphanous ghost. He asked me to lift up his knees one after the other, as he could not raise them by himself, and I heard the creaking of the bones of a fleshless skeleton.

He mentioned some delicate errands which he had at heart. He had entrusted them to me. He took my hand and thanked me for all I did for him. In his affectionate, proud and tender look, I saw his gratitude and his regret that he could not do them himself. What touched me most was his simplicity of tone, which meant: 'Anyway, it's quite natural between you and me, you know quite well I'd have done the same for you.' Indeed I know; and what a support I therefore lose in life, with the disappearance of this brave brother of my mother's! When all those moral supports come to fail us, we finally let go, and fall in our turn. . .

In order to prepare us for eternal separation from the people whom we believe essential to us, Providence sometimes arranges things so as to bring us despite ourselves to want some or other ending. The agony – we believe at times – is worse than death itself (and, when death comes, how we regret the agony!) for the poor man who is dying and for those who watch him suffer. . .[1]

Ajaccio, Saturday 17 February 1899

On Wednesday evening at nine o'clock I announced to Mother that I was leaving for Corsica. 'That's right,' she answered, 'I'm coming with you.' She took hold of my arm, drew me to the stairs, and walked down to the courtyard. I had all the trouble in the world to make her go up again and to settle her back in her chair. . . Poor dear darling! Who knows exactly what impression they give her, these successive departures of relatives and friends? I take care not to tell her the fatal news, but with that second sight with which she is endowed, like all inward-looking creatures, she feels Death hovering round her, and she feels a repercussion of it in her heart. . . And then the maternal instinct has survived in the Mater dolorosa, and, although I try to hide my cares from her, she reads my agonies and griefs in my eyes, my features, my attitude, the tone of my voice. I feel her anxious gaze weighing upon me, I hear the words she murmurs to herself; it seems as if this poor clouded creature has kept her clearsightedness where her children are concerned.

'I don't understand any more,' she says. 'You do understand. . .' She has abdicated her faculty of comprehension, and, since she no longer has the joys of the world, it would be fair that at least she no longer had its griefs; but she has the painful feelings of a nightmare which it is impossible to shake off. . . In certain lucid moments, which are sadder than utter darkness, she understands,

237

but, unwilling to accept Death, she does not let her mind rest on these funereal thoughts, and she resumes her vaguely painful dreams. . . At other times, however, she believes that everyone is dead, and when she sees someone again she cries out, almost with surprise: 'He's still alive!' And so, when I come home again after an absence, it is for her a resurrection. She embraces me so eagerly that I feel that she had thought that she had lost me like the rest; and she holds on to my arm so tightly that I feel she fears another separation. And people are surprised that I find it difficult to leave her! I have now been with her for seven months, and the parting is only the more painful – but this time it is a question of accompanying the body of her brother, whom she had called 'Honour in person' – and I am sure that she would approve of me.

At the station I found Mimy and Eugénie [Prince Napoleon's daughters, Maria [Mimy] Gotti and Eugénie de la Moskowa]. They were pale under their crêpe veils: they had just said goodbye to their husbands, whom they would have liked to accompany to Corsica. They both mourn their Father deeply, but grief expresses itself differently in each of them, according to their natures: it softens the valiant, energetic, gentle Mimy, while it frightens the cold Eugénie, and makes her rigid. I'm afraid that Eugénie deluded herself about the health of the man whom she loved most in the world, and this prostration, mixed with indignation against men and things, has something touching in its injustice. She turned away angrily from the most sympathetic people, and disgustedly pushed away the friendly hands which were outstretched to her. When I told her about the death of the Princesse de P. : 'Well, she was old, wasn't she?' she cried, with a shrug of the shoulders which contrasted with her usual reserve. Her Father, she thought, had been struck down in his very prime. He had seemed destined to live a long time yet, and to enjoy his daughter's happiness with the husband he had chosen for her – 'the only one,' she said, 'he could have chosen.'

So I leave with the two sons-in-law – and my Uncle's coffin locked up in a railway carriage – while a newly married couple take their places in a third-class compartment, escorted by a whole wedding party, who are rather lit up, and the gaily waved handkerchiefs, waved in celebration, stop in mid air, overcome with fear [sic], when the hearse passes mournfully in front of them, bearing the coffin.

In the sad light of dawn we reach Livorno. Napoleon Parisani, whom the Gabriellis have sent to represent them at the funeral, comes to meet us at the station and take us to the Hôtel du Japon. It is too early to walk round, too late to go to bed. We collapse into

238

armchairs in the reading room, which is cluttered up with the usual horrible and pretentious trivia, the sight of it has never shocked me more than it does now. Are there states of mind, perhaps, in which you need not only solitude, but a void around you? . . .

At five o'clock the faithful Pietri arrives from Cap Martin: sent by the Empress to escort the body of her favourite nephew to Corsica. He tells me that Her Majesty has requested him to bring me back to the Villa Cyrnos, where my room is ready for me. At six o'clock, at sunrise, we go to attend the removal of the coffin from its armoured train. The iron door swings back on its hinges and the interior of the carriage appears to us, all decked with flowers, like the Virgin's sepulchre in the painting by Perugino. There is a harvest scattered round the catafalque: two splendid garlands from the King, the wreaths from the two daughters, the palm from Mother, the sprays from friends – even a humble bunch of violets from [our faithful maid] Vittoria. We take all the ribbons off to hang them in the chapel, and we keep the palms and violets. The coffin is set on a hearse, and we make our way towards the harbour. There, with the aid of a crane, the precious burden rises up a moment, and hovers, eddying, in space, and comes down in a boat. We climb into another boat and we precede it on board the *Cyro*. There the coffin is hoisted up again, and lowered on to the bridge of the ship. It is once more under shelter, and it is soon covered with French and Italian flags, beween the folds of which we lay the palms and the flowers. As a crucifix was wanting, I sent for a cross of violets. Tricolour flags are hanging from the roof, all round, and isolate the Dead from the Living. A sailor is posted outside this improvised funeral chamber which is more like a military tent in which a soldier is taking his rest.[2]

Rome, 12 March 1899

I am home at last! . . . It is the sweetest, most calmative feeling that I know: to feel that I am beside her. . . At midnight I went into her room, she was half asleep, and let herself be kissed, but it was only this morning, little by little, that she drew me to her, and took my head in her hands – and, as she looked at me, her eyes filled with tears.[3]

9

On 12 May 1899 came the death of the dramatist Henri Becque. He had made his name with *Les Corbeaux*, that powerful early naturalistic drama, and his unfinished play, *Les Polichinelles* – a study of the financial world – was to have been his masterpiece. Primoli was moved by the thought of the unfinished work, and by the recollection of *Les Corbeaux*: its portrayal of insanity reminded him acutely of his own domestic tragedy.

Naples, 15 May 1899

The papers announce the death of Henri Becque. I remember his visit to Rome in 1893. I had occasion to see him several times, to take a photograph of him and to write a sketch of him in my diary – quoting a few of his terrible and deadly witticisms. He dies without having written his play *Les Polichinelles*, which he had been ruminating for years. A moment ago a black mass [of birds] alighted on the theatre in Pompeii where I was sitting, and it made me think of *Les Corbeaux*: those women in black who weep, and that wretched young girl who goes mad. . .

Even the joyful Matilde Serao does not have the power to cheer me, though her quick wit and her Neapolitan verse have the gift of putting me in good humour. It is true that she's no longer herself, she is so depressed by our great friend's coldness towards her.

La Duse is completely under the Poet's spell and in his clutches. [D'Annunzio] is dragging her on to a fatal slope where she is losing, one by one, all the fruitful seeds which Genius had planted in her noble soul. She has undertaken an Italian tour with the man who is said to be our finest actor, so as to present her author's work. By force of genius and determination she has forced them to accept a mediocre play called *La Gioconda*. But, encouraged by this unenviable success, Poet and Actress thought they could impose an absolutely senseless drama, with the derisory title of *La Gloria*, on the Neapolitan public. La Duse found herself booed and hissed. . . And while, on stage, she fought in vain against a sneering audience, while she defended her friend's work with her genius, heart and strength, what was he doing? 'Where were you during the battle?' Scarfoglio asked him. 'Me?' he replied, with nauseating cynicism, 'I was busy raping a nun! . . .' He had in fact hidden in the dressing-room of a little actress who was playing a sister of charity in the drama, and he was demanding consolation from her. Of course this crude remark was repeated to the unhappy mistress, who was fighting – fighting until she collapsed on stage for the Glory of the man who rewarded her by deceiving her in the wings.

Matilde told Eleonora brutally: 'Act Dumas if you want to make money for him, but don't confuse your love and your art. Don't act these plays: they are bad in themselves, and you perform them badly. They do you a material and artistic wrong.' In fact, Eleonora is too modern to represent the pseudo-antique . . . She is forcing her nature and her talent; she is contradicting herself.[1]

* * *

May saw another theatrical figure in Italy: Jules Claretie, sometime administrator-general of the Théâtre-Français. He and Primoli admired 'those Roman horizons . . . in the very place of Tasso's dreams.'[2]

Then summer came, and Primoli escaped the Roman heat. In July, he was invited on a cruise in the North Sea by the Empress Eugénie.

10

Bergen fjord, Saturday, 8 July 1899

When we left England the day before yesterday, I was in a comatose state between life and death. I only revived today, on the dawn of the third day, when the *Thistle* slowed down at the entrance to the Bergen fjord. I went up on to the bridge, and watched a boarding-party. At the sight of this little black boat, manned by men of another race – I was about to say of another age – muffled up to the eyes, and armed to the teeth, I had a vision of Norwegian pirates trying to set a ransom on the elegant English yacht. Instead of plundering us, the sailors hoisted up the pilot who was to guide us through the fjord, and they set him down on the bridge. This aged giant seems to be a hundred years old, and to be the incarnation of Time itself. . .

This first fjord I cross gives me the impression of a nature closer to Creation. It seems to me that, geologically, in this primitive soil, one would find more direct traces of prehistoric time, and I murmur that line from Hugo:

> La terre encore humide et molle du Déluge.

Light and darkness are still not equally divided, since months of utter darkness are followed by days of twenty-four hours in which the sun is shining at midnight. It is a Wagnerian scene completely impregnated with Scandinavian poetry, and in the crevices of these rocks, with their fantastic shapes, one looks for the sleeping Walkyrie, just as through the mists one sees them pass, astride the clouds. . .

A cloud of white birds wheel above the deck, uttering little childlike cries, . . . and they complete the picture by recalling the metamorphoses of human beings into winged creatures dear to the Poet of the Swan and Dove. And when, tired of losing itself in the clouds, the eye comes down again to the banks of the fjord, it finds,

242

coyly perched on the side of a green hill, a cottage, a church with a pointed steeple, a factory with its chimney, a villa with *down-windows* [i.e. sash windows], and flowers. . . It is the characters of Ibsen who rise up before my eyes: the ghosts drive out the gods, and the Walkyrie are replaced by Nora and Hedda Gabler. . . No landscape suggests literature more than a Norwegian fjord which encloses within its wild or cultivated shores all the literature of this *fin de siècle* personified by Wagner and Ibsen.[1]

It was here, off the coast of Norway, in this remote and haunted and seemingly primaeval part of Europe, that they found themselves abruptly involved in politics.

Bergen, Saturday 8 July 1899

We make our entrance into the port of Bergen. . . Three ships are anchored in the roads. The enemy flags confront each other: a German cruiser, the *Gneisenau*, and a French one, the *Iphigénie*. Both of them are full of midshipmen. A connecting link between the two, the pretty white yacht of the Prince of Monaco. The *Princesse Alice* is getting ready to leave for Spitzbergen with her crew of scientists and apparatuses, to make experiments. Prince Albert, philosopher, scholar and traveller, comes to see us and describes the scene that took place yesterday. He found himself involved in it, and had indeed prepared it, in accordance with the secret wishes of the two governments, who were tired of the sullen rancour of the last thirty years. They were trying to come together, perhaps to league against the common enemy, the universal conqueror, the one who holds Germany in check and has just humiliated France at Fashoda, the one who, says the Empress, seems to have inherited the mantle of the Romans: the Englishman.

The day before yesterday the Emperor William therefore sailed into Bergen on the *Hohenzollern*, and, having made sure of a good reception, Agamemnon the King of Kings went to pay an official visit to the *Iphigénie*. He behaved, of course, most graciously to the officers, midshipmen and sailors, and he departed leaving the republican crew under the spell of his imperial charm. That evening, delighted with his visit, he went to dine on the yacht of the Prince of Monaco, who had arranged the meeting for him, and rubbing his hands, he said to him: 'That's done it!' And from this neutral territory he despatched a telegram to the President of the Republic to congratulate him on these young French midshipmen and to express his satisfaction at finding himself with *friends* once again. Then he wrote a letter to the captain of the *Iphigénie* and asked him to come next day, informally, to drink a little punch on board the *Hohenzollern* with *some* of his crew. In this way they would meet some of Germany's hopes and make acquaintance with them. . . And, folding up his letter, William said to the Prince of Monaco: 'I've only invited *some* of the crew so as to let the captain make a choice. I don't want to force the ones who keep too bloodstained a memory of 1870, it would be too painful for them to board a German ship. I understand these patriotic feelings too well not to respect them.' And, handing his letter to the Prince's secretary, he said to him, smiling: 'Off you go, messenger of Love!'

So yesterday on the *Hohenzollern* they had a little dinner; the Emperor divested it of any official character, as he wanted it to be inspired by the most complete cordiality. These command performances are always somewhat embarrassed, and one is more aware of the wish and the determination to be pleasant than the spontaneous attraction between the guests and hosts. There was perhaps more animation among the officers, better prepared to play their part, than among the more primitive sailors. The latter looked at each other in embarrassment, could not understand each other, and smiled and clinked their glasses to order. The Emperor, however, had left nothing to chance. He displayed all those refinements of unexpected delicacy of which he has the secret. He had therefore arranged to receive the President's answer to his telegram at the appropriate time, and he had had the two telegrams posted up on the bridge. The two crews filed past them so that they could ascertain the good relationship between their governments. Having encouraged the sailors to fraternize with each other, William took his seat at a little table between the Prince of Monaco and the captain of the *Iphigénie*. Over the champagne, the Comte d'Eulembourg, German Ambassador to Vienna, brought his master a decoration and a telegram. The Emperor handed both of them to the French officer. 'Allow me,' he said, 'to offer you the Red Eagle to remind you of our happy meeting in the port of Bergen; and at the same time,' he hastened to add, to forestall the slightest hesitation, 'I am glad to show you the telegram by which at my request your Government permits you to accept this Order from me, and to wear it in memory of today.'

And this morning the *Hohenzollern*, saluted by the French and German flags, made its departure from the port of Bergen, very proud of its peaceful victory, and, like the Phantom Ship, it disappeared into the mists on its way to the North, where I very much hope that we shall meet it.[2]

Midnight struck on the clock on the *Thistle*, and we could still not tear ourselves from the bridge, the sky was so luminous. Up above they had forgotten to put out the sun, and it was casting its last rays on the glaciers and the sea. By this unusual light the Empress was reading *Au fond du gouffre*, which I had lent her. It interests her even without a connection with the Dreyfus Affair – because she likes 'novels which make progress and not the ones which mark time on the spot and never get on'. As for me, I was arranging my slides, because I had been taking photographs until 11.30, and the others, armed with binoculars, were watching the *Hohenzollern*. . . For an invasion disturbed the peace of the little port of Molde. At about ten o'clock the Captain came to point out a white *man-of-war* on the horizon, followed by a cruiser and a torpedo-boat. It could only be the Emperor William. In fact we saw it solemnly advancing, the cumbersome, massive, completely white warship which is indeed *Seiner Majestät Yacht*, on which one can imagine the man who embodies the military nation *par excellence*, and the all-powerful German Empire formed from the remains of its neighbours. On the bow of the colossal ship, on the bridge, was the theatrical silhouette of the Kaiser himself, wearing a helmet of dazzling whiteness, and draped in a pale cloak. The *Hohenzollern* went through the movements of a mastiff looking for its place, and it dropped anchor not far from us; beside it anchored the cruiser loaded with attendants and luggage, in the midst of which I made out a *Karriole* and a grey horse; and the dark torpedo-boat full of men blackened by the coal turned round and went away with a whistle, leaving a wake of blackish smoke behind it. Soon afterwards, in spite of the still luminous light from heaven, we saw an electric sun shining brightly at the top of the great mast. Beside it flew the white flag bearing the iron cross on the sceptre and the imperial sword; a ramp of light lit up along the gangway which came down from the ship to the sea, lighting up the descent of white-uniformed officers who were going ashore to leave and receive despatches. A petrol launch left the side of the cruiser and appeared to be coming in our direction: it was our yacht that she was approaching. One of the three sailors on board demanded in an imperious tone, in the Emperor's name, the names of the yacht, the owner and the passengers. The demands were brief, but there were long negotiations to get the answers; our captain decided to say '*Thistle* – Captain Fane – Comtesse de Pierrefonds'. The Empress wanted to add 'Asleep'. She was alarmed by the idea of this untimely visit. I persuaded her not to add the unfortunate word, by reminding her that it was unnecessary. Although the sun was determined to shine, it was nonetheless midnight – and it was not the moment, I thought, when a young Emperor visits an old Empress. 'Very well,' she told the captain, 'but in that case you will raise anchor and we will leave at the first light of dawn.' The Widow of Napoleon III did not feel that she was guaranteed against the encroaching amiability of the grandson of William I. On one occasion he had gone to seek her out at Farnborough. Whether it was to please his grandmother, or to satisfy his curiosity, or even because he obeyed an instinct of chivalrous courtesy, he asked her to receive him. The Empress could not refuse his wish; he was the grandson of the woman whose guest and friend she was, and she agreed to see him. He himself had the tact and delicacy not to appear before her in the uniform of the German officer who had conquered France, but to wear the English uniform which her son had worn. . . This time, no doubt, the young Emperor is preparing a master-stroke for tomorrow morning, and tonight he will ruminate the lapidary phrase with which he will greet her in the Norwegian fjord; but tomorrow morning, alas! the *Thistle* will be on her way to Trondhjem.

* * *

When we arrive in the port of Trondhjem we see the English fleet. The Emperor's plan is revealed to us, so we believe, because with this Prince of the unexpected one never knows what will happen next day. Everything leads us to think that he is faithful to his system of compensations, his diplomatic habit of establishing a balance, of holding the scales level with one another. Having given hopes to the French Government by his theatrical gesture to the *Iphigénie*, he wants . . . to visit the English fleet and throw a little soda on the champagne [*sic*]. He wants to drink to the Royal Navy: one of those toasts which will have no significance, but will nonetheless echo resoundingly all over Europe.

The Commodore comes to put himself at Her Majesty's orders [*sic*]. He tells me that at any moment he expects his Sovereign's terrible grandson, although he has not chosen to announce his arrival. In fact I seem to see it already: the white mass of the *Hohenzollern*, plated with gold, sparkling under this everlasting sun of July. He will come forward into the middle of the Fleet, it will salute him with salvoes of gunfire until he goes to visit each ship and call the sailors – these sailors, too – his friends. And then British respect will dissolve into Southern enthusiasm: Hip, hip, hurrah! for the greatest stage-manager of this dying century. He will leave republicans discomposed and a Caesar triumphant![3]

11

On the somewhat unexpected date of 31 May 1901, Primoli sent a postcard to Robert de Montesquiou: 'Happy century!'[1] He himself was far from happy:

> Until we are twenty we enjoy the tales that we are told: adventures, extraordinary travels, love stories; from 20 to 40 we live these tales, these travels, these novels, which start up joyfully at dawn and die away in a melancholy sky. After 40 we hardly take any interest except in the stories that we tell ourselves: histories most often created from our dreams and memories, from what might have been and what occurred. I have reached this stage in life, I obey this need of the soul which urges us to open our hearts – only too happy if our own natural relief can procure an hour of forgetfulness for those who seek sincerity. It is enough for us to be sincere for others to find themselves in us; but not everyone can be sincere.[2]

Primoli had just passed his fiftieth birthday. A few months later came the event which, he must have known, would be the greatest sorrow in his life. On 30 September, when, for nearly twenty years, she had lingered in a spiritual limbo, his mother died.

> I see her for the last time in her lovely room at Ariccia [so he was to write, ten years later] . . . She is lying motionless on her great lemon-wood bed, she is beginning to fall asleep in eternal sleep. . . And then I lie down quietly, myself, on the edge of her big bed, in the hope that she will bear me away on the long journey from which there is no return. And, as I had done at night when I was a child, I take the small white hand which is lying limply on the

sheet. . . I clasp it in mine, and bear it to my lips. . . When the soul had flown, this hand still remained, and I laid it on my eyes, which were full of tears.[3]

*　*　*

His bereavement was not unexpected, but it was devastating. It was, no doubt, this summer that he told Princess Mathilde: 'When I stop trying to forget, I am overcome again by grief . . . which perhaps only your affection can, at times, assuage.'[4]

Now, it seemed, he had no future but a continuation of the social round: he would be committed, for ever, to the unhappy introspection, the inner loneliness which he had known since his early manhood. He had lost the essential sense of being needed.

Paris, July 1902

I am always surprised, flattered and touched to find that I exist for somebody. I am well aware that I am useless in this world, and it is certainly not false pride which makes me talk like this. One of the losses I have known in losing my mother has been the loss of knowing that someone needed me – a feeling which gave me back my self-respect. Now that she has gone, I feel that I am no longer good for anything, and no longer useful to anyone, and that I only exist through memory.

I am worth much less than people say, but a little more than they believe. . .

And I often weep when I am all alone.[5]

Paris, 1902

And now it begins before my eyes: the procession of marriageable young girls and young women. Friends of mine have taken my isolation to heart, and they are changing the slides in the magic lantern. A nice setting for a few profiles of women.

Yesterday evening someone arranged a meeting for me with a little Parisian widow. She wasn't very pretty, but she was attractive and charming, lively and witty. She is a fanatical nationalist, and she let her joy overflow when I confessed that, having been a Dreyfusard, I had become indifferent again at the sight of the consequences of the affair, and refused to compromise with the Dreyfusards all the same. 'Oh Monsieur,' she cried, 'what pleasure you give me! You are the first foreigner I have heard who talks like this!' And the evening ended with reading poems by

Hugo, Théo, Sully Prudhomme, and Madame de Noailles' fine poem to France.[6]

An evening wasted. Yesterday evening I was fully aware of my old age [sic]. I found myself in Paris with absolute freedom, and banknotes in my pocket. Night had fallen, and the boulevards were dazzling with lights. Well, I didn't feel attracted by the aroma of a good restaurant, or by a poster for a fine performance, or by the heady perfume of the women, or by any whim, permitted or forbidden, which I could have allowed myself, since I am accountable to no one – alas! – for what I say and do. I dined in a modest restaurant, I took the common omnibus, and I went home to bed at 9.30 – alone![7]

One person clearly needed him.

Rome, 3 December [1902]

I am summoned to Paris by sad letters and urgent telegrams from my dear Aunt Mathilde, whose affection gives me the illusion that I am still good for something in this life. Her telegram said: 'I am waiting for you with open arms,' and her last note was just as cruel: 'Dear beloved Gégé, I'm still waiting for you, don't make me wait too long. I am alone and unhappy, and I don't believe in life. I embrace you, and hope to see you soon. Your old and desolate aunt, M.'

It is perhaps the first time that this adorable woman, who was made to love and to be loved, dares to tell herself – dares to write: 'I don't believe in life. . .' In another letter, she writes to me: 'Come and make me go on living!' And those heartfelt words are all the more touching when one considers that they come from someone who is simple, upright, and unaffected, averse to all fine phrases and fine writing.[8]

On 7 December he answered, on mourning paper: 'The thought of seeing you again and feeling your maternal embrace has decided me to leave Rome. . . Let us hold each other close, my dear Aunt, let us make society out of our two solitudes! I count on you – on you alone!'[9]

* * *

He counted, as always, on the Princess; but he needed, still, to

249

lose himself in the vortex of social life. In 1903 Fernand Gregh, the young man of letters, arrived in Rome. He and his wife had already met Primoli at Mme Arman de Caillavet's, in Paris: 'A charming, rather old-maidish man, who, [Anatole] France used to say, was as amazed as we should be to be a Bonaparte.'[10] Now they encountered him again.

> We had settled [Gregh remembered] in the foreign quarter, Piazza Trinità dei Monti, in the house in which Keats had died... At night, through the wide open windows, as I worked, I heard the eternal splashing of the fountains of Rome. This apartment had been inhabited, before us, by Siegfried Wagner... Every day, a man came from a neighbouring trattoria to bring us our lunch, and it was only in the evening that we dined at the restaurant for a few lira, including a delightful wine. Everything in Rome in those days cost virtually nothing, at least for the French, because of the rate of exchange. The food was so good that we sent for dishes from the restaurant, and gave a big dinner-party to which we invited Anatole France, Mme Arman de Caillavet, Comte Primoli, and writers and poets of the day.[11]

Primoli was glad to return their hospitality:

> Comte Primoli [continued Gregh] was avid to entertain all the famous visitors who were passing through Rome. A lover of the arts and of poetry, he gave them sumptuous and cordial hospitality in the palazzo which he had inherited from his mother, *née* Charlotte Bonaparte. One day we found ourselves with him in the lift which was taking us to the Comtesse Pasolini's. She had invited us to dinner. Primoli was holding a little package wrapped in tissue-paper, which he was carefully guarding against any collisions. 'Do you know what I've got here?' he enquired mysteriously, while the old quilted lift went up in its slow, majestic way – and at the same time he unfolded the paper. We saw a plaster object which looked like a goblet turned upside-down. 'I should say it was a cast,' I answered, 'the cast of a woman's breast.' 'You're quite right,' he replied, 'it's Pauline Borghese's.' And as I repeated, slightly taken aback: 'Pauline, your...?' 'Yes, my great-aunt. I'd promised it to Mme Pasolini, I'm going to put it on her table, and give her a surprise.' Enchanting Italy, so enamoured of beauty that a Bonaparte can bring his great-aunt's breast as a present for a woman friend!
> On another occasion, Primoli invited us to a big lunch at Frascati. Among the other guests, there were Anatole France, Mme

Arman, Réjane, and a young writer from South America, very much in love with Réjane who, I think, returned his passion. He was none other than Dario Nicodemi. We know that since then he has had quite a brilliant career as a dramatist, and was even president of the Society of Italian Dramatists; but at that time, at his début, he was unknown, so unknown that when Primoli gave everyone their places, he forgot his name and said to him: 'And you sit there – I mean you, the Argentine.' The Parisians were all enchanted to meet again, in this corner of the world which was hardly foreign for artists, but was, nonetheless, out of Paris. And so the conversation was as lively and sparkling as you could imagine.[12]

There was, as Gregh recorded, a more dramatic meeting.

One day, as he was piloting a very old lady who was hobbling with her stick though the great museums of the Eternal City, Comte Primoli came to seek me out to present me to her: it was the Empress Eugénie.
'Madame, may I present Gregh, the Poet?'
'Are you Greek, monsieur?'
Well, so as not to put the great lady in the wrong, and to simplify things, I answered yes, and the conversation ended.[13]

It was not their only encounter. Soon afterwards, the author of *La Beauté de vivre* witnessed a very curious scene which, he confessed,

I should hardly believe if I had not been present myself and even played a small part in it. . .
It was, again, during a visit to a museum, but this time in the open air, in the gardens of the Villa Albani. We were strolling through them, Mme Arman, Anatole France, my wife and I, stopping at the statues which had been unearthed from this illustrious soil, and breathed again in the very spot where they had long been concealed. There appeared in the distance, with the same Primoli, her habitual guide, the same old lady.
'Monsieur,' said Mme Arman, 'there's the Empress!'
'Let's be off,' said Anatole France. 'Primoli wants to present me, and I don't want it.'
'What harm would it do you?'
'No, madame, I won't have it.'
And he slipped away, from plinth to plinth, and vanished behind the statues.

251

But, despite the old lady's age, the couple gradually approached. . .

'My dear friend,' France said to me, 'do me a service: stand behind this plinth and warn me if she comes too close. I shall admire that fine group over there at my leisure.'

I took up my position. . . France was able to escape in time, and the couple, who were not going fast, gave up the thought of reaching him, and vanished. . . It will, I think, have been given to very few to witness such a curious scene: the Empress Eugénie pursuing Anatole France from statue to statue in the gardens of the Villa Albani.[14]

* * *

In his own conversations, now, with the Empress Eugénie, Primoli urged her to talk about the past. One day, at the turn of the century, as the *Thistle* cruised off Naples, she talked about the dramatic circumstances of her birth.

On 5 May 1826, five years to the day since the death of Napoleon, a violent earthquake shook Granada and sent the terrified inhabitants out of their shaking houses.

Among the people driven out of their homes was the young Comtesse de Teba, who was about to give birth to her second child, and no doubt her emotion hastened its arrival. She just had time to take refuge in a garden, and there, in a grove of rose-trees and cypresses, she brought into the world a little girl with blue eyes and golden hair. The stormy prelude of nature which preceded the first cries of the new-born child was the prologue to the most dramatic of all lives; this human being was predestined to glory and disaster: her life was to pass between the summit and the abyss. No one climbed higher and no one fell lower. . .

Thirty years after the fall of the Empire, the Empress Eugénie found herself on her yacht, the *Thistle*, in the gulf of Naples. A sudden storm had unleashed the elements, and Vesuvius was threatening. Although the Sovereign admired the great spectacles of nature, she evoked the scenes we have just recalled and she allowed herself to describe them: 'I cannot express the terror I feel at thunder and lightning. I was born during an earthquake: my mother had run to seek refuge in a grove of laurels and cypresses [*sic*], and it was under a tree that I came into the world: it was an omen of my destiny.'[15]

She had in fact been born in a tent in her parents' garden; but, not for the first time, Primoli embroidered history.

She talked, too, of her childhood. It was in 1839, on Stendhal's last visit to Paris, that Mérimée had introduced him to the Comtesse de Teba, now Comtesse de Montijo, and her daughters.

I asked the Empress [wrote Primoli] if she remembered Stendhal. 'Remember *Monsieur Beyle!*' she cried. 'He was the first man who made my heart beat – and beat violently! . . . He came to my mother's every Thursday; that evening, in honour of our great friend, we went to bed at 9 instead of 8, we didn't have dinner, we were so impatient to hear him! Whenever the bell rang we rushed to the door. . . At last we brought him back in triumph, into the salon, each of us holding one of his hands, and we settled him in his armchair by the fire. . . He used to take one of us on each knee: we didn't give him time to breathe before we reminded him of the victory where he had left our Emperor, the Emperor we had thought about all the week. . . He had inspired us with his fanaticism for the only man whom he admired. . . We wept and laughed and shuddered, we went mad. . . He showed us the Emperor radiant in the sun of Austerlitz, pale in the snows of Russia, dying at Saint Helena. . .

'My mother used to intervene and admonish us: "Leave him in peace!" . . . "It doesn't matter," he used to say, as he embraced us. "Only little girls understand great things; their approval consoles me for the criticisms of fools and bourgeois."

'When he returned to his post [at Civitavecchia] and we made our way back to Spain, a regular correspondence kept us in touch.'[16]

Grief had long brought the Empress closer to Princess Mathilde. In 1880, before she set out on her vist to the Cape, to see for herself where her son had died, she had sent Mathilde a portrait, by Isabey, of the King of Rome.[17] They had corresponded, sometimes tartly, about Bonapartist politics; but when, in 1883, she had learned of Prince Napoleon's imprisonment, Eugénie had remembered 'only one thing, that he bears the same name as I do. There are times,' she had told Mathilde, 'when dissidence must give place to unity.'[18] She had, repeatedly, asked Mathilde to Farnborough. 'I still hope,' she had written in 1885, 'that, despite your horror of the sea, you will decide to come Farnborough, it would be easy, when you are at Dieppe'[19]; and Primoli had assured his aunt, with a certain optimism: 'The Empress still hopes that I can bring you to Cap Martin!'[20] Eugénie had written to Mathilde on the death of Popelin: 'I myself have suffered so much that I share all suffering. . .'[21] She had sent her a telegram on the death of Dumas *fils*: 'Nothing replaces a faithful friend. I acutely feel your grief.'[22] Now, on 9 May 1903, from the Villa Cyrnos, at Cap Martin, she wrote to her:

I am distressed to see from your kind letter that you are despondent and sad. I understand that your solitude weighs upon you, and yet you are surrounded by faithful and devoted friends. Griefs . . . seem heavier as one gets on in life. I wish with all my heart that I could be with you more often, but, alas! my destiny has condemned me to a life of wandering![23]

12

It was with the Empress that Primoli spent much of the summer of 1903. This time, on her steam-yacht, the *Thistle*, they cruised in Italian waters. As he recorded:

> The *Thistle* left Spalato on Monday, 6 July 1903, . . . and was due to arrive in Venice next morning at ten o'clock. . . A gondola drew alongside the yacht, and I saw a whole bundle of letters and newspapers, and particularly the yellow envelopes which meant telegrams. . . These missives told me that my dear Aunt Mathilde had had a fall, and that she summoned me to Her at Saint-Gratien.[1]

She had fallen down the spiral stairs from her bedroom to her studio, and she had fractured her femur. She was very old and tired, and she had no overwhelming wish to live. She recognized that this would be the end.

Friends recognized it, too. On 21 August, from Hendaye, in the Basses-Pyrénées, Pierre Loti wrote to Gégé, at Saint-Gratien:

> I am delighted with the good news of the Princess which you are kind enough to send me. . . Please would you give Her Highness my best wishes for her complete recovery?
>
> I have one more request to make to you. . . I should like to keep a portrait of Her Highness; but, last month, I looked for one, in vain, in the arcades of the rue de Rivoli. If you could possibly get me the smallest photograph, you can't imagine how pleased I should be; but I realize I'm very bold to ask.
>
> In ten days or so I'm setting off for my beloved Orient again. . .[2]

He sailed on the *Vautour* for the Levant with a signed photograph of *la bonne princesse*.

On 22 September, Gégé returned to his notes:

. . . Here I am, all alone at St Gratien with my poor Aunt. She had a fall at the beginning of July, she fractured her femur. . . The doctors all tell her that she will never be able to walk again, and I have decided to devote myself entirely to the poor invalid.

Princess Clotilde arrived from M[oncalieri], Prince Louis from Tiflis, summoned by Louise Rasponi and Lucien Rocca – who were at St Gratien at the time of the accident – 3 July – but they have all left again, and I am staying on alone with my dear invalid. The Princess was so astonishingly young that in April I still saw her *décolletée*, doing the honours of her *salon*, she seemed to be twenty years younger than she was; but since her fall she has become her age, and her dear face has become the face of a woman of eighty. She is aware of the physical change which has taken place in Her, and her feminine coquetry suffers from it. . .

The Princess has never dyed her hair, but she touched up her hair with cosmetics [*sic*], and her false piece on top of her plaits and her real chignon gave the illusion of hair which was still young. The Princess felt such repulsion for white hair, that her old lady's-maid, who had no pretentions at all to youth and beauty, tinted her hair so as not to alarm her mistress. . . The Princess had a horror of everything which suggested old age and death: She didn't like the country in winter, she was saddened by the leafless trees. . .

And now, when she becomes aware of her state and age, she has fits of despondency which nothing can appease. . .

The Princess cannot eat any more, . . . She has grown so weak that I can see her fade, waste away and die. . . She is also suffering from acute rheumatism in her poor legs, which have been immobilized for nearly three months. . . The Princess wanted to give me little mementoes to show her gratitude: her bust by the Comte de Nieuwerkerke; a cast of her hand in Algerian marble; some bouquet-holders from the balls which were given at the Tuileries; some glass; her portrait drawn by Amaury Duval. . . But nothing is worth the look and the gentle smile with which She thanked me for having stayed with Her, for giving her the comfort of knowing that she is not alone.[3]

[1 October]

[When she left Saint-Gratien for Paris], we covered the stretcher with her sheets and with a blue silk counterpane which I had brought her from Rome. . . I walked beside her, holding her hand to reassure her as we came down the stairs. . .

The Princess wore her little white cambric nightcap, her grey hair [*sic*] was drawn in waves over her emaciated cheeks . . . She wore a violet dressing-gown . . . We made our entrance into Paris down the avenue de la Grande Armée.[4]

In his diary for 1903, Primoli enlarged on his notes.

Thursday, 1 October

It is the great day of departure. We must decide to leave St Gratien before the cold is upon us. The poor Princess is in anguish, not knowing how the journey will pass. . . The [ambulance-]coupé opens at the back, the nurses slide in the stretcher with the poor invalid: I have a vision of the coffin! . . . I try to hide it from the dear invalid by getting into the coupé first, to receive her. I sit down beside Her with Dr Berger. . . She looks at her park, she greets the gardeners, and the woman at the lodge who asks in tears as she opens the gates: 'Will she ever come back to this dear Saint-Gratien which she has created?' All the way to Paris, the little street urchins are crying out gaily: 'There's the ambulance!' and trying, with cruel curiosity, to have a look at the invalid. She holds my hand convulsively. . . We are shaken and tossed about, the journey has never seemed so long to me. . . She is not in pain, but she is apprehensive, and in anguish. The motor-cars, the bicycles, the railway, the big waggons. . . Everything alarms her. . . And then, at last, the fortifications! Paris! The Arc de Triomphe. She sees it, and blows it a kiss – the kiss of the Niece for the Uncle [Napoleon].[5]

* * *

Dear Princess [wrote Ernest Hébert, on 3 October],

We saw Gégé this morning. . . It seems, from what he told us, that you are glad you have returned to your Paris home. . .

I am so sorry not to be there when you come back. Alas, I am still confined to my bed for a few days; so it is only by letters that I shall be able to give Your Highness a sign of affection, dear Gégé will read them to you and answer me, and then Gaby will come and see you, dear Princess, and time, which bears away our joys, will also bear away our sorrows![6]

The letter remains among Primoli's papers; and among them, too, is a letter from Marcel Proust: a letter dated simply 'Tuesday' – which, perhaps, was written on 29 December 1903. Proust knew how Primoli had suffered from his mother's death:

. . .These dreadful memories were not enough. Reality had to give you, a second time, the sight of what had caused you such grief. I have been isolated for too long to know anything about the Princess's state except what one can learn from the concierge in the rue de Berry. But if the Princess is aware of her state – and I profoundly hope that this is spared her – how it must hurt her to think that she must leave you. She loved you so much that when I close my eyes and try to find, in memory, the most gracious image of the Princess, the one most full of charm, of smiling love, of tenderness, I think of her at the moment when she spoke your name, your *petit nom*, and said that you would be returning soon.[7]

* * *

Friday, 1 January 1904

The poor dear Princess is growing weaker every hour. . . She can hardly move her lips to kiss me. For nearly a week, now, she has lost the power of speech. And the *hôtel* is full of baskets of flowers for the New Year. Her face lit up with a sudden light of admiration when I took her a basket of red carnations from Masson. She still loves flowers, at the moment when people no longer love anything. Today she had to have an injection of morphia, She was in such pain. . . And when she came out of her sleep, I gave her a single long-stemmed rose sent by [President] Carnot. I said to her: 'Carnot offers you a rose: La France.' And the rose opened, and shed its petals on her face and on her emaciated hands. . . A sinister omen. I remember that recollection of radiant youth when, She used to tell us, men could not distinguish a rose-petal from her cheek. And now! . . .[8]

Saturday, 2 January

. . . Princess Clotilde wants to have her given the last sacraments. I send for the curé of Saint-Gratien. He arrives at 10 o'clock. She is barely conscious, but She hears and her eyes are open. I lean over her bed and smile at her, holding her attention throughout the rites so that she is not aware of the priest and the dismal formalities. . . I smile at her affectionately, and her eyes do not leave mine. . . Then she falls into a coma which seems to me the supreme sleep. . . I tell the friends who want to kiss her hands for the last time: Coppée, the Massons, d'Ocagne, . . . etc. The Empress. The servants hurry off. At 7 o'clock she draws her final breath.[9]

The will was opened, and I have the [satisfaction] to discover that my attentions were disinterested. I am not even mentioned in the will which Benedetti had made her write. In the codicil added in 1895 She leaves me all her papers: a sign of trust.[10]

Monday, 4

I fulfilled her wishes, and found a carnation and a rose to be buried with her in her coffin. I chose the rose 'La France', as a symbol of the country which she had loved all the more since she had been born in exile. She was put into her coffin, I laid the rose and the carnation on her heart, as she had wanted, with her crucifix and a medallion of the Emperor.[11]

* * *

That day, Proust wrote again to Primoli:

Cher Monsieur,

I went to the rue de Berry, and I asked to see you. They told me that it was impossible. Let me just tell you that I weep bitterly with you, because I loved the Princess with infinite respect – and because it hurts me so much to think that you are so unhappy, and with all one's heart one would wish you so much happiness, you with your grieving, wounded heart, whom one would like to see escape every cruel blow. For a long time I have foreseen the grief that [such a blow] must cause you. I suffered physically at the thought that you were going to suffer again, that all the sadnesses of your life would condense and weigh upon you, more heavily than ever, at the moment of this last misfortune. . . You have at least the comfort of knowing that you were the delight – the profound delight, the happiness – and also the charming gaiety, the perpetual entertainment – in the Princess's life. No one made her feel, as you did, the worth of gaiety and the charm of tenderness. It was you who always brought to her lips that exquisite smile we shall never forget. We shall all remain grateful to you, those of us to whom the Princess's happiness was dear, those who will always treasure the delightful, smiling image they will keep of her.[12]

Her funeral was held in the little village whose name had come to be inseparable from her own. On Thursday, 7 January, Primoli recorded in his diary: 'At 9 o'clock left by motor-car with the Empress Eugénie . . . for St Gratien.'[13]

Six

1

The death of Princess Mathilde marked the end of an age in Primoli's emotional life. He had lost the constant maternal figure which he had needed. He had lost, perhaps, a sense of significance, for she in turn had needed him as a confidant and escort, and as a son. By her death he had also lost the rue de Berry and Saint-Gratien, the brilliant setting for much of his existence. He had become, by this one event, the repository of the historic past.

Jules Claretie recognized that 'if Count Joseph Primoli, the inheritor of Princess Mathilde's papers, ever produces a volume of memoirs out of this pile of different testimonies, he will write one of the most valuable and most remarkable books of our time.'[1] Primoli welcomed the legacy as a sign of trust; but 'what I lack,' he wrote, predictably, 'is a confidant for my literary plans, my psychological observations, my memories, the anecdotes I have collected and want to make other people enjoy. In short, I have the need, the itch to write, and I lack the energy, the necessary will to hold the pen.'[2]

After the Princess's death, he needed a new base in Paris. He found an apartment at 19, avenue du Trocadéro (later the avenue du Président-Wilson). Jules Troubat, the former secretary of Sainte-Beuve, saw his opportunity. He offered to sell him a watercolour by Princess Mathilde: a painting of an Italian girl, which she had once given to Sainte-Beuve. He also offered Primoli a picture of the Princess with her dogs in the familiar park at Saint-Gratien. Sainte-Beuve had admired the view of the park from the dining-room window, and, proud of his affection, she had had this painting done for him.[3] Primoli filled his two salons, now, 'with a medley of disparate pieces of

263

furniture and unrelated things, where worthless trifles stood next to treasures beyond price. On the mantelpiece reclined a small version of the statue of Pauline Borghese, sculpted naked by Canova. On the walls hung kakemonos, bearing the signatures of writers. It was there that he received his friends from Paris, Rome and elsewhere.'[4]

*   *   *

One of the first must have been his beloved Eleonora Duse. In 1904 he noted:

> La Duse announces that she is now in Paris . . . She has been a friend for 25 years and I have a very real admiration and affection for her: she is the most honest man [sic] and the greatest lady I know. I left her in Rome, desperate, abandoned, and on the verge of suicide: she had even bought a pistol to make an end of it, because she found herself on the brink of material and emotional bankruptcy. And I find her revived, appeased, calmed and cured . . .
>
> Gratitude overflows from her heart . . . She feels the need to cry it out. It is the first time, she says, that she has known *material* gratitude. A great and generous Jew appeared: [Robert Mendelssohn], the husband of her friend [Giulietta Gordigiani]; he had a noble soul, and he made a noble gesture . . . She had contracted 200,000 francs of debts in order to stage the *Fille de Jorio* which her health no longer allowed her to perform; he paid her debts, he put her affairs in order, he gave her back the peace she needed if she was to go on living . . . And she said: 'That is life! For five years I worked to help a man of genius in whom I believed; it was someone else, who owed me nothing, who helped me . . . I wonder what I have done to deserve this deliverance? . . . I had told the *Other* [Gabriele d'Annunzio] that I was on the verge of bankruptcy and that I didn't know how to go on. In order to continue to support his work I had to revive *La Dame aux camélias* – 700 francs assured at the box-office. I had to ask him for his permission because I had contracted to perform his works exclusively. He agreed, but he didn't answer directly. So I gave the *Dame* because the performance would fill up a few holes . . . In the third act I received a telegram signed Gabriele: "Is it true that you have changed, that you have abandoned the mission?" This telegram was a blow which went straight to my heart . . . I answered, but how could I go on acting in the state in which he plunged me by this reproach? How would I have the strength to stay on stage, to

264

find the words and gestures? Well, overwrought as I was, I was Marguerite as I had never been, and I brought the audience to its feet.'[5]

On 15 April 1905, according to *L'Écho de Paris*, Primoli was the guest of another theatrical friend. 'Bald, and white-bearded, Count Joseph Primoli is dining this evening at Mme Emma Calvé's. With his twinkling eyes and quietly sceptical smile, he suggests a very worldly Eternal Father, with charming manners: an Eternal Father whom one could well see dancing in a cotillion.'[6] Proust was perhaps aware that Primoli was only fifty-three, and he read such comments with surprise. 'I don't know that Primoli will have been so pleased . . . It seems to me that his beard is fair even if it has turned a little white, and that he isn't in the least a venerable old man.'[7] Proust was fond of Primoli, and warmly admired him. Primoli, he assured a friend, might not be a Frenchman, but he was 'very worthy of being one'.[8] He was always worthy of inclusion in a gossip column. On 15 May, said *Le Figaro*, he dined at Francis de Croisset's with a friend of Proust's: the composer Reynaldo Hahn.[9] On 21 June Hahn announced to Proust that Mme de Pourtalès was 'coming *to take tea* on Saturday with her *two daughters* (!!) and Primoli (!!!).'[10]

Such coquetry was vain: there was not the remotest likelihood, now, that he would marry. He had chosen to lead a bachelor life, and it had been uncommonly brilliant; but he was increasingly lonely and introspective.

I am worth much less than people think and rather more than they believe [he confided in his diary in 1905].

I am anti-sceptical.

People praise me for being kind to my inferiors. There is no merit for me in this behaviour, because quite honestly I do not consider anyone inferior to myself. I feel that I am inferior to everyone because I lack determination, energy, courage, self-esteem, ambition and vanity, the will to live, etc.: all the qualities or failings which constitute a personality.

Hébert moved me to tears when he said that for him and my friends I remained the legitimate heir of Princess Mathilde, the only real one, the one who had inherited her spirit and her friends, the one who had gathered in the affection which she had sown. I no longer laugh except to make people laugh.[11]

* * *

That year he returned to Egypt; he had last been there in 1869 to watch the Empress open the Suez Canal. Now the Empress was old, deposed and in exile; and Théophile Gautier, for whom he had stolen the silver sprig of cotton from the cotton-field, had been dead for more than thirty years.

Primoli was all too aware of the passing of time.

Paris, March 1906

What I love about Paris, though I sometimes feel bewildered and confused there, . . . is that in Paris you learn how to use every minute: as soon as you have a moment to spare, you don't waste it, it is so rare and precious that you determine to use it. I have sometimes written a page in Paris when I had ten minutes to wait, while, in the country, all I did for a whole day was to *think* of writing. Here they say 'time is money', in other places they try to *ammazzare il tempo* . . . One should send young men to Paris to train their minds, just as one sends them to England to train their bodies: it is the platform for intellectual sport, and here you learn to return a word just as somewhere else you learn to return a ball . . . On the banks of the Seine you learn to catch an idea in flight, without needing to underline or even indicate it. Perhaps you are frivolous here, but you are prompt – *quick* – you judge superficially, but you judge fast. There is the reverse of the medal, of course, but it is still the medal of the right stamp. Do not let us confuse French wit with Parisian stupidity. One of them travels across the mountains and the seas – Molière and Beaumarchais – it is almost understood in Rome and in New York. The other does not go beyond the fortifications of Paris.[12]

He himself often crossed the seas. In 1906, the Comtesse de Behague invited him on a cruise on *Le Nirvana*. Among the other guests was the artist Jacques-Émile Blanche, son of the doctor who had treated Charlotte Primoli at his asylum in Passy. While the yacht was at Cowes, Blanche and Primoli were moved to see Queen Victoria's house at Osborne still untouched. It was five years since her death, and time had not yet replaced her real presence by a biographer's preposterous image.[13] Another guest on *Le Nirvana* was the poet and

266

novelist Henri de Régnier, a son-in-law of José-Maria de Heredia.

During the two months that we spent in the Mediterranean [he recalled], Primoli appeared to me every day just as he was, with his curiosities, his good nature, his little susceptibilities, the inoffensive manias of a fussy and artful confirmed bachelor, with his naïve tricks and his friendly kindnesses, with everything that made him a charming character in historical comedy, with his amusing quarrels with his valet Nereo. I remember him like this in Athens, Cyprus, Damascus, Constantinople, during the long conversations on board and the walks when we put into port, with his inseparable apparatus slung over his shoulder, his nonchalant, rather heavy gait, treading with a lazy step the rugged soil of the Acropolis or the smooth marble flagstones of the Green Mosque at Broussa.[14]

2

He remained, as he had always been, an asset to society. He was welcome for his gaiety. The *'little demon* of the household'[1] at Saint-Gratien had become the audacious raconteur, the joker who delighted the grandson of *le bon Théo* with his extravagant inventions. Dr Gautier had heard him, once, lamenting the damage which was done to works of art in wartime. The Government, he said, was to have the Louvre mounted on a gigantic lift, so that in case of danger the entire museum and its contents could simply disappear underground. Primoli's conviction, when he talked such nonsense, was so plausible that his victims did not see that he was joking until he himself confessed it. He had also inherited his father's taste for outrageous behaviour. One evening, at the rue de Berry, he had noticed the arrival of the Minister who represented Norway and Sweden. The diplomat had been accompanied by his ample wife. Primoli had bowed to each of her breasts in turn, and announced: 'My respects to Sweden . . . and to Norway.'[2]

And yet, for all his indolence, his indecision, for all his social frivolity, Primoli was deeply serious.

Beyond the vicissitudes of princes and the downfalls of régimes, he kept [so André Chaumeix was to write] a noble sense of the grandeurs of history. Everything merged and harmonized for him in the natural and honest love of what contributes to a country's glory. Independent of politics, he was content to be, with quiet pride, the survivor of a past, and, with sympathy, the witness of the present . . .

Italy, his native land, and France, his second native land, inspired him with an equal love. He often added that he felt a little more Roman in Paris and a little more Parisian in Rome. On all occasions, he remained the devoted servant of both countries. The Villa Médicis and the Palazzo Farnese counted him among their greatest friends, and no one more deeply appreciated the company of Mgr Duchesne. He liked to bring together the politicians, ambassadors and guests of every kind who chose to visit him in his palace by the Tiber or in his sunlit apartment in the avenue du Président-Wilson. Every year, come the month of May, he arrived in Paris and he often spent the whole summer there. Autumn or, at least, the Christmas festivities took him back to Rome. For many years, as long as his mother was alive, this rhythm was absolutely regular . . . He made no exception to the rule unless it was to answer the appeal of some of the countless friends who wanted to make him travel with them: especially the appeal of the Empress Eugénie, who invited him to Cap Martin or on her yacht. These absences scarcely troubled his existence, which was filled by his social life.

Although he resolutely stood apart from serious affairs, he was too informed, he heard too many conversations, not to have a useful word to say when occasion demanded. Never did he fail to work to strengthen the friendship between the two countries which he loved, and to bring to light what unites, not what divides . . .

Count Primoli took the most eager interest in literature. He had soon understood that, if he was not destined to play a political rôle which he did not want, he could be a cultural ambassador between Rome and Paris. This mission he accomplished with all the delicacy of a Latin, all the active goodwill of an amateur who had a genuine predilection for writers and artists . . . In the *salon* of Princess Mathilde, who had treated him as a nephew, he had known all the celebrities of the age. After the Princess died, he was anxious to continue what she had done so well, to keep his old friendships, and to add newcomers every year, welcoming everyone: courteous, mischievous, and perhaps – at least at times – amused. He liked to have people round him. He enjoyed visits, intimate meetings, piquant, motley social mixtures. It was his pleasure to entertain the most illustrious and the beginners, Gabriele d'Annunzio, Anatole France, Sarah Bernhardt, La Duse and the latest winner of the Prix Goncourt.

It needed all his personal qualities to preside successfully over these ceremonies. The centre of the gatherings was really himself, by the sole power of his somewhat caustic bonhomie, his perfect manners, his ingenious nonchalance, and the supreme gift of simplicity. He was of medium height, and corpulent like a

Venetian nobleman, fresh-faced, his beard well trimmed. His eyes were both childlike and kind under their heavy lids, and bright, with a gleam of malice. Although he was nobody's fool, he was indulgent and obliging, and one knew that he had a fund of great understanding and great kindness. He was capable, when he chose, of gravity. As soon as a subject seemed to him to deserve it, he expressed his opinion, without insistence, in his slow and very quiet way. He would say: 'I don't know, but it seems to me . . . ', and his opinion was always full of wisdom. And, without seeming to do so, he even taught a little lesson. A very young man, uninhibited at the end of an evening, was amusing himself by shaking a cushion, and he observed that it was old and losing its feathers. The Count, who was already old, said gently: 'Yes, it's old, and it's losing its feathers, . . . but you still lean on it.' But sayings of this sort were rare. He preferred to run on the surface of things. This sage, who had heard great affairs discussed throughout his youth, chose to spend his life among trivia, and he relished their delicious uselessness.

He was not being frivolous. History, which he had lived, had shown him the importance of small causes, the unexpected relations between facts, the complexity and contradictions of characters. When time had passed, there would be a division between what mattered and what didn't matter, great people and great events would impose themselves. But, for the present, everything was confused for the witness, everything was on the same level, and Count Primoli greeted everyone with a curiosity in which there was a touch of indifference and a sort of impossibility to choose. He enjoyed the variety of the subjects which held his attention. Like a good Roman, he knew all the philosophy that is contained in Italian comedy. He smiled as he showed his quilted furniture, all his bric-a-brac and trinkets, the most valuable mementoes of the Empire, and a wonderful drawing by Ingres. He felt some indefinable inner satisfaction in appearing lordly or childlike, as he chose, and, such as he was, he was endearing and people loved him.[3]

People mistrusted him [Ferdinand Bac continued, in his *Promenades dans l'Italie nouvelle*]. People mistrusted him, though they did not admit it. But they also loved him. He had a mischievous smile which was irresistible. Had he ever loved? Women knew that they risked nothing in his company, but they sought him out although they did not actually adore him. He was charming in the highest degree. Careerists were quick to open their ears in his salons and, if need be, to confide their cases of conscience in him.

He knew how to hurt without meaning to, and how to do a service without dwelling on it.

In Rome, one met Queens, and Princes of the Church, in his palazzo. He had the air of a Maecenas who disposed of the favours of world-wide diplomacy. He protected the chartists and the Prix de Rome. He decided dynastic successions and reconciled the Nations, sometimes mortally embroiling them. And then he smoothed out every difficulty, and confidently expected not to die before he had contrived . . . a meeting between the Pope and the grandson of Victor-Emmanuel . . .

He had the curious head of a Cardinal of the Barberini age, and the Romans called him *figlio di preti*. He had his unctuous, indulgent and rather dissembling side. Could he not intrigue like a woman, repeat anecdotes, recall the gossip of the town like a hairdresser? To make friends quarrel simply for the pleasure of reconciling them again was an art at which he excelled. Creating a misunderstanding, making Forain dine with Joseph Reinach – and, if he could have done so, Lenin with the Pope – were the sort of tricks he contrived. Into these little things he put all the secret diplomacy of a great political act.[4]

* * *

Maurice Barrès met the *figlio di preti* in the studio of Princess Lucien Murat, to whom he was sitting for his portrait. Primoli

> had summoned d'Annunzio to attend the sitting and to charm the few intimates who were admitted to this studio. It was a revival of the Italian customs of the Renaissance . . .
>
> Primoli, if I remember right, was posing in a red robe, and this colour emphasized the resemblance in his features to a Roman cardinal in the time of Barberini, Urban VIII . . . Like an Eminence, he liked to be surrounded, to have his Court. He had therefore been inspired to summon 'the divine Gabriele', who, for his part, seemed charmed with this occasion for conversation.[5]

Primoli cherished his friendships with d'Annunzio, and with Proust. Early in 1907, with the intensity of an invalid and a recluse, Proust wrote to him:

> . . .Thank you with all my heart for your kindness in sending me that postcard. It is too good of you to think about my health. There is no possible cure for me. But I must not complain too much, because it has earned me such a charming thought, and brought me, suddenly, a little foretaste of the charm of Rome, a little of the

charm which I had in sometimes seeing you. There are a great many pleasant thoughts which your delightful souvenir awakes in me. And it is the privilege of solitary souls, tranquil and drowsy, like my own, that a movement once awakened there spreads and prolongs itself indefinitely. And so the thought of all the happy hours which I can never spend in Rome discovering so many beautiful things under your guidance and in your company, will long remain with me and give me great pleasure.[6]

Despite the limitations of ill-health and geography, the friendship continued. On 1 July, when Primoli was once again in Paris, Proust scribbled: 'If you are doing nothing this evening (Monday), at about ten o'clock, it would be very nice of you to come and hear Risler in a small salon at the Hôtel Ritz which has been reserved in my name.'[7] Primoli, touched by the thought, invited Proust to come and see his autograph collection. 'Thank you a thousand times,' wrote Proust. 'Alas, I hardly leave my bed once or twice a month, and so far I have never succeeded in getting up during the day. If ever I manage to improve my régime and my hours, it would give me the greatest pleasure to take advantage of the delightful honour you offer me . . . '[8]

Primoli was understandably proud of his autographs. One evening that summer, he read Barrès

a long letter in a very fine and controlled hand in which the Empress, now a woman of eighty, said that she expected nothing from history, that she knew that she had been finally condemned, sacrificed to unjust prejudices which are stronger than truth. In any case they will never hear her protest, complain, recriminate . . .

At the same time Primoli read me a letter in which Marie-Louise says that she has just learned of the death of her son's father [Napoleon I], that she has never had cause to complain of him, – and, after this brief sentence, she adds at length that what she is sad about is that she has learned this from the papers, not from Vienna, and that she sees this as a grievous sign of her family's indifference.[9]

* * *

Primoli had his likes and dislikes among the Bonapartes. Years after he had died, and his palace had become the Museo Napoleonico, Ferdinand Bac paid a visit to the ground-floor rooms where Diego Angeli, the curator, did the honours to him.

I found an atmosphere [he wrote] no doubt deprived of its old somewhat Bohemian intimacy, but enriched by many souvenirs which had acquired new value through their perfect presentation. They had also brought out of the shadows a number of treasures which Primoli himself had buried. It was his limited way of taking revenge on the Dead. He took comic reprisals on relations whom he had disliked since his childhood, through an ever-fanatical conception of his patriotism – a conception which ill accorded with his open door.

So it was that he had hidden in a cupboard all the portraits of the King of Rome which had come to him from his family. Even before the War, he had not considered him as a Napoleon, and since 1914 he had called him 'the Boche'. He had also put away the portraits of Marie-Louise, whom he boldly proclaimed 'the greatest strumpet in Europe'. But by one of those delightful inconsistencies which were his charm, all this seemed to be to the benefit of Pauline Borghese, whom he held to be the most virtuous of women. With a kind of heroism, he seemed to ignore her famous excesses, and only to see her as a gracious cousin who, one day – for the love of art and, in fine, to please him – had taken off her clothes in front of Canova, and, after this exploit, had at once resumed all her imperial dignity.

This childishness, based on great historic conjectures, was not without its savour . . .

Diego Angeli handed me a triple folding mirror, a wedding-present from Pauline to her niece Charlotte Bonaparte. On the silver initials, encrusted on the back of the mirror, which was made of some rare wood, one could see that the giver had had the initial P erased, and replaced it with a C. This economic way of changing the initials on something which had belonged to her, in order to pass it on to her niece, gave us quiet amusement. This Pauline, who had lavished millions on her clothes and jewels, readily returned to the customs of the *petite bourgeoisie* whose thrifty schemes are justified by need. The Emperor's sister turned back to her little island, where the old women, with a familiar gesture, collected the crumbs of bread from the table to finish their meal, so that nothing should be wasted. So her mother had done, before the days of Glory . . .

We found ourselves beside Pauline's sofa, on which she had posed for Canova . . . The Duchess of Alba's, immortalized by Goya, was more comfortable. It is quite certain that, in the midst of

273

all these apotheoses, the Bonapartes had never acquired that sense of comfort which comes from further back. They were ready to feel uncomfortable with angular furniture, out of respect for the Eagles, crowns and bees, those legions of bronze symbols which they caressed with their hands. They lived for the gallery. In daily life, they behaved with alarming nonchalance as soon as they found themselves out of sight of the indiscreet . . .

Once upon a time, Joseph Primoli showed us these things with sighs of tenderness which seemed to say: 'You understand what I feel'. When he talked of Pauline or of Charlotte Bonaparte, he brought them together with the same affection. 'He knows so many things,' Prince Napoleon used to say of him, 'but he doesn't know them properly' . . .

All Primoli's preferences were given to Pauline, perhaps because she had sinned the most. When he took her little slippers out of a glass case, his almond-shaped eyes grew wet with the emotion of a lover. With these pious accents, the romanticism of Saint-Gratien adorned with flowers the memory of a legendary dissolute life . . .

In the room devoted to the Jeromes, one finds intimate profiles of Princess Mathilde and of her circle, the dreadful coxcomb Nieuwerkerke, and his 'substitute', Claudius Popelin, the honest enameller. She liked *musketeers* in all their aspects. And there one finds the portrait of the young Marie Abbatucci. Silence reigned in this little room. It held so many secrets and private dramas! A scent of faded roses hung about it.

The Museo Napoleonico only tells what it wants . . . A little more, however, than its donor. He liked academic, diplomatic tittle-tattle whispered on the sly. But he hated noise.[10]

Princess Mathilde with guests at Saint-Gratien: a vignette of the *fin de siècle.*

François Coppée. This photograph, taken in Rome beside a bust of Napoleon, emphasizes the poet's well-known likeness to the Emperor.

'As small as one of his pictures, with a long flowing beard.' Ernest Meissonier in Rome, *c.* 1889.

Gabriele D'Annunzio in the Piazza S. Pietro, *c.* 1895.

'The delightful musician of my twentieth year': Paolo Tosti (centre, with white hat) and the laughing Eleonora Duse. On the left is Matilde Serao, on the far right is, probably, Tristan Bernard. The photograph was taken in March 1897.

Eleonora Duse and Primoli. Paris, 1897.

Eleonora Duse in a
gondola. Venice, *c.* 1902.

On the *Delfino*, sailing to
Corfu: a study in the
picturesque.

'I aspire after Ariccia,…
meditation in isolation.'
The *piazza* in Ariccia.
Primoli's palace is on the
right.

Napoleon-Charles
Bonaparte, the last Prince
of Canino, with his
daughters Maria (Mimi)
Gotti and Eugénie de la
Moskowa.

'And people are surprised that I find it difficult to leave her.' Primoli with his afflicted mother at the Villa Taverna, Frascati.

The Villa Cyrnos, Cap Martin, 7 May 1912. Frederik VIII of Denmark (left) talks to Lucien Daudet. The Empress Eugénie, in black, talks to the Court Marshal of Denmark and the Comtesse de Wimpffen.

'An exquisite refuge against the sullen winter.' Primoli in his library in Rome.

Primoli in his apartment in Paris: 19, avenue du Trocadéro (later avenue du Président-Wilson). This photograph was taken in the latter years of his life.

3

He loved to live well. In the early years of the century, he had acquired an apartment in Paris. He had continued to entertain on a lavish scale, to indulge his love of books and bibelots,[1] to give handsome presents, to patronize the arts, and to travel widely. Princess Mathilde had wisely not bequeathed him any money, but he was happily spending a fortune which he did not possess.[2] Not content with his seaside villa at Fiumicino, his vast, dilapidated *palazzo* at Ariccia, he was building himself a new palace in Rome. On 22 October 1909, once again in Paris, he recorded:

Left home at 9 o'clock yesterday, and escaped my building, which is still invaded, after five years, by the workmen, builders and architects. Every morning I began by having a fit of anger which dissipated during the day, and in the evening I ended by giving in to the foreman's wishes . . . I perceived too late that I was not born to build. The word 'Lotta' inscribed on the turret of my palace in memory of my Eternally Lamented [mother], is only the name of the dearest departed and not [*lutter* – to struggle] – the motto of a life of constant battle. I am not a soldier or a leader. I can neither command nor obey. I cannot be determined: at least, I lack the perseverance of determination: the glimmers of independence, the flashes of revolt in the morning, are followed by evenings of submission, the numbness of faculties, exhausted by the struggle, the need of rest, indifference, apathy, sleep . . .

There are continual meetings between me and my architect. My merits and demerits combine to make me discontented twice over.

At first glance I grasp the weak point of a thing, the one which offends my aesthetic or practical sense: I recognize it, indicate it with anger or bitterness. Then reflection makes me calm again, my ingenuity tries to repair the irreparable, my accommodating nature seeks and finds the good side of it, and turns it to the best possible account, to such an extent that I finally prefer what they have done in spite of me to what I should have liked them to do . . . Third phase: whether he has been convinced by my reasoning or terrified by my anger, the architect has taken my observations literally, and, without warning, he has hastened to change things back to what I had originally wanted. And when I find them like this, I had become so accustomed to what I had deplored, that I am once again disappointed and discontented. And so I have decided to escape these alternatives which wear down my health and spoil my character, to escape my building and not to come back until it is finished.

I am one of those who hesitate to take the catalogue of the exhibition when I go in, preferring the unexpected and the unknown, and then decide to buy it as they leave the exhibition – when it can only be a souvenir, a useless souvenir! Couldn't this little fact symbolize and specify a certain category of indecisive people, the multitude of whom are legion?[3]

*　*　*

It was a shrewd, unflattering self-portrait; and when Ferdinand Bac came to write his life of Princess Mathilde, he drew another portrait of Primoli which was equally observant and uncharitable.

Because of his mischievous wit, his amusing familiarities, his desire to please and *belong to the house*, and because of his ready compliance, he was, among the young Napoleonides, the one who always had his place. Still very young in the days of the Empire, he had been dazzled by this premature friendship with 'his aunt's poets', and he followed *le bon Théo* round wherever he went. A spoilt child, who often degenerated into an *enfant terrible*, he dared almost everything, because he was sure that he would be forgiven.

He was a *relation* but not *family*, as Countess Benedetti said, very rightly, with her subtle sense of distinctions. If the Princess ventured a somewhat severe reprimand, he accepted it compliantly. Feline, cultivated, witty, inquisitive and a story-teller, he knew how to see and hear, to arouse, provoke and conclude. He was not only uninhibited, he was also affectionate and sensitive, he neglected only the fragile friendships, but cultivated and cherished the others. In a word, people were always delighted when he arrived. They were not always sorry when he left. His verbal audacities and the far-fetched encounters he liked to arrange often gave more pleasure to him than they did to those who served as his puppets.

After the death of the Princess, he hastened to spend more time with the Empress. Her milieu naturally pleased him less, because she hated practical jokes and she understood nothing about paradoxes. He lavished attention on her and he was a real delight in her household.[4]

Réjane, on a European tour, arrived in Rome to find 'her old friend, Joseph Primoli, the inseparable companion of the Empress Eugénie'.[5]

He himself, with affectionate admiration, recalled the Empress in the early years of the twentieth century.

The Empress kept her simple habits into her extreme old age – if indeed one can call it old age: the wonderful and valiant survival of the woman who had been everything and was henceforward nothing.

In 1910 the Comtesse de Pierrefonds (she sometimes used this name) was staying at the Hôtel Continental in Paris, at the time of the disastrous flooding of the Seine.

The desperate hotel manager asked to speak to her.

'Madame,' he said, 'my hotel is three-quarters empty, and all my clients are leaving me. On account of the floods, I cannot give them the comfort that they expect. Your Majesty is almost alone here. Her presence still keeps a few foreigners here, because they dare not complain where the Empress is resigned. But if She leaves me, my last clients will leave, and I shall be obliged to shut the hotel. I therefore beg Her Majesty still to be patient, and to forgive me if I am obliged to deprive Her of the comfort which She is entitled to, more than anyone.'

'Don't worry,' she answered. 'I shall stay here until the end of my visit. Don't trouble about my material well-being: I can do without everything. Did I have a telephone or a lift, electricity or central heating when I was living at the Tuileries? And I lived there for eighteen years!'[6]

4

In November 1910, once again, Primoli found himself at Farnborough. He was there with Lucien Daudet, the novelist's son; and Lucien, who viewed him with a mixture of affection and mistrust, sent his mother an account of the visit. His letters later appeared, undated, in *Dans l'ombre de l'Impératrice Eugénie*.

> What lovely sunshine this morning, although it's winter! From my room (the same one as before) I can only see a vista of autumnal mauve and orange, and through the open window I can only hear one bird. It is very early. An old gardener, who is very old, is picking up leaves, one by one, in HM's private garden, with surprising slowness and care.
>
> An enchanting welcome yesterday evening. They had sent the motor-car to the station for me . . . I found HM alone with Primoli and that old Englishman [sic] whom I have often mentioned to you, Sir Donald Ma[c]kenzie Wallace, who was with Lord Dufferin in India.[1]

Sir Donald had also been in charge of the foreign department of *The Times*, and he was the author of books on Egypt and Russia. He was a frequent visitor to Farnborough Hill. 'Yesterday,' continued Daudet, 'Primoli went to London for *déjeuner*, Pietri was still suffering from gout . . . So I spent the day alone, so to speak, with HM, who was really *wonderful*.'[2]

He observed his fellow-guest with less admiration:

> How curious Primoli is! Sometimes paternal, sometimes icy.
>
> After dinner, I intimated that I knew that someone had said that the Empress didn't like me any more, but I said that I hadn't

278

believed it, I knew that *She always did her commissions herself.*
'When did they tell you this nonsense?' she asked, with a smile.
'Oh, a long time ago, Madame! Before I leave for Cyrnos this spring
. . . ' She laughed, and looked at Primoli, who discreetly lowered
his eyes. And then, charmingly, she patted my arm.[3]

Further visitors arrived. The Earles escaped the notice of the
Empress's biographer, and they remain, alas, unidentified.

Arrival of the Earles, the Empress is very fond of them . . .
    Primoli told me that Carpeaux was very vulgar (it's surprising
for a man whose work, genius apart, is the very opposite of
vulgar). At Saint-Gratien, he played boules at the bistro with the
servants, which embarrassed Princess Mathilde! . . .
    Yesterday we went without HM to see Princess Christian of
Schleswig-Holstein. A beautiful old house in Windsor [Great]
Park, among the deer and pheasants. A warm and delightful
welcome from the Princess, who is as good as she is nice . . . Much
affected by her brother's death [Edward VII had died on 6 May].
Apparently it was on the evening of Rostand's play [*Chantecler*]
that the King contracted the illness which was to prove fatal to
him. He had to leave the theatre before the end of the performance
. . . A charming, old-fashioned drawing room, very pretty chintzes,
all of it extremely Old England and Queen Victoria. A canary was
hopping about in a cage. It was raining. The Princess was very sad
as she talked about it all again . . .
    Primoli shows the most constant, most touching attention to the
Empress. And then, he knows how to make her laugh, even when
she doesn't want to![4]

On 14 November Prince Napoleon, the son of Prince
Napoleon and Princess Clotilde, married Princess Clementine
of the Belgians. The event roused the Empress's bitterness
about Bonapartist politics. Next day, at Farnborough, Lucien
Daudet recorded:

Yesterday I got up, as usual, at about half-past six. From half-past
eight till ten, I read a little and thought about this plan for a book
on HM. At ten o'clock Primoli and I took the Earles back to the
station – they had prolonged their weekend by a night. Then a few
errands in Aldershot. We came back here at quarter to eleven. We
didn't see HM, who appeared in the morning-room when it was
time for *déjeuner*. She looked sad and tired, and complained that

she had coughed a lot last night. We went into the dining-room in silence. Then, in the middle of *déjeuner*: 'When are the trains to London?' '2.10 at North Camp Station, Your Majesty,' answered old Bristol, who is an accurate repository of all information. 'Then I'm going to London . . . You're coming, Joseph . . . And you, too, *le petit* . . . ' . . . We rushed through our coffee, and Primoli and I flew upstairs like lightning to change our clothes completely (morning coat, etc.) in six minutes. (North Camp is quite a long way and there was no longer time to have a special train at Farnborough Station). HM got into the motor-car. 'Get in quickly!' This to Primoli. 'And Luciano? Where is he?' 'Here, Madame.' – 'And my little bag! My little bag!' Mme Pelletier [Aline Pelletier, who had been in attendance since the last two years at the Tuileries] rushed up with the little bag . . . At last we set off, the chauffeur sped to North Camp. The train was leaving; they stopped it when they saw HM. They opened a compartment for her, where we were by ourselves, and the Empress talked until we got to London. To begin with, she went through her old faithful friends, Admiral Jurien de la Gravière in the front rank, then through others who, alas, were less faithful. As Primoli and I grew indignant: 'Oh no, you mustn't be indignant . . . I used to be indignant myself, once upon a time, I used to say "why did so-and-so desert me, why did he abandon us? Why? We had always been good to him . . ." . . . It's different, now . . . I weigh the pros and cons, and think: "Why should he have been heroic? He had a wife and children . . . " I admit, I did feel hate at first, . . . and then, for a long time, I felt contempt . . . For some years, now, I have felt indulgence . . . One comes to that . . . '

Primoli and I looked at one another. She was *sublime* in her grandeur and resignation, and she was still so simple, speaking so gently: always that moderation . . . A little while later, she looked at the countryside. 'God knows I love England, but, all the same, to end my days in this mist . . . You don't make your own life, you see: life makes and unmakes you . . . ' In her town clothes: a long dress, a little black bonnet, a veil, in a corner of the railway carriage, she was as beautiful as Fate.

As soon as we reached London, we took a taxi-cab and went straight to Maples', a great resource at moments of exasperation. She looked, she chose, she bought, she went upstairs, she came down, she remembered that something was missing in a particular room, she went up again; Primoli and I were done for! At last we had tea, still at Maples'. She was now refreshed by her very tiredness, she was much enjoying herself, she thought the toast was excellent, she was laughing at everything, the waitress, the tea, the woman with the excessively solemn manner in charge of the lavatory! We were delighted, Primoli and I, to see her brightened up and pleased with her escapade. 'What a nice little outing! I haven't moved around so freely for a long time!' she said at last, as we left Maples'.

On the way back, at Waterloo Station, the carriages were crowded, and eight of us were packed into a compartment for six. No one recognized her. She was absolutely *incognito*. And then we understood: It was yesterday, Prince Napoleon's wedding at Moncalieri, and it was the eve of her own saint's day. She needed physical agitation to calm her emotional turmoil. In a low voice, haunted by memories, sitting between Primoli and me – we tried to leave her enough room – she recalled that Saint Eugénie's Day when Prince Napoleon had refused to propose her health at Compiègne, on the pretext that he could not speak extempore. Then, another day, in Corsica, he had spoken to the electors about 'this woman, raised up to the throne by an amorous caprice . . . ' Sitting close to her, I felt her trembling. 'Never . . . Never has a woman been treated as I have been! . . . ' And people say and believe that she's insensible and indifferent! . . . My God! . . .

Primoli left this morning. I got up at six o'clock to accompany him to the station. We parted from each other affectionately, and we embraced.[5]

They were soon to meet again. In the spring of 1911, Lucien duly paid his visit to the Villa Cyrnos, at Cap Martin. 'Primoli is here,' he reported on 25 March, 'complaining about his health, and, nowadays, in spite of his beard, he looks very much like the First Emperor. The Earles are here, as nice as ever, . . . Pietri, whom I like more and more . . . In the evening, we all went to Monte-Carlo to hear *Déjanire* in the Prince of Monaco's box.'[6]

281

5

The social life continued, in France and Italy. In 1911, when Jacques-Émile Blanche and his wife came to winter in Rome, it was Primoli with whom they dined on the evening after their arrival.

Count Primoli [recorded Blanche] had recently moved into his new palace. It was near the Ponte Sant' Angelo, on the banks of the Tiber, where thirty-five years earlier he had welcomed me to the tumbledown and melancholy house that his family had owned. I had also seen him at Ariccia, near Tivoli, in a villa in still worse repair which had belonged to his mother, a Bonaparte. She was not then in her right mind, and she had created an atmosphere like that of an Ibsen drama.

Gégé was more French than Italian by temperament . . . In Rome he was an unofficial ambassador of France, and his palace became a centre for artists. He brought about unexpected meetings, seating people who had quarrelled next to one another at luncheon-parties. Gégé was an *enfant terrible*. It amused him to put indiscreet questions to his guests; they had either to laugh them off or to leave the table. One day, when Eleonora Duse was his guest of honour, he had also invited Gabriele d'Annunzio's secretary. It was just after the much-advertised break between the author of *Il Fuoco* and Eleonora. Gégé turned to her, and said point-blank:

'Madame, I have put d'Annunzio's confidant next to you. I thought that you would like to hear where the traitor is hiding his latest mistress.'

The great actress, who was then quite inconsolable, . . . preserved her dignity; and, going into the dining-room, she said to the major-domo:

'Please change the card that bears my name; I shall sit at the foot of the table.'

D'Annunzio's secretary was told, when he came, that La Duse was there, and he left.

All Rome talked about the way in which Gégé had been snubbed, but the bad joke was only one of many which were forgiven him because of his genuine and practical kindness; the friendship between Eleonora Duse and Gégé did not suffer.[1]

It was a tribute to her affection and, even more, to her tolerance.

* * *

He continued to earn friendship and understandable mistrust. He remained entertaining, disarming and unpredictable. On 9 May 1912, once again from the Villa Cyrnos, Lucien Daudet wrote to his mother:

> . . . Primoli arrived on Monday, embraced me, repeated a thousand times how much he had enjoyed my book, and then said to Joachim (who repeated it to me): 'Lucien! I love him like a son!' Oh, how I dislike what HM calls 'exaggerations'! One always pays for them, and Primoli will soon curse me and detest me with no more reason . . .
>
> He arrived just in time to come to the *déjeuner* which HM gave on Tuesday for King Frederik VIII and Queen Louise of Denmark. The King has short thin whiskers, a military appearance, a quick, intelligent glance, an affable and understanding expression on his fine, worn features. Not at all frozen and freezing like the King of Sweden, and he seems to be happy where he is. But it's strange to think that he's the brother of Queen Alexandra, because he isn't like her in the least . . .
>
> The *déjeuner* (which was very good) was also – unexpectedly – very nice and even entertaining. The Empress was brilliant, Gégé very droll, and the King (who is witty) seemed to enjoy himself as if he had not been royalty. After *déjeuner* we all went on to the terrace (luckily it wasn't raining!) and the King spoke to me almost at once, and asked me if I knew that most of Papa's books were translated into Danish, and very popular . . . In the meanwhile, Primoli was taking photographs as hard as he could go.[2]

Within the week, on 14 May, Frederik VIII died suddenly in Hamburg, on his way back to Denmark. These pictures were the last to be taken of him.

* * *

Count Primoli, wrote Arthur Meyer, the journalist, in his memoirs, 'occupies a considerable position in Rome. He has been adopted by Parisian society, where he has only friends.'[3] Among his friends was Jules Claretie: journalist, man of letters, and sometime administrator-general of the Théâtre-Français. Claretie admired Primoli the philatelist, who sold his stamp collection 'for over one hundred thousand francs'.[4] He also admired Primoli the photographer. 'I even have a photograph in which,' he told Victorien Sardou, 'you are seen chatting with Dumas in front of these famous sphinxes [at Marly-le-Roi].'[5] He recalled 'Count Joseph Primoli, an artist down to his fingertips, down to his Kodak,' taking photographs in the courtyard at the Conservatoire, at the time of the annual *concours*.[6] Above all, perhaps, Claretie was impressed by Primoli the bibliophile, who had discovered all the works of Stendhal, 'annotated, with critical comments, by H. Beyle himself, in the back-shop of a reading-room at Civitavecchia. He could rightly say that this find alone would make him a wonderful library.'[7] But there were other priceless books: among them a first edition of *Clara Gazul*, with a note by Stendhal: 'This book is by M. Mérimée, a young man of twenty-six, very melancholy.'[8] In October 1912, Claretie recorded with awe:

At the Comédie [-Française] one can see the *Molière* from St Helena, which was presented to us by Count Primoli.

This *Molière* from St Helena bears the stamp of the library at Longwood and the ex-libris of its last owner: *Ex-Libris Joseph-Nap. Com. Primoli* ... It had in fact long adorned that extraordinary library where Stendhal rubs shoulders with Flaubert and Dumas, in the Palazzo Primoli, on the banks of the Tiber.[9]

The Molière was a fair exchange for the Légion-d'honneur, which Primoli was given this year.

There could have been no better ambassador between Rome and Paris, no envoy more devoted to Italy and France. 'He was endlessly hospitable,' wrote Bac, in a waspish mood, 'and he went about his mission of bringing nations together rather like Miss World.'[10] Others were kinder. In 1913, the artist Albert Besnard returned to Rome, to take charge of the Villa Médicis. He found Primoli 'most welcoming, agreeable and amusing, and very French although he was very eloquently Italian. One will never,' he wrote, 'pay adequate tribute to the power and skill and diplomacy with which Primoli preserved the traditions of friendship between France and Italy during the War. No one could have conceived how they were endangered.'[11]

On the last day of 1913, Primoli wrote to Mme Poincaré: 'I send the most respectful and the most sincere good wishes from the depths of my heart to you, Madame, and to the dear President . . . '[12] A few months later, the Great War began.

6

In the first days of August [Primoli reported to Mme Poincaré], I came to England to be with the Empress. I knew that she was alone and in agony, and that she felt she was once again climbing the grievous Calvary of 1870. I understood what She must be suffering, and I hoped, by sharing her patriotic anguish, to help her, now she is 89, to survive these cruel trials . . . We have installed a hospital in a wing of the house, and the Wounded who are brought to us keep us in touch with the battlefields with their descriptions, illustrated by their wounds! . . . We live on anguish and on hope, but no one in England doubts the final victory.

For five months my heart has beaten with yours, and my thoughts have not left you . . .[1]

In the meanwhile England and France fought on, without Italian support, and Primoli was deeply grieved at the division between the two countries which he loved. On the last day of the year, from Farnborough, he explained to the President's wife:

At this tragic moment I hesitated to send you my faithful annual remembrance, but, on reflection, it seemed to me that it has never been more necessary to send fervent wishes for the glory and the happiness of France. One wish alone should spring from every heart: that the new year may bring the Allies their final victory over the common enemy, and that, at home, the Country may keep its Unity and Peace.[2]

* * *

The most Parisian of Romans continued his social life beside the Tiber. Early in 1915, Albert Besnard recorded:

286

To Count Primoli's; to his library, where there is always a crowd. The men kiss the hands of the ladies, who greet them in that warm Roman voice . . .

The lofty rooms are well designed for entertaining. You feel free to circulate, leaf through a book, isolate yourself and even shine. For the master of the house, as we know, is urbanity itself, and a veritable allegory of Indulgence. In the midst of the books, in front of the [Napoleonic] pictures, Past and Present meet without bitterness. On the walls there are the faces of women, aunts or grandmothers, mothers or sisters, whom David's brush has saved for ever from oblivion, waiting, one might say, to join in the conversation. And as they all resemble the master of the house with their very dark and rather forbidding eyes, they are the visible link which joins the past to the present. It seems as if one hears *the women* of former times talk through the lips of *the women* of today. Indeed, at this fireside one enjoys the warmth of Intelligence . . . This library is an exquisite refuge against the sullen winter, in any case a protection for old intimacies and for those which are in their early stages . . .

I really don't know what the foreigners' stay in Rome would be like if this palace did not exist.[3]

After Primoli had died, Gabriel Faure confirmed such feelings:

When I dedicated my first book on the Eternal City to him, I put: 'To Count Primoli, without whom Rome would no longer quite be Rome for me' . . . The richness of his conversation – he had known so many things and so many people! – was equal to the richness of his collections and his library. He proudly showed the Napoleonic treasures which he had amassed. No dwelling place saw such a procession of illustrious personalities from all over Europe: crowned heads, diplomats, society figures, prelates, writers, famous actors and actresses. The *déjeuners*, in one of the salons, or on the terrace from which one saw the Tiber and the dome of St Peter's, count among the exquisite hours of my Roman visits.[4]

Jacques Bainville, in *La Guerre et l'Italie*, remembered 'that great friend of France, . . . a neighbour of the Tiber', and his palazzo, 'a wonderful retreat, . . . where the welcome has incomparable charm, a palace so rich in books and works of art that one would brave all the ardours of the Roman sun without fear, and even with pleasure.'[5]

* * *

287

For Primoli, the social life continued to conceal regret. He longed for Italy to join the Allied cause.

When the First World War broke out, all Italians were afraid that Germany and Austria would be victorious. They feared, above all, that Austria would destroy Italian unity, which had been so painfully and recently achieved. By the terms of the triple alliance, Italy was only obliged to support Germany and Austria if they should be attacked, and that had clearly not been the case. Yet England and France had both been critical of Italy, and there was little eagerness to support them, even if Italy had been in a position to do so. Antonio Salandra's government, which succeeded Giovanni Giolitti's, therefore pursued the policy which was known as 'sacred egotism'. It consisted in building up Italian military power while keeping other countries in doubt as to Italy's intentions.

On 24 May 1915, Italy joined the Allies. She entered the war largely as a result of the massive demonstrations organized by d'Annunzio, Mussolini and others who were longing for action. The revolutionary socialists wanted war, while Giolitti and the parliamentary socialists wanted peace. The war party won because King Victor Emmanuel III and his new Prime Minister, Salandra, also wanted war.

Everyone who knew Primoli [wrote André Chaumeix], knew the anguish which he felt during the war. The day when Italy ranged itself on the Allied side, he felt a joyful pride: he could bring together the two nations which he loved in the same wishes and the same hopes, and, later, he could celebrate their victory. And then one became aware that this idle descendant of an illustrious race had kept the cult of glory strong and deep in his heart; one knew the blood that flowed in his veins.[6]

I do not forget [he wrote himself to President Poincaré, that July], that, on my last stay in Paris, where you gave me such a cordial welcome, . . . you alone had absolute confidence in the threatened alliance. You told me that the only danger was an [Italian] ministerial crisis. In fact it occurred, but it was avoided thanks to the energy of the King, supported by Salandra, Sonnino and Martini, and above all thanks to the nation, who were revolted by Giolitti's treachery. He was treating with the enemy over the heads of the government and even the Crown. One must also remember d'Annunzio's contagious enthusiasm, which carried the multitudes away. This unexpected volte-face will be among the strangest enigmas in our history. The previous day, 300 deputies offered their support to Giolitti; in the Senate, sixty members at most out of 400 were in favour of intervention, and next day Salandra had to guard Giolitti's departure so that he was not lynched by the crowd. It was at that moment that I arrived in Rome. I had left London impassible. I crossed a Paris which was grave and silent, moving, and aware of the tragedy of the moment . . . I found Rome en fête, decked with flags since the morning, and illuminated at night.[7]

King Victor-Emmanuel had marked the alliance by offering the President the Order of the Annonciade. Primoli sent Raymond Poincaré his congratulations. 'I have found an old book,' he added, 'on the statutes of the Order . . . Do me the great pleasure of accepting it as a tribute from a friend of twenty years and an ally of two months.'[8] It was indeed twenty years since they had first met; and, as Poincaré reflected: 'This evocation of the past recalls, for an instant, before my eyes, the smiling image of Princess Mathilde. Under the auspices of Count Primoli and M. Maurice d'Ocagne, she readily welcomed writers and artists at her table, and in their shadow there hid a young Minister of Public Instruction, who was a little out of his element.'[9]

Colette was clearly out of hers when, in July 1915, she found herself in Rome as a war correspondent for *Le Matin*. 'Count Primoli's palazzo,' she recorded in her *Journal intermittent*. 'An Italian hotch-potch of things all unrelated to one another. A terrible dinner, eight courses and as many wines . . . Tea at Primoli's; M. de Giers and Monseigneur Duchesne: the latter talks about *Dialogues de bêtes* and sleeps with his cats. People say there's a formidable stench in his lodgings.'[10]

Colette was followed, that winter, by a more sympathetic visitor, Paul Claudel. On 28 December, at the Palazzo Primoli, he talked to La Duse, who was full of fire and life.[11]

* * *

Primoli's sympathy for writers and men of letters was genuine [so Henri de Régnier wrote in *De mon temps* . . .]. He liked to mix with them, compare their appearance and character with their works, he was greedy for anecdotes about them, and capable of doing them good turns . . . He had known everyone who mattered in literature.

On the beams of his ceiling, in his Roman palace, he had inscribed the names of his literary friends, even the humblest, and when I visited him there, . . . I ascertained that mine figured among them. However literary he was, he rarely revealed himself as an author: a few pages of recollections in the *Revue de Paris*, and *Sur les pas de Stendhal à Rome*, in the collection 'Les Amis d'Édouard', which gave him a place among the beylists.[12]

On 6 October 1917, in the *Revue hebdomadaire*, he published 'La Princesse Mathilde et le Maestro Sauzay'. The article, he said, was part of a book in preparation on Princess Mathilde and her friends; it was followed, in time, by 'La Princesse Mathilde et le Duc d'Aumale', and two articles on 'La Princesse Mathilde et Théophile Gautier'. But, despite the good intentions, the chiffonier full of documents in the avenue du Trocadéro, and the archives in the via Zanardelli, he could not bring himself to write the book.

He remained, as ever, a benevolent cultural attaché, linking the two nations which he loved. In the spring of 1918, Gabriel Faure arrived in Rome. He accompanied the French representative to the inter-allied conference. Primoli asked him to *déjeuner*.

At table [Faure remembered], I found myself next to General Stefanik, who asked me to come next day to the presentation of the colours given to the Czech regiment formed in Italy . . .

I remember another *déjeuner* attended by the most diverse guests. I can read the names on the back of the menu, which I kept: Mgr Duchesne, Barrère, Albert Besnard, Prince and Princess Ghika, the Marquise Rossi, the Comtesse Morosini (the one whom the Italians call *bellissima*), Gorki's son, Louis Bertrand, Jean Carrère, and Pietro Misciatelli, who had just published his fine book on the Siamese mystics. But, that day, I did not profit as I should from the conversations, especially after *déjeuner*, when everyone assembled in the corner of the salon under the Leonardo da Vinci which Primoli was so proud of. I was giving my first lecture in Rome at the end of the afternoon.[13]

* * *

In the spring of 1919, Primoli found himself again at 19, avenue du Trocadéro; and there he continued to cultivate his gratifying friendship with the President of the Republic and his wife.

Madame [goes a letter of 21 March],

Since you have been kind enough to allow me to ask you to tea in my modest apartment, honoured not long ago by your presence – and since I have at last got a little coal! – I take the liberty of reminding you of your most gracious promise . . . [14]

No doubt Henriette Poincaré found time to sit beside his fire. On 5 April he wrote to her: ' I cannot leave Paris without thanking you for the kindnesses with which you have showered me during my stay . . . I expect to come back somewhere about June . . . '[15] In June he was once again in France; and, always at the centre of events, he watched the signing of the Peace which ended the Great War.

Madame [this again to Mme Poincaré],

On my return from Versailles, where I had the joy of attending the signing of the Peace Treaty, I feel that I must leave at the Élysée the homage of the profound and respectful gratitude which we owe the President for this glorious conclusion which He has prepared by his noble and patriotic attitude since the first days of the War.

I beg you to allow me, Madame, to express my respectful affection.

Your most devoted servant,
PRIMOLI[16]

* * *

The 1914 War [recorded Ferdinand Bac] had left him in the exalted state of d'Annunzio's harangues. He hated the Germans intensely, like those hysterical women who – a long way from the Front – gobbled up atrocities as hungrily as they devoured petits-fours . . .

His aversion later led him to invent the acts of scorn which he would have liked to perform for Prince de Bulow, who frequented his palace – and whom he readily visited himself . . . The Peace of Versailles left him overwhelmed with glory, while in Rome he rightly blamed the way in which the Allies had treated Italian valour.

As for the March on Rome, he greeted it from the wings, in an attitude of expectancy which was very prudent. It was an attitude which was not without fear for his social position and for his glass cases. He had had so little to complain of in the Past. What good would there be in his Future? When a fascist guard-house was set up under his roof, he was privately convinced that the end of the world had come. But he greeted the Blackshirts with that slightly acidulated smile which made his nostrils curl and left the door open to all suppositions. As he had adapted himself to the best, so he finally came to terms with what he thought the worst, and he went on living, going gently down the slope of life. He was always afraid for the morrow, which nonetheless left intact all the treasures which he had inherited. As he had planned, he bequeathed them to his two countries . . .

He hesitated constantly in the choice of his executors. Full of superstitions about his 'last wishes', he was reluctant to set them down, for fear of seeing Death arrive too soon. And so he had given the correspondence inherited from Princess Mathilde to five or six friends, only to take it back again . . . He had never been able to accept, without grief, the thought that a day would come when he would have to abandon everything. Constantly divided between Paris and Rome, he had sought an arrangement which would let him divide his palace and his library between France and Italy.

In the end, things turned out for the best. When, for the first time since the War, I crossed the threshold of this palace where a beadle had once greeted us by striking the floor with his wand of office, I recalled the hospitable donor, that lay Eminence who had – like all the Bonapartes in exile – gone through several countries and had left in none of them the memory of a great citizen.[17]

7

It was in Paris, in 1919, that Primoli met Marie-Louise
Pailleron. She found him

a charming old man, full of memories ... In his apartment [she
recorded] I saw a very curious correspondence between Mme de
Staël and King Joseph Bonaparte. 'In the first letters,' said Primoli,
'it was a question of love, because this woman with countless
lovers had loved King Joseph. I think the fact is not generally
known.' But Count Primoli burnt those particular letters. He was
constantly afraid of shocking or of compromising; this is actually
the reason why he did not publish his own memoirs ...

On the mantelpiece of his Paris salon he had set the act of
marriage between Napoleon I and Marie-Louise, complete with all
the signatures. I also saw a chiffonier six feet high, full of letters
signed Stendhal, Flaubert, Théophile Gautier. Each drawer was
very deep, and must have been three feet long ...

Count Primoli had known Sainte-Beuve. One day I asked him
when he had come closest to him.

'At Princess Mathilde's,' he answered, 'and, talking of that,
here's a recollection. One morning, at Saint-Gratien, I found
myself at *déjeuner* with him. I was a child, a young and
unimportant boy at the far end of the table. The conversation was
led by the Princess, who was full of verve; it seemed to me to be
very animated. They were talking about Chateaubriand, and
discussing the question of René's love for his sister. You
understand?'

'Of course.'

'All right, but you can imagine that I myself couldn't grasp why
the guests were getting so excited about a question which, to me,
Gégé, seemed quite unimportant. Finally, Sainte-Beuve called out,
and asked me, *mischievously*, what I thought about it. I replied,

293

in my utter innocence, that I found it perfectly natural that Chateaubriand [*sic*] should have loved his sister, and the question wasn't worth all that conversation. Then the Princess said: 'A very good answer, Gégé, come and kiss me!'[1]

To Marie-Louise Pailleron the ageing Primoli talked, also, about Dumas *fils*, and the passions which he had aroused in women who saw his plays. Primoli was, so he confessed,

a very young man before the war of 1870, with a great love of literature and a passion for the theatre. At that time he, too, was ardently following the dramatic triumphs of Dumas *fils* . . .

After *Les Idées de Mme Aubray* (1867), he could contain himself no longer, and he wrote the author a letter so touching, so overflowing with youthful fervour, that, accustomed though he was to such incense, Dumas was interested by the form of this letter – signed only with a Christian name – and remained convinced that only a woman could have written it. Flattered, and roused by a certain curiosity, he replied *poste restante*, as he had been asked to do. Primoli, enchanted, and still hiding behind a pseudonym, replied in his turn. A correspondence duly began between the delighted young man and Alexandre Dumas. A charming correspondence, Primoli assured me, 'and, on Dumas' side, full of the liveliest wit and the most diverting ideas'. No doubt about that. Perhaps (but Primoli did not mention this to me), since the dramatist believed that he was writing to a woman, it also had an amorous, even gallant tone, which must have made it all the more extraordinary.

Then came the war [of 1870], which interrupted this exchange of letters. The years which followed brought the two correspondents close together. Primoli was introduced to Dumas. 'He took a liking to me,' Primoli told me. 'Of course he didn't suspect anything. And it's curious, but I think it's natural: the more he trusted me, the more ashamed I became of having duped him . . . Finally, full of remorse, I confessed to Alexandre Dumas that his *lady correspondent* was the young man who stood before him, and was sorry that he had deceived him, and, as you can imagine, I returned his letters to him.'

'What a pity!' I said to Primoli. 'Dumas must have burnt them?'

'Of course. And I must confess that he seemed rather displeased to have been kept in error for so long. Dumas was more afraid than most of being *conned*.'[2]

* * *

As Ferdinand Bac suggested, the most important legacy that

Princess Mathilde bequeathed to Primoli 'was, with her papers, his mission to prolong his rôle as familiar at Farnborough or Cap Martin, with the widow of Napoleon III.'[3] Among the Poincaré Papers is a note from Primoli to Mme Poincaré, sent from the Villa Cyrnos (telephone 056) where, once again, he was staying with the Empress. 'On my way to Rome I have stopped at Cap Martin, to spend Holy Week here ... '[4] Another note to Mme Poincaré is sent from the avenue du Trocadéro. 'Alas! Madame, I am leaving for England on Thursday morning. I had a telegram from the Empress saying that She wanted to see me – and, as she has entered her 93rd year, one dares not keep her waiting.'[5]

In 1920, as he recorded, when she was ninety-five,

she expressed a wish to undertake a journey to Spain and to be operated on for cataract. The doctors strongly opposed both her plans, and said that at her time of life she would be exposing herself to two mortal dangers . . . She answered their observations and her friends' fears by saying: 'I feel the need, before I die, to see my country once again, and to breathe the scent of the orange-trees in Seville.' Perhaps, for her, these flowers represented her youth before the grandeurs and catastrophes, her *prehistoric* youth, as she called it, smiling. Perhaps she wanted, one last time, to intoxicate herself with the pure fragrance of a distant past, the only one that she could evoke without recalling the sad vision of the dear departed . . . She left for Spain and closed her eyes there. She had reopened them, just for a moment, long enough to see her native land again and to read a few lines of *Don Quixote*. Then, once more, she closed them, this time for ever.[6]

On 11 July 1920, she died in Madrid; her body was taken back to England, and on 20 July she was buried at Farnborough with her husband and son.

My dear President [wrote Primoli to Raymond Poincaré],
   I cannot leave Paris to accompany the Empress to her last resting-place without telling you how touched I have been by your sympathy. For me it is a hearth growing cold, a hearth where I was always sure of finding a good welcome, and warmed myself with thoughts of the Past. Let me say that the Empress never allowed your government to be attacked in Her presence. She remembered how hard it had been in her own day to achieve the blessing of

295

unity, and what harm the opposition had done during the Empire. At least she has died happy with la Revanche – with the revenge which France has won under your rule, and no personal thought ever clouded her patriotic joy.

Please give my respects to Madame Poincaré – and count me among your most faithful friends.

PRIMOLI[7]

* * *

The Empress, as Bac remembered, had

> made full use of [Gégé's] pleasant and attentive company. It was a pity that his long service as benevolent chamberlain, his daily devotion and entertainment, were only rewarded by a worthless picture: a legacy which was rather like a grudge. He did not even touch it. Discreet but embittered, he sent it to the Musée de la Malmaison. So it was that, at one stroke, he lost his long admiration, hardly mentioned her again, and even let people judge her fairly without feeling obliged to castigate the bold.[8]

He had stood guard for a long time, and he had severely censured other people's comments on the Empress.[9] He had marked a passage in Princess Mathilde's memoirs 'unfair and wrong – to be burnt'.[10] After the Empress's death, he himself decided to publish some recollections. Although they were abridged, she would doubtless have preferred not to know them.[11]

Seven

1

In Rome, in the early days of Mussolini, Jean Ajalbert, the man of letters, called on Primoli in his palace in the via Zanardelli.

It was open to all French friends, just as his apartment in Paris was open to all his Italian acquaintances. He had run into debt by building it, in the building epidemic which had raged in the city – largely described by Zola [in his *Rome*]. I had met him at a Goncourt Sunday, where he photographed the familiar visitors at the Grenier, in a photograph which is often reproduced: a collection of top-hats and enormous overcoats in the last days of Naturalism, in about 1885–1890; he had received me in Rome in 1905. After 1908, we saw one another regularly, at Malmaison, with Frédéric Masson. He was one of my immediate advisers in the rebuilding of the consulate, where he brought the Empress Eugénie to meet 'the anarchist curator'. For his palazzo he had chosen a site in fhe old dell' Orso quarter, with a boundless view over the Tiber and the expanses which are covered, now, by the Palace of Justice and so many other new buildings. He was an attentive and delightful master of the house – nothing was left to chance, although it gave the appearance of being improvised. He contrived unexpected seating arrangements at his table: great ladies and actresses, poets and financiers, prelates and Jews. The fare was simple and carefully chosen, that of a gourmet who let no one else fetch the specialities which he brought back from his chosen suppliers. 'You should be less concerned with what you eat than with whom you eat,' Epicurus said. Both food and company were appropriate at Primoli's table. He knew how to stage a performance, just as he knew how to set off his guests. They all of them came away enchanted, and the foreigners left with invitations for the whole of their stay. So it was that people entered the most exclusive princely, ecclesiastical, political and artistic life, with this *Sesame* who was so courteous and witty: this Sesame from whom one hoped to have the piquant observations of an observer well known in so many different milieux . . . Who had he not known, what had he not seen? But, nonchalant and disabused, without a minute to himself in his unremitting social life, did this charming idler keep the time for, did he not always postpone until tomorrow, the writing of a diary, for which the Goncourts had given him the taste? . . . It was our masters in Auteuil who also inspired him in his will, in which he left his worldly goods to youth.[1]

He had wanted to found a sort of Académie-Goncourt: d'Annunzio called it the Accademia dell'Orso, or La Primola. Finally, to realize the dream of his life, the spiritual union between his two countries, he bequeathed his Museo Napoleonico, on the ground-floor of his palace, to the municipality of Rome.[2] The Fondazione Primoli was established to promote Franco–Italian understanding.

* * *

Rome, February 1922

Prince and Princess de Bulow have just left me. Amiable though they are, I cannot help feeling slightly uncomfortable in the presence of the former Chancellor of the German Empire . . . He wanted to be agreeable, and he was interesting. He maintains that his Emperor never wanted war; in which case it seems to me that he cannot be forgiven for having made it. He told me some touching anecdotes about Queen Victoria, a great queen, but a perfect *housekeeper* [*sic*].

Yesterday I read a few 'odd pages from an intermittent diary' to some over-indulgent listeners. My friends congratulated me, and they particularly praised me for having been able to write for so long just for myself, without any ulterior thought of publication . . . Well, whatever people have said to me, I know that I have been very wrong, and I couldn't advise anyone to have this excessive reserve. The result of my abstention is that I have constantly seen the grass cut under my feet, the grass which was turning mouldy in my drawer. If my notes are published too late they will seem faded and dated. The anecdotes and the witticisms which I gathered at first hand have since become known, and if I publish them in turn I should appear to have them at second hand. One

300

must serve things hot, and never forget that a warmed-up dinner is always worthless.[3]

* * *

He kept his diary and his notebooks, classified the papers which Princess Mathilde had bequeathed him: her correspondence with Théophile Gautier, Flaubert, Renan, Sainte-Beuve . . . He could have been, single-handed, the memorialist of an era, from Octave Feuillet to Maupassant, from Winterhalter to Bonnat. He turned increasingly towards the past. He still lacked the concentration to write a book, but he published Renan's letters to Princess Julie and Princess Mathilde, Mérimée's letters to Princess Mathilde, and some of his own memoirs of Princess Mathilde and the Empress Eugénie. They were an engaging contribution to history. He was capable, too, of pure invention. *Caprice de Prince* was an imaginative exaltation of the love-affairs of Napoleon III; and Primoli sometimes saw the Empress as the heroine of a novel by Mérimée, sometimes as a legendary character, and sometimes as the great lady which she actually was, conscious of her rôle and of her political mission. He gave a more complete and more accurate portrait of Princess Mathilde. In November 1925, with deep affection, he published some of his recollections of her:

> . . . Perhaps the person who has best described her eyes is the extraordinary Marcel Proust, who had frequented the rue de Berry when he had hardly left the lycée, and had asked the Princess to dictate her memoirs to him. She made the mistake of not taking him seriously, because of his extreme youth, but in his *Jeunes filles en fleurs* [sic] he has left a few snapshots of her, taken from life, more like her than the official portraits which were drawn by her familiars:
>
>> I remember [he writes] how the charming eyes of Princess Mathilde took on a different beauty as they rested on some or other image left on her retina and in her memory by some great men, some great sights of the beginning of the century, and it is that image, emanated from them, which she saw and we shall never see. I had a feeling of the supernatural when, at such moments as this, I met her gaze: that gaze which, in a short and mysterious line, in an action of resurrection, joined the present to the past.

301

Does she not sum up a whole century of literature [Primoli continued], this woman, born on the eve of the Emperor's death, celebrated at fifteen by Jules Janin and Alexandre Dumas *père*, in her middle years by Sainte-Beuve and Théophile Gautier, Flaubert and the Goncourts, and at eighty by Marcel Proust?

Personally, I always see her as she appears in the living pastel by Lucien Doucet, who surprised her at work and recorded her utterly absorbed in her task, as attentive as the Erasmus of Holbein.[4]

In the 1920s, presumably with Primoli's authority, some of her memoirs appeared in the *Revue des Deux Mondes*.

* * *

In Paris, an extraordinary Bonaparte, he had always cultivated his friendship with the President of the Republic. 'He called Poincaré *my dear friend*,' observed Ferdinand Bac, 'and he said he was *at home* at the Académie. He was persuaded that he created "Immortals" and that he nominated ambassadors. Anyhow, he gave the idea that he helped them.'[5] Bac was, presumably, jealous of such influence. In the meanwhile, Primoli invited Raymond Poincaré, 'Monsieur le Président and most illustrious Friend', to lunch at the Cercle Interallié, to meet an admiral, a general, Maurice Barrès and Paul Bourget.[6] He continued, happily, to receive Mme Poincaré, to dine at the Élysée, and to enjoy the Presidential box at the Opéra.[7] Visitors to the avenue du Trocadéro – now renamed the avenue du Président-Wilson – delighted in his conversation, and, when they dined, they enjoyed the thoughtful or amusing present each of them would find under his napkin. But, as Henri de Régnier observed, 'time had passed, his health had deteriorated, and it gave him cause for anxiety. His stoutness, his increasing baldness and his white beard indicated old age, an old age which emphasized the Napoleonic features of his fine, serene Italian face. Through the Primoli there appeared the Bonaparte.'[8]

He was in his seventies, now, and his friends were dying. The death of Eleonora Duse, in 1924, was a great sorrow to him. He himself was slowly fading.

The last time I saw Comte Joseph Primoli [recalled the socialite André de Fouquières], it was in his *pied-à-terre* in what is now the avenue du Président-Wilson. I found him distant and as if apart. His great friends had gone . . .

It is to Primoli that Paris owes having known La Duse, the incomparable interpreter of d'Annunzio. She had been a great friend of his. Her death had deeply distressed him and he told us, the Princesse de la Moskowa and myself, who were listening as he sadly unwound his thread of memories:

'She has gone before me, she is showing me the way.'[9]

The last time I saw him [added Henri de Régnier], some time before his departure for Rome, I was struck by the change which had taken place in him, and I had the feeling that I should not see him again, and that I should not again hear the 'Gégé is in Paris' which had so often signalled his arrival. However, he was still making plans, among them that of finally writing his Memoirs. This proposal led us to recall certain figures and events from the past. Since the name of Princess Mathilde had arisen in our conversation, I reminded him of the evening in the rue de Berry when he had brought a gramophone record from Rome: a record of Leo XIII giving his benediction. He had made us listen to the venerable Latin words strongly accentuated by the sepulchral, nasal voice of the Sovereign Pontiff. The record had been heard by a circle of men in evening dress and women with bare shoulders and their bosoms generously displayed, kneeling piously before the magic box from which, an echoing ghost, there emerged the Papal *Benedicat vos*.

At the thought of this, a mischievous smile lit up the wan face of the favourite nephew whom the Princess 'forgave', with amused indulgence, for the clever tricks of an old spoilt child, and sometimes for the faults of an *enfant terrible*.[10]

Monsieur le Président [he wrote, now, to Raymond Poincaré],

I am so sorry to leave Paris without having the great pleasure of seeing you. As soon as I arrived, Madame Poincaré had the kindness to invite me to dinner, but my state of health is compromised by continual haemorrhages, and it does not allow me to go out in the evening . . .

Goodbye, my dear President. I hope to see you next year.[11]

The letter, which is undated, seems to be Primoli's farewell to France.

2

His illness had been apparent at least since the beginning of 1925. On 30 March that year, on a postcard of the Palazzo Primoli, he had scribbled to Gabriel Faure:

> My dear friend, thank you for your charming book. It found me in bed, where I have been kept for the past 5 weeks by a serious disorder of the liver, in my moments of respite I have read several chapters which have delighted me. Most affectionate thanks.
> PRIMOLI[1]

On 18 May, Paul Claudel called at the palazzo, and 'saw Count Primoli dying, serene and noble. He is dying like a gentleman. When I left he asked to embrace me. Surrounded by the portraits of all his dead friends who have preceded him. Not talking about himself, but uniquely about other people. Had a good lesson in dying.'[2]

He lingered on for two more years.

> Palazzo Primoli [recorded Ajalbert] . . . I saw him dying there, in 1927 . . . Confined to his bed, he received no one, now, except his intimates . . . His old valet recognized me, and insisted on presenting my card, and I was shown in . . . He was emaciated, with a waxen complexion, and his eyes were glazed – but he still had that musical voice, and that smile, despite his suffering.
>
> 'My dear friend . . . What, Mme Ajalbert is with you? . . . I should like to meet her, if it doesn't worry her coming into this sickroom . . .'
>
> What courtesy!
>
> 'I should have liked to show her Rome . . . But you know it as well as I do . . . My motor-car will be at your disposal . . .'

And so he offered it to everyone, because he would always do anything for his friends; he would have needed a dozen motor-cars for them.[3]

He died, in his palace near the Tiber, on 13 June 1927. He was seventy-six. In Paris, and in Rome, there was deep and genuine regret. For half a century he had been among the most representative and most familiar characters of an age which was henceforward part of history.

* * *

Writing in the *Revue des Deux Mondes*, to which Primoli had more than once contributed, André Chaumeix, the editor, paid a shrewd and poignant tribute to him:

The readers of the *Revue* have not forgotten the charming studies which he published here in recent years. They were simple accounts, vivaciously told, anecdotes, recollections of the literary or political world of the Second Empire: odd pages from a book of Memoirs, which Count Primoli could have written better than anyone, and which he left in a fragmentary state, a little out of indecision, a great deal out of delicacy, and also as the result of a melancholy and resigned inclination for the unfinished.

He had been the witness of too many events not to feel the futility of many things and not to have a certain fatalism. Born in the Papal States, brought up in Paris during the Second Empire, he saw, in his youth, the foundation of the Kingdom of Italy and the fall of Napoleon III. He entered life at the moment when the world that he had known, the world for which he had been formed, suffered a profound change. And so, at the very moment he reached manhood, he found himself an exile, as it were, in his epoch, divided between his concern for old loyalties, and his liking for the new age, which attracted his enquiring mind. It was his merit and his distinction to reconcile the two with good grace and much tact . . .

He could be, single-handed, the memorialist of an era . . . He complained mildly that he had been irresolute, that he had had a singular destiny which had lacked the simplest comforts, the ones which the human condition so readily gives, or imposes: a family and an occupation. His real treasure and his real delight had been friendship. All Paris was sad to learn, a few weeks ago, that Count Primoli was ill and was leaving his apartment in the avenue du Président-Wilson, that he would not come to Paris this summer,

305

then that he would not come to Paris again . . . Few men, when they depart, have left so many people with the feeling that they have just lost a friend.[4]

Notes

ABBREVIATION

References to Primoli or to the Primoli Papers relate to the archives which the author consulted at Spoleto. These documents have since been transferred to the Fondazione Primoli in Rome.

One

1

1. Spaziani (ed.): Joseph-Napoleon Primoli: *Pages inédites*, 127–8
2. Ibid., 128
3. Ibid., 131
4. Ibid., xv

2

1. Bac: *Promenades dans l'Italie nouvelle*, I, 80
2. Primoli: 'Autour du mariage de l'Impératrice'. (REVUE DES DEUX MONDES, ler novembre 1924, 71)
3. Ibid., 71–4
4. Princess Mathilde: *Mémoires* (Primoli)
5. Primoli: op. cit., 83–4
6. Ibid., 98–103. Recalling the ruby velvet dress, Primoli wondered 'if it was in memory of that day that the Emperor, who took little interest in his wife's clothes, insisted that the Empress always had a red dress in her wardrobe'. Ibid., 102, note

3

1. Primoli: 'La Princesse Mathilde et Théophile Gautier'. (REVUE DES DEUX MONDES, ler novembre 1925, 73 sqq.)

2. Primoli: *Souvenirs, Pensées, Poésies, 1864*, 102, 105
3. Primoli Papers
4. Primoli: *Souvenirs, Pensées, Poésies, 1864*, 3–4
5. Ibid.
6. 26 octobre 1864. Goncourt: *Journal*, VII, 18
7. Primoli: op. cit., 37–40
8. Blavet: *La Vie Parisienne . . . (1884)*, 16
9. 13, 14 août 1865. Goncourt: *Journal*, VII, 101, 102–3, 103
10. Spaziani (ed.): *Pages inédites*, 29–30

4

1. Primoli: 'L'Impératrice Eugénie et le Tsar Alexandre II. Souvenirs'. REVUE DES DEUX MONDES, 15 septembre 1922

5

1. Primoli: 'La Princesse Mathilde et Théophile Gautier', I. (REVUE DES DEUX MONDES, ler novembre 1925, 82–4)
2. Ibid., 84
3. Ibid., 84–6
4. Ibid., 86
5. Primoli Diary, 1867. Vol. II, 92 sqq.
6. Ibid., 101–2
7. Ibid., 110–1
8. Ibid., 115 sqq
9. Primoli: 'La Princesse Mathilde et Théophile Gautier', II. (REVUE DES DEUX MONDES, 15 novembre 1925, 329 sqq.) The conversation is recorded in the diary for 1867, pp. 131–2, where it is dated 2 October. In October 1868, Primoli added a postscript to this entry. 'I have had a letter from Princess Mathilde: "Gautier is still delightful, and I am going to get him a secure position, which he needs."' She failed to persuade the Emperor to give him a sinecure, and she finally made him her own librarian. 'She did me the honour of consulting me a good deal about it,' Primoli noted, 'perhaps she was afraid that Théo would be too proud to accept this sinecure ... Gautier accepted with gratitude, and said that he would rather owe something to her than to anyone else.' (Primoli Diary, 1867, p. 133)

10. Primoli: op. cit., 331 sqq.
11. Ibid., 335–6

6

1. Primoli: 'Lettres à la Princesse Julie'. (REVUE DES DEUX MONDES, 15 juin 1924, 729)
2. Sainte-Beuve: *Lettres à la Princesse*, 341–3
3. 28 juin 1868 (Primoli)
4. Primoli Diary, IV, 19 sqq.
5. Ibid., 26 sqq.
6. Ibid., 50 sqq.
7. 'Lettres de Mérimée à la Princesse Mathilde'. (LA REVUE DE PARIS, 15 juin 1922, 690)
8. Primoli Diary, IV, 74–5. Princess Mathilde's portrait of Mérimée is now at the Musée Carnavalet.
9. Primoli Diary, IV, 84
10. Ibid., 38
11. Ibid., 143
12. Primoli: 'La Princesse Mathilde et Théophile Gautier', I. (REVUE DES DEUX MONDES, ler novembre 1925, 75–8)

7

1. Primoli Diary, VI. Avril-octobre 1869
2. Undated letter (Primoli)
3. Primoli Diary, VI. Avril-octobre 1869
4. Ibid.
5. Primoli: 'La Princesse Mathilde et Théophile Gautier', I. (REVUE DES DEUX MONDES. ler novembre 1925, 47–55)
6. Primoli Diary, VI. Avril-octobre 1869
7. Richardson: *Théophile Gautier: his Life and Times*, 232–7
8. Primoli: 'La Princesse Mathilde et Théophile Gautier', II. (REVUE DES DEUX MONDES, 15 novembre 1925, 349, 350)
9. Ibid., 350, 351
10. Ibid., 353–6
11. Richardson: *Théophile Gautier: his Life and Times*, 236–7
12. Primoli: 'Lettres à la Princess Julie'. (REVUE DES DEUX MONDES, 15 juin 1924)

13. Ibid., 725–6. In his diary for 1867, Vol. II, p. 39, Primoli had noted: 'Mme de Metternich. She is Talleyrand with a heart. In the morning she's a good fellow; in the evening she's a wit. Everywhere she is the Ambassadress.'

8

1. Primoli Diary, VII. Février – juin 1870
2. Ibid., 12
3. Ibid., 22
4. Ibid., 74
5. Richardson: *Princess Mathilde*, 179
6. 30 avril 1870. Primoli Diary, VII, 109
7. Ibid., 118–9, 120, 124, 125
8. Ibid., 142–3
9. Primoli Diary, VIII. *Notes intimes. Politique et Voyages. 1870*
10. Ibid.
11. Spaziani (ed.): *Pages inédites*, 88–9
12. 14 septembre 1870 (Primoli)
13. 12 octobre 1870 (Primoli)
14. Spaziani (ed.): op. cit., 89

Two

1

1. Vasili: *La Société de Rome*, 571
2. Ibid., 571–3
3. Primoli Diary, X, 116
4. Ibid., 127
5. 17 décembre 1872 (Primoli)
6. Bac: *Sous la République*, 216–8
7. Primoli: 'La Princesse Mathilde et Théophile Gautier', II. (REVUE DES DEUX MONDES, 15 novembre 1925, 362–5)
8. Spaziani (ed.): *Pages inédites*, 3, note

2

1. 9 janvier 1873 (Primoli)
2. 9 January 1873. Buckle (ed.): *The Letters of Queen Victoria*. Second series. Vol. II, 236
3. Primoli: 'Caprice de Prince'. (LA REVUE DE PARIS, 1er octobre 1923, 482)
4. Ibid.
5. Primoli: 'L'Impératrice Eugénie et le Tsar Alexandre II. Souvenirs'. (REVUE DES DEUX MONDES, 15 septembre 1922, 304 sqq.)

3

1. Besnard: *Sous le ciel de Rome*, 77

2.   Spaziani (ed.): *Pages inédites*, 4
3.   Ibid., 4–5
4.   Ibid., 5–6

4

1.   20 décembre 1876 (Primoli)
2.   2 mars 1877 (Primoli)
3.   Primoli: 'L'Enfance d'une Souveraine. Souvenirs intimes'. (RE-VUE DES DEUX MONDES, 15 octobre 1923, 780–2)
4.   Ibid., 783–8

5

1.   16 juillet 1877 (Popelin)
2.   22 juillet 1877 (Primoli)
3.   Lundi [octobre 1877]. Flaubert: *Correspondance*, 8e série, 88
4.   31 janvier 1878 (Primoli)
5.   Dated only 1879 (Primoli)
6.   4 juillet 1879 (Primoli)
7.   Mme Octave Feuillet: *Souvenirs et correspondances*, 390–1. This was Primoli's answer to Feuillet's letter of condolence to the Empress Eugénie.

6

1.   Primoli: *Princesse Mathilde. Souvenirs. Saint-Gratien, 15 7bre–15 8bre 1879*, 3 sqq. (Primoli Papers)
2.   Primoli Papers
3.   Flaubert: *Lettres inédites à la Princesse Mathilde*. Préface, i sqq. (Primoli Papers)
4.   Flaubert: *Correspondance*, 5e série, 168; Primoli Papers
5.   Charlotte Primoli's autograph book. (Primoli)

1. Primoli: *Princesse Mathilde. Souvenirs. Saint-Gratien, 15 7bre–15 8bre 1879*, 17–18 (Primoli Papers)
2. Ibid., 19–21; see also Goncourt: *Journal*, XII, 48, 49
3. Primoli: op. cit., 22 sqq.
4. Ibid., 43–4
5. Ibid., 56–7
6. Ibid., 99 sqq.
7. Ibid., 106
8. Primoli Diary, 1879. On 6 September, from Saint-Gratien, Primoli had written to his parents: 'On Tuesday the Princess is taking me to visit the château de Maintenon, we're having *déjeuner* on the train, it's quite an event, but she has now been ruminating this 12-hour journey for several years.' (Primoli)
9. Primoli Diary, 1879

1. Flaubert: *Lettres inédites à la Princesse Mathilde*, xxv–xxvi
2. Primoli: *Notes. Saint-Gratien. Septembre 1880*
3. Ibid. The Princess told Primoli that Feydeau had once asked her to intervene to save his wife, who had been accused of shoplifting.   ·
4. Primoli: op. cit.
5. Ibid.
6. Primoli: *Notes. Paris. Décembre 1880*. On 19 November, Arnold Mortier had recorded another expedition: the Princess and Primoli had attended the revival of *Un Père prodigue*, by Dumas *fils*, at the Vaudeville. (Mortier: *Les Soirées parisiennes de 1880*, 402)
7. Primoli recorded that 'Mme Gaby Hébert, who is pretty, good, gentle, intelligent, sympathetic and frank, . . . is forty years younger than her husband.' For Hébert's relationship with the Princess, see Richardson: *Princess Mathilde*, 49, 140–1
8. Primoli: *Notes. Paris. Décembre 1880*
9. Ibid.
10. Ibid.
11. Ibid.
12. Ibid.
13. Ibid.

14. For other versions of the break with Nieuwerkerke, see Primoli's Diary, VII, février-juin 1870, 121–2, and pp. 137–9 of the present book. There is a detailed account of events in Richardson: *Princess Mathilde*, 158 sqq.
15. 7 mai 1881 (Primoli)

9

1. Primoli: 'La Duse'. (LA REVUE DE PARIS, ler juin 1897, 497–8)
2. 11 mai 1881. Ibid., 498–500
3. Ibid., 500
4. Ibid., 500, 501
5. Ibid., 501
6. Spaziani (ed.): *Pages inédites*, 99–101
7. Primoli Diary, October 1879
8. 30 décembre 1881 (Primoli)
9. Goncourt: *Journal*, XII, 140
10. Ibid., 147–8
11. Daudet: op. cit., 106

10

1. 20 janvier 1883 (Primoli)
2. Primoli Diary, 1883
3. Ibid.
4. Ibid.
5. Ibid.
6. Ibid.
7. Ibid.
8. Ibid.
9. Ibid.
10. Ibid. Gustave Popelin had in fact left his father, in 1870, to stay with Dumas *fils* during the Franco-Prussian War.
11. Goncourt: *Journal*, XIII, 17
12. Hugo, Comtesse Clémentine: *Rome en 1886*, 306
13. Primoli Diary, 1883
14. Ibid.
15. Ibid.

16. Spaziani (ed.): *Pages inédites*, 7
17. Ibid.
18. Spaziani (ed.): *Con Gégé Primoli nella Roma Bizantina*, 33
19. Spaziani (ed.): *Pages inédites*, 7–8
20. Ibid., 8
21. Ibid., 8–9
22. Ibid., 9–10
23. Ibid., 10
24. 28 septembre 1883 (Primoli)
25. Spaziani (ed.): *Pages inédites*, 11. It is not clear whether Primoli's allusion to his nursing refers to the final illness of his brother, or to that of his father, who was to die later this year.
26. Ibid.
27. Ibid.
28. Ibid., 11–12
29. Ibid., 12
30. Primoli: 'La Duse'. (LA REVUE DE PARIS, ler juin 1897, 503–5)
31. Undated. Ibid., 505
32. Spaziani (ed.): *Pages inédites*, 12
33. Ibid.
34. Ibid.
35. Ibid., 13
36. Ibid.
37. Ibid.
38. Ibid.
39. Ibid., 14

Three

1

1. Spaziani (ed.): *Pages inédites*, 14
2. Ibid., 14–15
3. Ibid., 15
4. Ibid.
5. Primoli Diary, 1884 (Primoli)
6. Spaziani (ed.): op. cit., 15
7. Ibid., 15–16
8. Primoli Diary, 1884 (Primoli).
9. Spaziani (ed.): op. cit., 16
10. Ibid.
11. Primoli Diary, 1884 (Primoli)
12. Ibid.
13. Spaziani (ed.): op. cit., 17
14. 15 novembre 1885 (Primoli)
15. Hugo, Comtesse Clémentine: *Rome en 1886*, 306

2

1. Primoli: 'La Duse'. (LA REVUE DE PARIS, 1er juin 1897, 506–8)
2. Ibid., 508
3. Ibid., 508–9
4. Ibid., 509
5. Ibid., 510–1
6. Ibid., 514–5

3

1. Spaziani (ed.): *Pages inédites*, 19
2. Ibid., xxv–xxvi
3. Bourget: *Cosmopolis*. Letter of dedication, 16 November 1892, iv
4. Spaziani (ed.): op. cit., 28
5. Spaziani: 'Lettere inedite di Maupassant al Conte Primoli'. (*Studi in onore di Vittorio Lugli e Diego Valeri*. Parte seconda, 925)
6. Ibid.
7. Ibid., 925–6
8. 9 juin 1885 (Popelin)
9. Tienot: op. cit., 38; Vallas: op. cit., 66, 67–8
10. Tienot: op. cit., 41
11. Spaziani (ed.): 'Lettere inedite . . .', 930–1
12. Ibid., 931
13. Ibid., 932
14. Thwaite: *Edmund Gosse. A Literary Landscape*, 274
15. Ibid.
16. Calvé: op. cit., 46, 57–8
17. Ibid., 49
18. Barrès: op. cit., III, 381, note
19. Blanche: *La Pêche aux Souvenirs*, 64
20. Lumbroso: op. cit., 566–8
21. Richardson: *Princess Mathilde*, 288
22. Spaziani (ed.): op. cit., 28–9

4

1. 11 juillet 1888 (Primoli)
2. Primoli: *Notes intimes. Fragments quotidiens. 15 juillet–7 septembre 1888*. (Primoli)
3. Primoli Diary, 17 juillet 1888 (Primoli)
4. Primoli Diary, 19 juillet 1888 (Primoli)
5. Primoli is adapting a passage from Daudet's novel, *L'Immortel*, 273–4; Princess Mathilde has become the Duchesse Padovani, Saint-Gratien is Mousseaux, but it is clear whom Daudet had in mind.
6. Primoli Diary, 19 juillet 1888 (Primoli). The quotation comes, again, from *L'Immortel*.
7. Primoli Diary: loc. cit.
8. Primoli Diary, 20 juillet 1888 (Primoli)

9. Ibid., 22 juillet 1888 (Primoli)
10. Ibid., 27 juillet 1888 (Primoli)
11. Ibid., 1er août 1888 (Primoli)
12. Ibid., 28 août 1888 (Primoli)
13. Ibid., 29 août 1888 (Primoli)
14. Ibid., 5 septembre 1888 (Primoli)
15. Goncourt: *Journal*, XV, 148, 149
16. Primoli Diary, 7 septembre 1888 (Primoli)
17. Ibid., 8 septembre 1888 (Primoli)
18. Ibid.
19. 6 octobre [1888] (Primoli)
20. 9 novembre 1888 (Primoli)
21. Undated letter. (Primoli)

5

1. 1er juin 1889. Primoli Diary, 1889, 32 (Primoli)
2. Undated, but apparently the same date. Ibid., 37 sqq. (Primoli)
3. 4 juin 1889. Spaziani (ed.): *Pages inédites*, 23
4. 12 juin 1889. Primoli: op. cit., 65–6 (Primoli)
5. [Juin 1889.] Ibid., 82 (Primoli)
6. [Juin 1889.] Ibid. (Primoli)
7. 16 juin 1889. Ibid. (Primoli)

6

1. Primoli: 'La Princesse Mathilde et le Duc d'Aumale'. (LA REVUE DE PARIS, 1er août 1922, 476–9)
2. Spaziani (ed.): *Pages inédites*, 23–4
3. Ibid., 24–5, 26
4. 1er juillet 1889. Primoli Diary, 1889, 85 (Primoli)
5. Primoli: *Notes intimes, 1889* (Primoli)
6. Ibid.
7. Ibid.
8. Ibid.
9. Ibid. See also Goncourt: *Journal*, XVI, 126
10. Primoli: *Notes intimes, 1889*, 137–8 (Primoli)

1. Primoli: *Notes intimes, 1889* (Primoli)
2. Rolland: *Printemps romain*, 111–2
3. Spaziani (ed.): *Pages inédites*, 26–7
4. Rolland: op. cit., 316
5. Ibid., 338, 339
6. Goncourt: *Journal*, XVII, 92
7. 18 octobre 1886 (Primoli)
8. 12 novembre 1886 (Grandjean)
9. 12 octobre 1890. Bibliothèque Nationale. Lettres adressées à Alexandre Dumas *fils*. Papiers Dumas, Tome V, ff 204 sqq.
10. Spaziani (ed.): *Pages inédites*, xxxii–xxxiii

Four

1

1. 30 octobre 1890. Spaziani (ed.): *Pages inédites*, 27
2. Spaziani (ed.): op. cit., 128
3. Primoli Diary, IV, 26 sqq. (Primoli)
4. Ibid.
5. 30 janvier [1890] (Primoli)
6. 20 septembre [1890] (Primoli)
7. ler octobre [1890] (Primoli)
8. 25 octobre 1890 (Primoli)
9. 2 novembre [1890] (Primoli)
10. Primoli Diary, 1890 (Primoli)
11. Primoli Diary, 11 décembre 1890 (Primoli)
12. Ibid., 19 décembre 1880 (Primoli)
13. 15 décembre 1890 (Primoli)
14. 3 janvier 1891 (Primoli)

2

1. 26 mars 1891 (Primoli)
2. 4 septembre 1891 (Primoli)
3. 3 décembre 1891 (Primoli)
4. 17 mai 1892 (Primoli)
5. Primoli Diary, 1892 (Primoli)
6. 25 juin 1892 (Primoli)
7. 7 juillet 1892 (Primoli)
8. 15 juillet 1892 (Primoli)
9. 20 juillet 1892 (Primoli)

10. 1er août 1892 (Primoli)
11. 7 août 1892 (Primoli)
12. 15 août 1892 (Primoli)
13. 19 août 1892 (Primoli)
14. 22 août 1892 (Primoli)
15. 7 octobre 1892 (Primoli)
16. Primoli Diary, 1892 (Primoli)
17. Mme Alphonse Daudet: *Souvenirs autour d'un groupe littéraire*, 174, 175

3

1. 12 février 1893 (Primoli)
2. Spaziani (ed.): *Pages inédites*, 30–1
3. Ibid., 31
4. Ibid., 31–3. On 3 August 1900, when she had once again resented some published comments on the Emperor, Primoli wrote to her: 'You are still the Princess of Taine's P.P.C.' (Primoli)
5. Spring 1893? Entry numbered 59 in Primoli's notebook (Primoli)
6. This letter is inserted in Primoli's notebook under the date of 26 February 1892, but it was no doubt written later. It is numbered as entry 43.
7. Spaziani (ed.): op. cit., 35
8. Ibid., 35–6
9. Ibid., 36–7
10. Primoli Diary, 1893 (Primoli)
11. Ibid.
12. Ibid.

4

1. Hermant: *Souvenirs de la vie mondaine*, 169–71
2. Smyth: *Streaks of Life*, 9
3. Ibid., 11–12
4. Spaziani (ed.): *Pages inédites*, 40 sqq.
5. 12 octobre 1893 (Primoli)
6. 13 octobre 1893 (Primoli)
7. 19 octobre 1893 (Primoli)

8. Spaziani (ed.): *Pages inédites*, 42–3
9. Ibid., 44–6
10. Ibid., 46

5

1. Goncourt: *Journal*, XIX, 190
2. Primoli Diary, 1893 (Primoli)
3. Primoli: 'La Princesse Mathilde et le maestro Sauzay'. (REVUE HEBDOMADAIRE, 6 octobre 1917, 5–7)
4. Primoli Diary, 1893 (Primoli)
5. Spaziani (ed.): *Pages inédites*, 50
6. Primoli Diary, 1893 (Primoli)
7. Spaziani (ed.): op. cit., 52
8. 18 décembre 1893. Goncourt: *Journal*, XIX, 201
9. Spaziani (ed.): op. cit., 53–4

Five

1

1. Spaziani (ed.): *Pages inédites*, 56–8, 58–9
2. Ibid., 59
3. Ibid., 59, 60
4. Buckle (ed.): *Letters of Queen Victoria*, 3rd series, II, 400
5. Primoli: 'La Duse'. (REVUE DE PARIS, ler juin 1897, 525–6)

2

1. 8 novembre 1894. Goncourt: *Journal*, XX, 147, 148
2. 11 novembre 1894. Ibid., XX, 148–9
3. 14 novembre 1894. Ibid., XX, 150
4. 28 novembre 1894. Ibid., XX, 157, 158–9, 159
5. Arrighi: 'Zola à Rome'. (REVUE DE LITTÉRATURE CONTEMPORAINE, juillet–septembre 1928, 496)
6. Ibid., 496–7
7. Ternois: *Zola et son temps*, 503–4, note 3
8. Quoted by Ternois: loc. cit.
9. Ternois: *Les Amitiés romaines d'Émile Zola*, 531
10. Goncourt: *Journal*, XX, 160
11. Ibid., XX, 163
12. Primoli Diary. In a note in 1868, Primoli refers to 'the immense, unbelievable good that she does' (Primoli)
13. 22 décembre 1894 (Primoli)

3

1. Primoli: *Notes intimes*, 1895 (Primoli)
2. 22 mai 1895. Goncourt: *Journal*, XXI, 55
3. Régnier: *De mon temps . . .*, 22–4
4. Spaziani (ed.): *Pages inédites*, 60–2
5. Ibid., 62–4
6. 20 novembre 1895. Goncourt: *Journal*, XXI, 132
7. 27 novembre 1895. Ibid., 134, 135. The play, by Bornier, was *Le Fils de l'Arétin*.
8. Spaziani (ed.): op. cit., 66–8
9. ler décembre 1895. Goncourt: *Journal*, XXI, 137–8
10. 4 décembre 1895. Ibid., 140
11. Primoli Papers
12. Spaziani (ed.): op. cit., 68

4

1. Primoli: 'La Princesse Mathilde et le Duc d'Aumale'. (LA REVUE DE PARIS, ler août 1922, 480–1)

5

1. Prévost: preface to *Le Jardin secret*. *Marcel Prévost et ses contemporains*, II, 257
2. Ibid., 258–9
3. 26 avril 1896. Goncourt: *Journal*, XXII, 9
4. 27 mai 1896. Ibid., XXII, 28, 29
5. [1894] Primoli Papers
6. Primoli Papers; and Richardson: *Princess Mathilde*, 294
7. Castillon du Perron: *La Princesse Mathilde*, 276
8. Primoli Papers
9. 7 septembre 1898 (Primoli)

6

1. Spaziani (ed.): *Pages inédites*, 111 sqq.
2. Ibid.

7

1. Lelièvre: op. cit., 99–100
2. Tosi: op. cit., 262
3. Ibid., 319
4. Spaziani (ed.): *Con Gégé Primoli nella Roma Bizantina*, 59
5. Primoli: 'Eleonora Duse'. (REVUE DE PARIS, ler juin 1897, 530–2)
6. Ibid., 486–7, 488–90
7. Ibid., 520–1
8. Lelièvre: op. cit., 122, and 124, note

8

1. Spaziani (ed.): *Pages inédites*, 70–2
2. Ibid., 73–5
3. Ibid., 76

9

1. Spaziani (ed.): *Pages inédites*, 77–8
2. 2 juillet 1899. Claretie: *La Vie à Paris, 1899*, 188

10

1. Spaziani (ed.): *Pages inédites*, 80–1
2. Ibid., 81–3
3. Ibid., 83–5

11

1   31 mai 1901. Papiers Montesquieu. B.N. N.A. Fr. 15233 f 19
2. Spaziani (ed.): op. cit., 88
3. Ibid., 143
4. 29 mai [1902?]. (Primoli)
5. Spaziani (ed.): op. cit., 89
6. Ibid., 89–90
7. Ibid., 90
8. Primoli Diary, 3 décembre 1902 (Primoli)
9. 7 décembre 1902 (Primoli)
10. Gregh: *L'Âge d'or*, 178
11. Gregh: *L'Âge d'airain*, 18
12. Ibid., 19–20
13. Gregh: *L'Âge d'or*, 207
14. Gregh: *L'Âge d'airain*, 22–4
15. Primoli: 'L'Enfance d'une Souveraine. Souvenirs intimes'. (REVUE DES DEUX MONDES, 15 octobre 1923, 756)
16. Ibid., 770–1
17. 12 mars 1880 (Primoli)
18. 20 janvier 1883 (Primoli)
19. 15 novembre 1885 (Primoli)
20. 5 septembre [——] (Primoli)
21. 8 juin 1892 (Primoli)
22. 29 novembre 1895 (Primoli)
23. 9 mai 1903 (Primoli)

12

1. Primoli Papers
2. Primoli notes
3. 21 août [1903] (Primoli Papers)
4. Undated letter, and letter of 11 January [1904] addressed to Primoli; letter of 25 August [1903] addressed to Princess Mathilde (Primoli Papers)
5. 4 septembre 1903 (Primoli)
6. 22 septembre 1903. *Notes. Dernière maladie de la Princesse Mathilde* (Primoli)
7. ler octobre 1903. Ibid.
8. Primoli Diary, ler octobre 1903 (Primoli)
9. 3 octobre 1903 (Primoli)

10. Mardi [29 décembre 1903] (Primoli)
11. Primoli Diary, 1904 (Primoli)
12. Lundi [4 janvier 1904] (Primoli)
13. Primoli Diary, 1904 (Primoli)

Six

1

1. 8 janvier 1904. Claretie: *La Vie à Paris, 1904*, 3
2. Spaziani (ed.): *Pages inédites*, 92
3. Troubat to Primoli, 25 mai 1904 (Primoli)
4. Régnier: *De mon temps*, 27
5. Spaziani (ed.): op. cit., 90–1
6. *L'Écho de Paris*, 23 mai 1905
7. Proust to Mme Straus. Vendredi [28 avril 1905]. Proust: *Correspondance*, V, 120
8. Proust to Robert Dreyfus [mai 1905]. Ibid., V, 148, and note, 149
9. *Le Figaro*, 16 mai 1905
10. Proust: *Correspondance*, V, 244
11. Spaziani (ed.): op. cit., 92
12. Ibid., 92–3
13. Blanche: *More Portraits of a Lifetime*, 173
14. Régnier: op. cit., 26–7

2

1. Bac: *Intimités du Second Empire*, III, 158
2. Castillon du Perron: op. cit., 273–4
3. Chaumeix: op. cit., 225–6
4. Bac: *Promenades dans l'Italie nouvelle*, I, 75–7
5. Barrès: loc., cit.
6. [Early 1907?] (Primoli)
7. [ler juillet 1907] (Primoli)
8. [Juillet 1907] (Primoli)
9. 10 juin 1907. Barrès: op. cit., V, 265
10. Bac: op. cit., I, 79–86

3

1. On 15 October 1903, Primoli wrote to Féli Gautier about subscribing to his new book on Baudelaire (Taylor Institution, Oxford. MS 8° F 40/205)
2. Castillon du Perron: op. cit., 294
3. Spaziani (ed.): *Pages inédites*, 93–4
4. Bac: *Princesse Mathilde*, 216–18
5. Porel: *Fils de Réjane*, I, 121
6. Primoli: 'L'enfance d'une Souveraine. Souvenirs intimes'. (REVUE DES DEUX MONDES, 15 octobre 1923, 767)

4

1. Daudet: *Dans l'ombre de l'Impératrice Eugénie*, 106
2. Ibid., 107
3. Ibid., 108
4. Ibid., 109–10
5. Ibid., 111–13
6. Ibid., 153, 154, 156

5

1. Blanche: *Portraits of a Lifetime*, 266, 267–8
2. Daudet: op. cit., 221–4
3. Meyer: *Ce que je peux dire*, 117
4. 22 avril 1904. Claretie: *La Vie à Paris, 1904*, 101
5. 4 janvier 1907. Claretie: *La Vie à Paris, 1907*, 3
6. 23 décembre 1904. Claretie: *La Vie à Paris, 1904*, 398, 399
7. 9 mars 1906. Claretie: *La Vie à Paris, 1906*, 74–5
8. 16 décembre 1906. Claretie: *La Vie à Paris, 1906*, 415
9. 18 octobre 1912. Claretie: *La Vie à Paris, 1911–1912–1913*, 260, 260–1
10. Bac: *Promenades dans l'Italie nouvelle*, I, 74
11. Besnard: op. cit., 155, 155–6
12. 31 décembre 1913. Papiers Poincaré. B.N. N.A. Fr. 16022 ff 232–3

1. 31 décembre [1914]. Papiers Poincaré. B.N. N.A. Fr. 16022 ff 234–7
2. Ibid.
3. Besnard: op. cit., 233–4
4. Faure: *Mes Alyscamps*, 62–3
5. Bainville: *La Guerre et l'Italie*, 218
6. Chaumeix: loc. cit.
7. Quoted by Poincaré on 17 July 1915. Poincaré: *Au Service de la France*, VI, 327
8. Ibid., 327–9
9. Ibid., 329
10. Colette: *Journal intermittent*, 13, 16
11. Claudel: *Journal*, I, 346. Ibid., 344, 348, 349
12. Régnier: op. cit., 25–6
13. France: op. cit., 64
14. 21 mars 1919. Papiers Poincaré. B.N. N.A. Fr. 16022 ff 242–3
15. 5 avril 1919. Papiers Poincaré. B.N. N.A. Fr. 16022 ff 244–5
16. The note was sent from the Cercle de l'Union Artistique, 5, rue Boissy d'Anglas, and dated 'samedi 28 juin 19 5h'. Papiers Poincaré. B.N. N.A. Fr. 16022 f 248
17. Bac: *Promenades daus l'Italie nouvelle*, I, 76–9

1. Pailleron: *Le Paradis perdu*, 149–50
2. Ibid., 147–8
3. Bac: op. cit., 218
4. Undated. Papiers Poincaré. B.N. N.A. Fr. 16022 ff 272–3
5. Papiers Poincaré. B.N. N.A. Fr. 16022 f 260. The note is undated, but the Empress had been born on 5 May 1826, and had entered her 93rd year on 5 May 1918.
6. Primoli: 'Autour du mariage de l'Impératrice'. (REVUE DES DEUX MONDES, ler novembre 1924, 76, note)
7. Juillet 1920. This letter, on mourning paper, may be dated between 11 July, the date of the Empress's death, and 20 July, the date of her funeral at Farnborough. Papiers Poincaré. B.N. N.A. Fr. 16013 ff 268–9
8. Bac: op. cit., 218
9. Ibid.

10. Primoli Papers

11. Bac: loc. cit.; and see Primoli: 'Autour du mariage de l'Impératrice' (REVUE DES DEUX MONDES, ler novembre 1924, *passim*); the
ending was distinctly unchivalrous.

Seven

1

1. Ajalbert: op. cit., I, 49 sqq.
2. Ibid. Primoli made his will on 19 March 1926; the Fondazione Primoli was established by royal decree in 1928. See also Spaziani (ed.): *Pages inédites*, xxxvii–xxxix
3. Spaziani (ed.): ibid., 94–5
4. Primoli: 'La Princesse Mathilde et Théophile Gautier', I. (REVUE DES DEUX MONDES, ler novembre 1925, 75–8)
5. Bac: *Promenades dans l'Italie nouvelle*, loc. cit.
6. Undated. Papiers Poincaré. B.N. N.A. Fr. 16022 ff 270–1
7. Undated. Papiers Poincaré. B.N. N.A. Fr. 16022 ff 256, 259, 274
8. Régnier: op. cit., 27–8
9. Fouquières: op. cit., 111–2. Eleonora Duse died on 20 April 1924.
10. Régnier: op. cit., 28–9
11. Undated. Papiers Poincaré. B.N. N.A. Fr. 16013 ff 273–5

2

1. Bibliothèque Nationale. Cent Lettres à Gabriel Faure. N.A. Fr. 16418 f 91
2. Claudel: *Journal*, I, 674
3. Ajalbert: op. cit., 51–2
4. Chaumeix: op. cit., 223–6

Select Bibliography

Books

English books are published in London, French books in Paris, Italian books in Rome, unless otherwise stated.

AJALBERT, Jean, *Mémoires à rebours (1935–1870)*. I. Règlements de comptes. (Denoël & Steele, 1936.)

ANGELI, Diego, *I Bonaparte a Roma*. (Milano. A. Mondadori, 1938.)

[ANNUNZIO, G. d'], *Gabriele d'Annunzio à Georges Hérelle*. Correspondance, accompagnée de douze sonnets cisalpins. Introduction, traduction et notes de Guy Tosi. (Éditions Denoël. 1946.)

BAC, Ferdinand, *La Princesse Mathilde*. Sa vie et ses amis. (Hachette. 1928.)

Promenades dans l'Italie nouvelle. Tome I. Rome. (Hachette. 1933.)

Intimités du Second Empire. III. (Hachette. 1932.)

Intimités de la IIIe République. 3 tomes. (Hachette. 1935.)

BAINVILLE, Jacques, *La Guerre et l'Italie*. (Arthème Fayard. 1916.)

BAPST, Germain, *Histoire des joyaux de la couronne de France, d'après des documents inédits*. (Hachette. 1889.)

BARRÈS, Maurice, *Mes Cahiers*. 14 tomes. (Plon. 1929–1957.)

BECCHETTI, P., & PIETRANGELI, C., *Roma tra storia e cronaca dalle fotografie di Giuseppe Primoli*. (Edizioni Quasar. 1981.)

Tevere et Agro Romano dalle fotografie di Giuseppe Primoli. (Edizioni Quasar. 1982.)

BESNARD, Albert, *Sous le ciel de Rome*. Souvenirs. (Les Éditions de France. 1925.)

BLANCHE, J.-E., *Portraits of a Lifetime*. The Late Victorian Era. The Edwardian Pageant. 1870–1914. Translated and edited by Walter Clement. (Dent. 1937.)

More Portraits of a Lifetime. 1918–1938. Translated and edited by Walter Clement. (Dent. 1939.)

BLAVET, Émile, *La Vie Parisienne*. La Ville & le Théâtre (1884). Préface de François Coppée. (Boulanger. 1885.)

BOURGET, Paul, *Cosmopolis*. (Lemerre. 1893.)

BUCKLE, G.E. [ed.], *The Letters of Queen Victoria*. Third Series. Vol. II. (Murray. 1931.)

CALVÉ, Emma, *Sous tous les ciels j'ai chanté . . .* (Plon. 1940.)

CASTILLON DU PERRON, Marguerite, *La Princesse Mathilde*. (Amiot-Dumont. 1953.)

CLARETIE, Jules, *La Vie à Paris, 1896*. (Bibliothèque Charpentier. 1897.)

    La Vie à Paris, 1899. (Bibliothèque Charpentier. 1900.)

    La Vie à Paris, 1904. (Bibliothèque Charpentier. 1905.)

    La Vie à Paris, 1906. (Bibliothèque Charpentier. 1907.)

    La Vie à Paris, 1907. (Bibliothèque Charpentier. 1908.)

    La Vie à Paris, 1910. (Bibliothèque Charpentier. 1911.)

    La Vie à Paris, 1911–1912–1913. (Bibliothèque Charpentier. 1914.)

CLAUDEL, Paul, *Journal*. 2 tomes. Introduction par François Varillon. Texte établi et annoté par François Varillon et Jacques Petit. (N.R.F. Gallimard. 1968–9.)

COLETTE, *Journal intermittent*. (Fleuron. n.d.)

CRISPOLTI, F.C., *Scene di vita quotidiana a Roma dalle fotografie di Giuseppe Primoli*. (Edizioni Quasar. 1980.)

DAUDET, Alphonse, *L'Immortel*. Moeurs parisiennes. (Lemerre. 1888.)

DAUDET, Mme Alphonse, *Souvenirs autour d'un groupe littéraire*. (Charpentier. 1910.)

DAUDET, Lucien, *Dans l'ombre de l'Impératrice Eugénie*. Lettres intimes adressées à Madame Alphonse Daudet. 6e édition. (N.R.F. Gallimard. 1935.)

FAURE, Gabriel, *Mes Alyscamps*. (Les Horizons de France. 1948.)

FEUILLET, Mme Octave, *Quelques années de ma vie*. 4e édition. (Calmann-Lévy. 1894.)

    Souvenirs et Correspondances. (Calmann-Lévy. 1896.)

FLAUBERT, Gustave, *Lettres inédites à la Princesse Mathilde*. Préface de Monsieur le Comte Joseph Primoli. Étude de Madame la Princesse Mathilde. (Conard. 1927.)

    Correspondance. Nouvelle édition augmentée. 5e série (1862–1868). (Conard. 1930.)

    Correspondance. Nouvelle édition augmentée. 8e série (1877–1880). (Conard. 1930.)

FOUQUIÈRES, André de, *Cinquante ans de panache*. (Pierre Horay-Flore. 1951.)

GREGH, Fernand, *L'Âge d'or*. Souvenirs d'enfance et de jeunesse. (Grasset. 1947.)

L'Âge d'airain. Souvenirs, 1905–1925. (Grasset. 1951.)

GONCOURT, Edmond & Jules de, *Journal. Mémoires de la vie littéraire*. (Monaco. Les Éditions de l'Imprimerie Nationale. 1956–)

HERMANT, Abel, *Souvenirs de la vie mondaine*. (Plon. 1935.)

HUGO, Comtesse Clémentine, *Rome en 1886*. 2e édition. (Rome. Imprimerie Nationale. 1886.)

LELIÈVRE, Renée, *Le Théâtre dramatique italien en France, 1855–1940*. (Armand Colin. 1959.)

LERNER, Michael G., *Maupassant*. (Allen & Unwin. 1975.)

LUBBOCK, Percy [sel. and ed.], *The Letters of Henry James*. 2 vols. (Macmillan. 1920.)

LUMBROSO, Albert, *Souvenirs sur Maupassant*. Sa dernière maladie, sa mort. 2 tomes. (Rome. Bocca frères. 1905.)

MEYER, Arthur, *Ce que je peux dire*. (Plon. 1912.)

MORTIER, Arnold, *Les Soirées parisiennes de 1880*. (Dentu. 1881.)

OLLIVIER, Émile, *Lettres de l'exil, 1870–1874*. (Librairie Hachette. 1921.)

ORMOND,Léonée, *George du Maurier*. (Routledge & Kegan Paul. 1969.)

PAILLERON, Marie-Louise, *Le Paradis perdu*. Souvenirs d'Enfance. (Albin Michel. 1947.)

PAINTER, George, *Marcel Proust. A Biography*. 2 vols. (Chatto & Windus. 1959, 1965.)

PASQUALI, Costanza, *Proust, Primoli, la Moda*. (Edizioni di Storia e Letteratura. 1961.)

PIETRANGELI, Carlo, *Giuseppe Primoli. Fotografo europeo*. (Edizioni Quasar. 1982.)

POINCARÉ, Raymond, *Au Service de la France*. Neuf années de souvenirs. 10 tomes. (Plon. 1926–33.)

POREL, Jacques, *Fils de Réjane. Souvenirs*. 2 vols. (Plon. 1951–2.)

[PRÉVOST, Marcel], *Marcel Prévost et ses contemporains*. 2 tomes. (Les Éditions de France. 1943.)

PRIMOLI, J.-N. *Une promenade dans Rome sur les traces de Stendhal*. Inédits de Stendhal. (Abbeville. Imprimerie F. Paillart. Les Amis d'Édouard. No. 45. 1922.)

PROUST, Marcel, *Correspondance*. Texte établi, présenté et annoté par Philip Kolb. (Plon. 1970–)

RÉGNIER, Henri de, *De mon temps . . .* (Mercure de France. 1933.)

RICHARDSON, Joanna, *Théophile Gautier. His Life and Times*. (Reinhardt. 1958.)

Princess Mathilde. (Weidenfeld & Nicolson. 1969.)

[ROLLAND, Romain], *Printemps romain*. Choix de lettres de Romain Rolland à sa mère (1889–1890). (Albin Michel. 1954.)

SAINTE-BEUVE, C.-A., *Lettres à la Princesse*. 3e édition. (Michel Lévy frères. 1873.)

SMYTH, Ethel, *Streaks of Life*. (Longmans, Green & Co. 1921.)
What Happened Next. (Longmans, Green & Co. 1940.)

[SPAZIANI, Marcello], *Joseph-Napoléon Primoli. Pages inédites*. Recueillies, présentées et annotées par Marcello Spaziani. (Rome. Edizioni di Storia et Letteratura. 1959.)
Gli Amici della Principessa Matilde. (Edizioni di Storia e Letteratura. 1960.)
Con Gégé Primoli nella Roma Bizantina. (Edizioni di Storia e Letteratura. 1962.)

TERNOIS, René, *Zola et son temps*. Lourdes–Rome–Paris. (Société 'Les Belles Lettres'. 1961.)

THWAITE, Ann, *Edmund Gosse. A Literary Landscape*. (Secker & Warburg. 1984.)

TIENOT, Y., & ESTRADE-GUERRA, O. d', *Debussy*. L'homme, son œuvre, son milieu. (Lemoine. 1962.)

VALLAS, Léon, *Claude Debussy et son temps*. (Albin Michel. 1958.)

VASILI, Comte Paul [*pseud.*], *La Sociéte dé Rome*. Édition augmentée de lettres indites. (Nouvelle Revue. 1887.)

VITALI, Lamberto, *Un fotografo fin de siècle. Il conte Primoli*. (Torino. Giulio Einaudi. 1968.)

Articles

ARRIGHI, Paul, *Zola à Rome*. (REVUE DE LITTÉRATURE CONTEMPORAINE, juillet–septembre 1928.)

BOYER, Ferdinand, *Le Musée Napoléonien du comte Joseph-Napoléon Primoli*. (NAPOLÉON. REVUE DES ÉTUDES NAPOLÉONIENNES, mars-avril 1925.)

CHAUMEIX, André, *Le Comte Primoli*. (REVUE DES DEUX MONDES, ler juillet 1927.)

DOMINIQUE [i.e. Marcel Proust], *Un Salon historique. Le Salon de S.A.I. la Princesse Mathilde*. (LE FIGARO, 25 février 1903.)

MATHILDE, Princesse, *Souvenirs des années d'exil. I, II, III*. (REVUE DES DEUX MONDES, 15 décembre 1927, ler, 15 janvier 1928.)

[MÉRIMÉE, Prosper], *Lettres de Mérimée à la Princesse Mathilde*. (LA REVUE DE PARIS, 15 juin 1922.)

PRIMOLI, J.-N., *La Duse*. (LA REVUE DE PARIS, ler juin 1897.)

  La Princesse Mathilde et le maestro Sauzay. (LA REVUE HEBDOMADAIRE, 6 octobre 1917.)

  Gustave Flaubert chez la Princesse Mathilde. Souvenir d'une soirée à Saint-Gratien. (LA REVUE DE PARIS, 15 novembre 1921.)

  La Princesse Mathilde et le Duc d'Aumale. (LA REVUE DE PARIS, ler août 1922.)

  L'Impératrice Eugénie et le Tsar Alexandre II. Souvenirs. (REVUE DES DEUX MONDES, 15 septembre 1922.)

  Caprice de Prince. (LA REVUE DE PARIS, ler octobre 1923.)

  L'enfance d'une Souveraine. Souvenirs intimes. (REVUE DES DEUX MONDES, 15 octobre 1923.)

  Lettres à la Princesse Julie. (REVUE DES DEUX MONDES, 15 juin 1924.)

  Autour du mariage de l'Impératrice. (REVUE DES DEUX MONDES, ler novembre 1924.)

  La Princesse Mathilde et Théophile Gautier. (REVUE DES DEUX MONDES, ler, 15 novembre 1925.)

[RENAN, Ernest], *Lettres à la Princesse Mathilde*. (REVUE DES DEUX MONDES, ler avril 1925.)

RICHARDSON, Joanna, *Proust and the Princess*. (THE TIMES LITERARY SUPPLEMENT, 17 October 1968.)

SPAZIANI, Marcello, *Le Comte Joseph Primoli, témoin de son temps (1851–1927)*. (ANNALES DE LA FACULTÉ DES LETTRES D'AIX, Tome XXXII. 1958.)

Lettere inedite di Maupassant al Conte Primoli. (STUDI IN ONORE DI VITTORIO LUGLI E DIEGO VALERI. Venezia. Neri Pozza. 1961. Parte seconda.)

TERNOIS, René, *Les Amitiés romaines d'Émile Zola*. (REVUE DE LITTÉRATURE COMPARÉE, octobre–décembre 1947.)

Index

343

and Empress Eugénie, 70–2; P. in love?, 73–4; his dissatisfaction with life, 73, 74–5; in Spain with EE, 76–7, 78; on the death of the Prince Imperial, 84–5; with Flaubert and Goncourt at Saint-Gratien, 86; Flaubert's private audience with PM, 86–92; Alfred de Musset, 93–4; Ernest Hébert, 96; Sainte-Beuve, 98; Alexandre Dumas *fils*, 99; Claudius Popelin, 99; the advent of Eleonora Duse, 101–12; Sainte-Beuve at Compiègne, 102–4; the Popelins in Rome, 106–9; admiration for Guy de Maupassant, 109; appreciation of Matilde Serao, 109–10; the marriage of Gabriele d'Annunzio, 110–11; Goncourt's latest novel, 112; appreciation of La Duse, 112–15; father's death, 119; mother's illness, 120, 122 and *passim*; relationship with Dumas *fils*, 68, 120–1, 294; visits Goncourt, 121; La Duse and *Denise*, 123–6; friendship with Anatole France, 127; friendship with Paul Bourget, 127; friendship with Maupassant, 127–8, 129–30, 131–2; and Claude Debussy, 128–9; and Henry James, 129, 130; and Emma Calvé, 130; Mme Franklin Grout, 131; on the wedding of Princess Laetitia and the Duke of Aosta, 133–6; on Popelin's illness, 133; PM's private life, 136–42; Marie Abbatucci, 141–2; Alphonse Daudet's novel, *L'Immortel*, 143–4; PM's visit to Turin, 145, 146; Paris Inter-

national Exhibition, 1889, 148; PM again discusses her private life, 148–51, 152–3; Ernest Meissonier's marriage, 151; Musset and George Sand, 151–2; the Duc d'Aumale and PM, 154–6; visits Maupassant, 157; at Saint-Gratien, 158; at Farnborough, 158; photographs Thomas Edison on the Eiffel Tower, 159; the Shah of Persia at Saint-Gratien, 159–60; PM and Popelin, 160; in Venice, 161–2; described by Romain Rolland, 162–3; and marriage of Jeannine Dumas, 183–4; thoughts about marriage, 162–3, 167; increasing affection for PM, 167; asks to write her life, 168; Daudet's second betrayal of PM, 169–70; photographs Prince Napoleon, 170; death of Prince Napoleon, 171; death of Popelin, 171; grief of PM, 171 sqq.; entertains Sarah Bernhardt, 176–7; recollections of Hippolyte Taine, 177–8; in Paris with EE, 178; visits Daudet, 179; a performance of Wagner, 179; Gounod at Saint-Gratien, 179–80; PM describes her childhood, 180–1; visits studio of Jacques-Émile Blanche, 181; introduces Abel Hermant to PM, 182–3; described by Ethel Smyth, 183; on the Kaiser in Italy, 184–5; Marshal MacMahon, 187; conversation with Émile Ollivier, 188–90; reflections on the new year, 201; La Duse at Windsor, 203–4; Goncourt's *Grenier*, 205; Émile Zola in Rome, 205–7; Réjane, 207–8;

described by Henri de Régnier, 209–10; Daudet at the *Grenier*, 210–11; Dumas' last visit to PM, 211–12; Goncourt's interview, 212; death of Dumas, 213; the Duc d'Aumale at the rue de Berry, 217–18; described by Marcel Prévost, 220–1; Paolo Tosti, 224–9; d'Annunzio, 230–1; admiration of La Duse, 231–4; death of his uncle, 235–9; Henri Becque, 240; La Duse and d'Annunzio, 240–1; a cruise with the Empress, 242–6; death of Charlotte Primoli, 247–8; thoughts on old age, 248–9; described by Fernand Gregh, 250–2; the Empress Eugénie, 252–4; last illness of PM, 255–8; death of PM, 258–9; P's new pied-à-terre in Paris, 263–4; friendship with Marcel Proust, 265, 271–2; a Mediterranean cruise, 266–7; described by André Chaumeix, 268–70; and by Bac, 270–1, 272–4, 276–7; P's new palace in Rome, 275–6; an anecdote of the EE, 277; visits her at Farnborough, 278–81; and at Cap Martin, 281; described by J.-É. Blanche, 282–3; photographs Frederik VIII of Denmark, 283; described by Jules Claretie, 284; appreciated by Albert Besnard, 286–7; friendship with President and Mme Poincaré, 285 and *passim*; and the First World War, 286–91; entertains Colette, 289; and Paul Claudel, 289; publishes articles, 290; described by Gabriel Faure, 287,

290; and by Marie-Louise Pailleron, 293–4; death of EE, 295–6; described by Jean Ajalbert, 299–300; recollections of PM, 301–2; failing health, 302; described by André de Fouquières, 302–3; and by Henri de Régnier, 303; last illness, 304; death, 305; appreciation, 305–6

Primoli, Luigi (grandfather of P): marriage, 3; death, 4

Primoli, Luigi (brother of P): birth, 14

Primoli, Napoleon (brother of P): birth, 14, death, 108

Primoli, Pietro (father of P): character, 17; appearance, 17; marriage, 4; settles in Paris, 14; at PM's, 16, 17; returns to Italy, 58; death, 119; P. recalls, 17

Primoli, Teresa (grandmother of P): marriage, 3

Rolland, Romain: discusses P, 162–3

Royal Military Academy, Woolwich: Prince Imperial attends, 70–1

Sainte-Beuve, C.-A.: and PM, 15, 28, 98, 102–4; and Princess Julie, 36

Saint-Gratien: described, 14–15, 95–6 and *passim*

Sauzay, Professor: teaches piano to PM, 193–5

Sedan: Napoleon III surrenders to Prussians at, 56

Serao, Matilde, 109–10, 115, 119

Smyth, Dame Ethel: on cruise with P and EE, 183

Sophie, Queen of the Netherlands: 40, 58, 59, 64